USE OF RATIONAL EMOTIVE BEHAVIOUR THERAPY (REBT) WITH EAST AFRICAN IMMIGRANT WOMEN IN TRIESTE, ITALY

by

Teresa W. Ngigi

BEd., Marist International College, 1995
MSc., Grand Canyon University, 2009

A Dissertation

Submitted in Fulfilment of the
Requirements for the Degree of

Doctor of Philosophy
In Psychology

Intercultural Open University Foundation

March 2015

ABSTRACT

Global movement caused by various reasons including wars, natural disasters, and a search for a better life, is causing a remarkable demographic shift around the globe. By 2013, there were an estimated 232 million immigrants in the world according to Rapporto Onu (2013). This number has increased steadily because the trend continues.

Italy, being the entry port leading to other European Union countries, happens to receive a large number of immigrants every month, especially in spring, early summer, late summer, and early fall (Rapporto Onu, 2013). This is remarkably challenging Italy's status quo. Immigration has become a pressing issue in Italy and as the number of legal and illegal immigrants' increases, new needs arise. One of these pressing needs is the integration process of these immigrants. Professional counsellors are therefore being challenged to expand their understanding and knowledge of techniques and approaches that are effective with diverse cultures.

A review of literature reveals that there is little research devoted to counselling immigrants in general, and, as will be seen, counselling as a profession in Italy is at its initial stages, therefore not much has been accomplished in the field.

This qualitative, phenomenological and heuristic study interviewed six East African immigrant women who have been in Italy for not more than six years, in order to assess their mental health needs and how Rational Emotive Behaviour Therapy (REBT) could or could not be used as a tool in counselling them. The purpose of this study is to determine whether REBT can be used as a counselling tool with this population. This study is also aimed at contributing towards helping mental health practitioners gain awareness of complex issues of immigrants, develop cultural competency, acquire skills, and help promote the mental health of immigrants. From the study, it suffices to note that REBT could be a good starting point in counselling immigrants, but an integration of other theories may be needed in order to meet the complex needs of these immigrant women. Cultural sensitivity is crucial in this process.

ACKNOWLEDGEMENTS

I would like to immensely thank God for the inspirations, strength, support, and graces that I have experienced throughout the process of my program. Being a believer, I know I would not have accomplished anything without His power and strength. He did for me what I could not do for myself.

I would also like to extend my heartfelt gratitude and recognition to my dear family members, especially my husband, Gianni, for supporting me when I decided to embark on this program, supporting me in both light and dark moments, waiting on me during the long evening hours of study, and rejoicing with me when I received positive feedback for my work, and being by me in all my ups and downs. I would also like to express my deepest appreciation to my two children, Harriet and Carsten, young as they are, they played a role in supporting me to continue with my program. Even during the times they would have preferred me to spend more time with them, they respected my space and allowed me to do what I needed to.

My deep appreciation to my Doctoral team mainly Dr. Sandra Hurlong and Dr. John Toothman for their unfailing support and encouragement throughout the program, their professional approach in everything, and their boundless availability every time I needed them. Their wise counsel always provided security to me and gave me impetus to go ahead.

My supervisor, Ambra, has been very instrumental in enlightening me and offering her critique at the right moment. She has worked very professionally and supported me in my darkest moments.

Special thanks to Caritas Italia for their help and availability in providing support in different ways. Without their help, interviews would have been very scarce.

The ladies who volunteered to be interviewed and who shared their deepest experiences offered a priceless contribution, were it not for them, this work would not have been complete. Their resilience in times of difficulties is extremely admirable and I learned so much from them.

And last but not least, I would like to thank my extended family, my friends, and all those who in one way or another contributed towards the success of my studies in whatever ways. May God reward each and every person who was directly or indirectly involved.

CONTENTS

ABSTRACT III

INTRODUCTION 1

    Purpose of Study 1

    Significance of the Problem and Justification for Studying it 3

    Working Definition of Terms. 3

    Research Gaps and Motivations. 5

    Scope of Project Population 6

    About the Author. 7

CHAPTER ONE. Literature Review 9

    1.1. Immigration in Italy. 12

    1.2. The Counselling Profession in Italy .15

    1.3. Immigrants Counselling 18

    1.4. Mental Health Needs of Immigrant Women 24

    1.5. Cross-Cultural Counselling 26

    1.6. Multicultural Counselling and Therapy 32

    1.7. Trauma Healing and Recovery. 37

    1.8. Rational Emotive Behaviour Therapy (REBT). 53

    Literature Review Chapter Conclusion. 63

CHAPTER TWO. Research Methodology 67

    2.1. Project Inspiration 67

    2.2. Research Team 68

2.3. Procedures...69

2.4. Participants..69

2.5. Limitations of Study...............................71

2.6. Delimitations...71

2.7. The Research Process.............................72

2.8. Conducting Research 73

2.9. Steps Followed in Conducting This Research (Schweigert, 1992) 74

2.10. Approach Methods in Research.........................77

2.11. Data Sources..81

2.12. Interview Process.................................83

2.13. Ethics in Research...............................85

Chapter Conclusion....................................87

CHAPTER THREE. Participants' Personal Narratives and
the Integration of REBT Within The Common Themes and Patterns 89

Introduction...89

3.1. Some General Characteristics of East African Culture. 91

3.2. Interviews 101

3.3. Common Themes and Patterns 104

Chapter Conclusion....................................124

CHAPTER FOUR. Preference of Rebt Over
Other Psychological Theories.................................127

Introduction...127

4.1. Psychodynamic Theories.........................128

4.2. Existential Theories 132

4.3. Cognitive Behaviour Theories 139

4.4. Family Systems Theory 147

4.5. Group Counselling Theory 148

4.6. Cross Cultural Theory 151

4.7. Multicultural Counselling and Therapy 152

4.8. Counselling Immigrant Women 153

4.9. Integration of REBT with other Therapies for Effective
Counselling. 156

Chapter Conclusion. 158

CHAPTER FIVE. Reflections, Conclusions,
and Suggestions for Further Research 161

Introduction 161

5.1. Impact on Narratives 161

5.2. Implications for Multicultural Social Work Practice. 162

5.3. Recommendations for Professional Counselling in Italy 164

5.4. Recommendations for Further Research 165

5.5. Interventions that could be Used in Counselling. 167

5.6. Limitations of Study. 168

General Conclusion. 169

BIBLIOGRAPHY 171

APPENDIX 201

Interview Reports. 201

Narrative 0VVN1. 201

Narrative OJN2 204

Narrative ONNK3 208

Narrative OAC4 211

Narrative OAK5. 216

Narrative OMK6 218

Demographic Information. 220

Interview Questions 221

INTRODUCTION

In the recent years, Italy has seen the number of immigrants from many parts of the world increase steadily. According to Adnkronos International (29th January, 2014), Italy's population stood at 61, 121, 366 as of 1st July 2014, the total number of immigrants being almost 5 million. The majority of these immigrants come from European countries, followed by African immigrants (Dossier Immigrazione, 2014). Immigration has become a pressing issue in Italy and as the number of legal and illegal immigrants' increases, new needs arise. One of these pressing needs is the integration process of these immigrants. This process affects not only the immigrants alone, but also the entire society. Whether these immigrants settle well or not is no longer the immigrants' only issue, but a national affair. Irrespective of what motivated the immigrants to move to Italy, the fact is that they are here and so finding ways to help them settle well is paramount to national security.

Most of these immigrants have left their countries in search for a better life, and therefore their integration process is paramount to achieving this goal.

This study is based on whether Rational Emotive Behaviour Therapy (REBT) could be a useful counselling tool in empowering East African immigrant women in their integration process in Trieste, Italy.

PURPOSE OF STUDY

Global immigration is affecting the world's demographic reality. The movement of human race from one country to the other has its effects on the personal, social, political, and economic reality. Immigrants carry, along with them, their heritage with all its various forms, and these factors call for attention in order for the integration process to be beneficial for both the immigrant and the host.

The mental health needs of individuals new to Europe and USA are often difficult to discern due to lack of literature focused on their needs (Yoshihama & Horrucks, 2002) and due to cultural and language barriers (Fan,

1999). This writer considers counselling as one of the ways that could be used to empower immigrants in their integration process.

In order for counselling to be effective, mental health workers need to understand the culture and experiences of the immigrants, and how these experiences affect both the immigrant and the mental health worker.

Immigrants often encounter problems including discrimination and prejudice as seen from the interviews. Black Africans experience discrimination more blatantly than other immigrants due to the skin colour according to the experience of this writer in working with immigrants in general.

It has been noted by a number of researchers that Western psychology may not be well equipped to serve immigrants, due to the tendency to *"medicalize"* human suffering (Summerfield, 1999, Williams & Calnan, 1996, no. 1609-1620), and due to the disregard of the cultural differences in response to adversity (Gozdziak, 2004). Religious and spiritual approaches are given less attention in counsellor training programs and therefore fall short of adequately preparing counsellors to understand clients' religious beliefs (Eng, 1998). Ethnographic approach helps enhance cultural competence (Gozdziak, 2004).

The Project Demonstrating Excellence in this study is based on how Rational Emotive Behaviour Therapy (REBT) could be used as a counselling tool and technique with East African Immigrant women seeking integration in Trieste, Italy. Being a conventional western counselling skill, its relevance with East African immigrant women living in the west is explored.

This study examines the lived experiences of East African immigrant women through a phenomenological approach. It is hoped that the knowledge gained will enhance mental health professionals' sensitivity to and awareness of the needs of these individuals and that it will also provide information that may improve the reception of newcomers by the receiving community.

This study will be an opening to further research on counselling techniques and their relevance to multicultural communities in Italy, considering that multiculturalism in the Italian context is a fairly new phenomenon and not much has been done in the field. In general, counselling itself is a relatively new discipline in Italy and it is still in the phase of development in that Italy has been slow in recognizing its need and importance (Remley, Bacchini, and Krieg, 2010). Italy is more open to psychology and psychotherapy and other forms of therapy in dealing with life issues than it is to counselling. The study will therefore attempt to lay the basis for a comprehensible evaluation of Rational Emotive Behaviour Therapy for therapists as well as the local service care providers, in order to offer a framework for counselling immigrants using effective multicultural counselling techniques.

The study is also open to further scrutiny in that the needs of immigrant women keep changing depending on various circumstances, calling for different approaches to different situations and realities.

SIGNIFICANCE OF THE PROBLEM AND JUSTIFICATION FOR STUDYING IT

As a result of this research, information and data will be gathered and compiled in order to explore how REBT could be applied in counselling East African immigrant women in their integration process in Trieste. The research focuses on exploring the experiences of these women and how their needs can be addressed using REBT. This information will attempt to provide a better understanding of culture and traditions, and be used as an initial tool towards designing ways of supporting these women in their difficulties. This could lead to an experience of a sense of belonging and empowerment, as the women are enabled to find meaning in participating actively in their own development as well as the good of the society which they are a part of.

WORKING DEFINITION OF TERMS

For the purpose of this study, the following working definitions are used.

TRAUMA

Trauma is the brain's response to serious injury including frightening thoughts and painful feelings that can produce extreme behaviour (U.S. Department of Health and Human Services, 2006). Michenbaum (1997) further defines a traumatic event as *"so extreme or severe, so powerful, harmful, and/or threatening that it demands extraordinary coping efforts"*. It happens when one experiences a threat to their life or the life of loved ones, while feeling helpless about it.

CULTURE

Culture is the characteristics of a particular group of people, defined by everything from language, religion, cuisine, social habits, music and arts (Zimmerman, 2012). Culture is therefore seen as the collective programming of the mind which distinguishes the members of one category of people from another. It is a combination of *"ethnographic"* variables such as ethnicity, nationality, religion, and language, as well as demographic variables of age, gender, social, economic, educational background, and a wider range of formal or informal memberships and affiliations (Pederson, 1990).

CULTURAL COMPETENCE

Knowing the cultural values and indigenous interventions of the client system and using them in planning and implementing services (Fong, 2001).

RECOGNITION

This is a phenomenon that addresses issues of identity and difference—a concept that reveals the other's *"foreignness"*.

RESILIENCE

This is the human capacity for growth through adversity (Lindy & Joseph, 2005), the ability to bounce back and cope in the face of challenges and difficulties (Soussou et. al. 2008). It refers to the capacity to withstand stress and catastrophe. It's not a congenital trait, but one that a person gains through life experiences.

ETHNO-PSYCHIATRY

Ethno-psychiatry refers to indigenous conceptions about mental states and mental illness in different cultures (Encyclopaedia 69). It is also a practice that models acknowledgement through a type of clinical listening that is political and therefore in disagreement with the policing mechanisms of the state, which claims to know the *"other"* through categories such as victim, migrant, and political refugee (Giordano, 2014).

REFUGEE

Someone who, owing to a well-founded fear of being persecuted for reasons of race, religion, nationality, membership of a particular social group or political opinion, is outside the country of their nationality and is unable or owing to such fear, is unwilling to avail himself or herself of the protection of that country; or who, not having a nationality and being outside the country of his former habitual residence as a result of such events, is unable or owing to such fear, is unwilling to return to it (UN General Assembly, 1951).

IMMIGRATION

This is the entrance of a person into a new country for the purpose of establishing permanent residence. An immigrant therefore is a person who leaves their country to settle permanently in another one (free web dictionary), motivated by various reasons.

EMPATHY

The ability to imagine oneself in another's world and understand the other's feelings, desires, ideas, viewpoint, actions, reactions, and worldview. It is walking in another person's moccasins (John Powell, S. J.)

RESEARCH GAPS AND MOTIVATIONS

Immigrant women, due to various reasons, personal or otherwise, may often not receive the help they need in order to abet their integration process, and the local authorities may find it hard to address their needs adequately for lack of the required, necessary tools. These women may also be struggling with their own personal issues, including identity crises, besides the integration problems they are likely to face.

The ability to integrate into the community may often be taken for granted by the local authorities as well as the local community, and techniques that may not necessary be multicultural in nature may be applied to those in need of counselling services. For this reason, these women may experience isolation, groping in the dark in search of ways to make themselves at home despite all odds. Sometimes these women are likely to settle for realities that they are uncomfortable with—through pure compliance, while their felt needs may not be adequately addressed. This situation may create an attitude of helplessness and consequent resentments, as reported by some of the women interviewed, hence the inability to be themselves and the augmentation of a sense of loss and defeat, to say nothing of the consequences of unproductivity and the toll their lack of health takes on the social welfare.

As the issue of immigration becomes more and more a global reality, it needs to be adequately addressed and research will assist this process. Among the immigrants in Italy, the number of women is more than 50% that of men (ISTAT: 2011). These women come from diverse parts of the world, and there is a significant number from English speaking Eastern Africa (Kenya, Uganda, Tanzania, Somalia, and Ethiopia) scattered all over Italy. It is not uncommon to find most of these women experiencing a sense of loss in the new environment, where they experience a hostile reception, and where they live in constant fear of being repatriated or not obtaining the relevant documents to help them settle and earn a living legally. Some of these may have gone through traumatic experiences, and may be carrying a baggage of unresolved issues which are bound to interfere with their wellbeing, to say nothing of the possibility of reliving the traumatic experiences of the past. These factors call for focused, multiculturally oriented counselling techniques, and Rational Emotive Behaviour Therapy as a technique is explored in regard to its effects on the counselling needs of these women.

Often times, integration is a slow and painful process, marked with a surfeit of difficulties along the way, starting from the basic ones namely climate, language, food, relationships, and social system, and on to the different laws, rules, and regulations. Most of these immigrants are self-conscious about racism, since they stick out visibly, while being aware of their differences.

A number of studies have been carried out and publications are available on the issue of the plight of immigrants and multicultural counselling approaches in different countries, and this study will build on these studies, as will be evidenced in the literature review. Cultural influences may be quite pervasive, widespread, and powerful in forming the basis of *"being"* for ordinary people, yet, remain elusive for those researchers who have sought to understand them (Kitayama and Marcus, 2000). This study therefore assesses Albert Ellis' specific counselling approach, and its adaptation to this particular context.

SCOPE OF PROJECT POPULATION

The target group in this research is English speaking East African immigrant women who have been in Italy for not more than 6 years, whose age ranges from 18—45 years old. As seen later in the chapter on methodology, this group was selected particularly because it is English speaking, and above all, because the researcher is an East African immigrant herself, and has always empathized with other immigrants who struggle in their settlement process, seeing as she struggled to settle down herself. Different organizations helped in identifying participants as detailed in the chapter on methodology. Since this group shares cultural characteristics, it was found to be a good ground to determine whether REBT could be a useful tool in the counselling process.

ABOUT THE AUTHOR

The author of this study is an African from East Africa, Kenya. She was born and brought up in Kenya, in a large family composed of 10 siblings. The family was a middle class family, and both parents had their respective occupations. The mother figure was extremely industrious and always creative. She was involved in various activities including business, community, and church activities. She was a woman of deep faith, and God in the family was central. The parents' Catholic faith was communicated, if not inculcated, into all the siblings and everyone went through the church initiation process. This writer was always inspired by the life the mother lived. Home was always open to everyone, and the gate was always left open. The family values of hospitality and generosity were communicated constantly through the example of the mother. The father figure instead was hardly present, and when he was, he always functioned as the normative parent. Relationship with the father was one of fear and avoidance, and he was approached only when it was extremely essential to do so. Needless to say, values passed on from the mother were more effective because she was always present to journey with her children despite being very busy and submissive to her husband.

Through the inspiration of the mother, this writer had the constant desire to be of help to others, especially the less fortunate, and even in high school, she could go out of her way to uplift other people and reach out to those in need. This is where the desire to be involved in the social wellbeing originated from. This writer then studied in Kenya, United Kingdom, and USA, and has been exposed to various realities concerning the difficulties immigrants go through in a foreign land. For this reason, she developed an interest in the issues of immigration due to her lived experiences, studies, and interactions with other immigrants.

Her personal traits, assumptions, biases, and epistemological position regarding the study have influenced the study data collection and its interpretation in the following ways:

Gender and ethnicity—these two helped the immigrant women feel comfortable because the researcher exercised empathy, acceptance, genuineness, and patience. The fact that she could understand the languages spoken made it easier for them to express themselves easily, and hence a good mutual understanding was established.

Religious beliefs—This writer is a Christian (Catholic) and this encouraged the participants to talk about their religion and spirituality which is an important cultural aspect of the day to day life. Faith features in almost every sentence of these immigrants, and it has played a major role in helping them in their resilience. This writer therefore was sensitive to the spiritual heritage that was shared, despite the ladies belonging to different professions of faith (Catholic, Protestant, and Muslim). Prayer was an integral part of these ladies' life, and this was given utmost respect.

Experience as a Counsellor and a mental health worker—This writer has been practicing for several years and her experience inspired and influenced the selection of the common themes and patterns detailed in a later chapter. The main theme was based on the search for meaning, inspired by Victor Frankl's book *"Man's search for meaning"* (1992), and, having worked extensively in promoting social change, the whole interview experience was such a rich encounter that she felt so much at home carrying it out as well as participating actively in the life experiences of these ladies.

This author had the assumption that the phenomenological approach would be an effective way of discovering the experiences of the participants and that a small number of detailed accounts of their experiences would lead to valuable information for counselling professionals (Baker, 2007).

The entire study experience has been an extremely enriching one for the writer, who builds on other people's cultural heritage, which is a childhood trait that was passed down from her mother. The author's struggles received a new light from the struggles of the ladies, and the writer had to change her perspective more than several times, when faced with different powerful realities lived by these ladies. This study is first and foremost an inspiration to the writer in her personal as well as professional growth.

CHAPTER ONE

LITERATURE REVIEW

This literature review addresses the issue of immigration in Italy and explores the role of immigrant counselling profession in Italy. Mental health needs of women immigrants are also addressed. Cross-cultural and multicultural counselling are prerogative for this research, and therefore attention is given to these factors. Since trauma is one of the most common characteristics of immigrants settling in Italy, as is shown in the interviews conducted, trauma experience and healing are also explored. Finally, Albert Ellis' Rational Emotive Behaviour Therapy (REBT), which is the subject of the research—is reviewed in relation to the needs of the immigrants.

The counselling profession in general has a long history; however, counselling theories have been developed within a certain context to answer specific contextual felt needs. So far, theories have been developed to answer to the needs that arise within the Western culture. Chambers and Smith (1995) affirm that a *"hermeneutic approach to therapy emphasises that individuals are thoroughly embedded in and shaped by culture, and if people are not aware of that, their perspective is limited by the horizon of their moral visions. Others' outlook and behaviour can appear pathological, mistaken, distorted, or even evil"* (pg. 226).

The issue of immigration is neither simple nor easy. As Chung (2010) asserts, during pre-migration, immigrants may encounter economic, political, and cultural restrictions, wars or political persecution, family loss or personal violence through war, oppression due to ethnic minority, among others. However, as Drozdek and Wilson (2004) affirm, for whatever reasons, immigrants leave their homeland and migrate to a new land, therefore they experience many losses including home, possessions, homeland, customs, and social roles as they leave their country and move towards a new land. For this reason, their felt needs are significant, and they need to address these needs if settling is going to be a fulfilling process. They continuously have to deal with challenges of adaptation and acculturation to life in the new country.

The immigration process is not an easy path and due to the unique stressors during pre-immigration and departure, transit, and settlement states, immigrants and refugees are at risk of developing mental health problems (Potocky-Tripodi, 2002).

While working with immigrants, Chung (2010) stresses that it is essential to take into consideration factors such as barriers to mental health services, culture, resiliency, and spirituality. These factors may include age, legal status, and language, among others. One of the main barriers, according to National Child Traumatic Stress Network (2005), is lack of mental health services in the native language of the immigrant.

A qualitative study of seven ethnically diverse health care providers by O'Mahony and Donnelly (2007) revealed that immigrant women face difficulties when accessing mental health services due to culture, stigma, and unfamiliarity with Western medication. Research from the past decade in the areas of migration and development has demonstrated that individuals' migration related choices are related to their family members' needs and that migration affects migrant's origin countries (Mazzucato and Schans, 2011).

In their research, Eisenhauer et. al. (2012) confirmed that most of the women interviewed have long struggled for survival, oppression, conflict, discrimination, and migration itself. Their resilience is evident as demonstrated by their ability to adapt. Eisenhauer et. al. (2012) further argue that these women confront cultural differences, language barriers, lack of technical job skills and education, and difficulty in adjusting to a new society. Lack of understanding of the lifestyle and the functioning system in the host country makes adjusting much more complicated. Issues are further complicated if immigrants do not speak the host country's language (s). It is therefore quite difficult and intriguing to elicit information from these women because after years of oppression and trauma, they become passive in nature (Eisenhauer et. al. 2012).

The term *"lifestyle migration"* has been used to refer to an increasing number of people who take the decision to migrate based on their belief that there is a more fulfilling way of life available for them elsewhere (Benson and O'Reilly, 2009). Benson and O'Reilly (2009) further argue that migration is often described using a language like *"getting out of the trap"*, *"making a fresh start"*, *"a new beginning"*, among others. This leads to immigrants seeking the greatest good in life. This concept implies dissatisfaction with the current life, hence the desire to change and become better. This could create the basis for therapeutic work with the immigrants. Rational Emotive Behaviour Therapy aims at improving life and making it worthwhile, therefore this foundation might be helpful in therapy due to the immigrant's disposition towards change.

Lifestyle migration is therefore a search, a project, rather than an act, and it encompasses diverse destinations, desires, and dreams (Benson and O'Reilly, 2009). Concerning immigrant's narratives, Benson and O'Reilly (2009) affirm that these narratives may not often reflect objective reality: the presented advantages of life in the destination are often romanticised accounts, while the immigrant's representations of the ills of their home society are often overstated. However, when all is said and done, the relocation of immigrants can be defined, according to Benson and O'Reilly (2009), as indicative of a fundamental desire for change in lifestyle, signifying a break, a contrast, a turning point, and a new beginning. This is confirmed by Chatty (2013) who posits that the question about why some people decide to move in situations of war and extreme coercion and others choose to remain, go underground, and risk political imprisonment, torture, or even death, is intriguing. At times the risks at hand are much higher than it may occur. While interacting with the many immigrants who travel in very risky conditions to Italy, one of them told this writer that she was faced with imminent death while in her own country, so she argued that she would not want to wait for death to find her, it would be a greater honour for her if she died while working towards a solution to her problems, hence her decision to embark on that long, risky, and uncertain journey on a dinghy.

Chatty (2013) goes further to say that a distinction is made between push and pull factors: the push factors consist of economic and political insecurity in the sending country, while pull factors include perceived opportunities for political asylum, family reunion, or economic benefits in the receiving country.

Errington (2007) notes that immigration, the decision to go or not to go, is a family affair, and is rooted in a matrix of familial relationships. This decision within families, family finances, and prospects in the new world are debated within the family. Specific questions of who goes where and when, and the consequences on those left behind are all a family affair (Yeoh and En, 2013).

11. IMMIGRATION IN ITALY

Immigration has influenced the political system in Italy in a significant way. As early as the year 2004, Wang and Freeland affirmed that the wave of immigrants is presenting new challenges to each receiving country in areas such as national immigration policy and daily interaction with the new immigrants (Wang and Freeland, 2004). Immigrants are often portrayed as a threat to national and supra-national identities, security, and cultural and religious values (Giordano, 2014). According to ANSA (2014), Italy has the highest immigrant population growth in Europe. This is not without its socio-political consequences. In fact, the interior Minister Angelino Alfano (2015) declared that as long as he remains interior minister, he will never approve a law that would make even one Italian youth lose their job to an immigrant (Africa News, August 2014).

Immigrants began to enter Italy in the early 1980's, but the flow increased sizeably in the 1990's, and skyrocketed in the year 2000 (Reyneri, 2007). According to the National Institute of Statistics—Istituto Nazionale di Statistica - (ISTAT 2007), in the early 1990's, between 50,000-70,000 immigrants arrived in Italy. In the later 1900's, 156,000, and beyond 236,000 after 2001. By 2004, 36% of all the immigrants were women (Reyneri, 2007).

Italy suffers from the seriousness of immigration and sees it as a tragedy. Italy never adopted an open-minded and proactive migration policy due to the perverse connection between underground economy (black economy—mercato nero) and unauthorised immigration (Reyneri, 2007).

According to Human Rights Today (August, 2014), Italy is one of the main gateways to Europe and has since become a top destination of international immigration routes.

More than 75,000 immigrants arrived in Italy, Greece, Spain, and Malta in the first half of the year 2014 (Africa News, August 2014). Italy had a total number of 63,884 immigrants in 2013, Greece 10,080, Spain 1,000, and Malta 227. These include women and children. By August 11, 2014, 90,879 immigrants had arrived in Italy since January 1, 2014 (Africa News, August 2014).

In the first half of 2014 alone, 800 immigrants lost their lives while crossing from Libya to Italy, while in 2013, 600 of them perished. In 2012, 500 immigrants drowned in the deep seas en route to Italy (Africa News, August 2014). Some of these lost their lives through drowning, suffocation, and suspected multiple stabbing (Africa News, August 2014). Rescued immigrants reported handing over their life-savings to smugglers in order to travel in unseaworthy and overcrowded dinghies, packed into a few meters of space with no food, water, or life jackets (Africa News, August 2014).

In 1998, the law on immigration (law 39), popularly known as Martelli Law, was revised and became Turco-Napolitano Law (law 40), conceptualized to better regulate flows of immigrants to Italy, to facilitate the grouping of immigrants' families, and to strengthen the programs aimed at integrating foreigners into the Italian society (Giordano, 2014).

ISTAT (2014) demonstrates that the non European Union (EU) residents holding a residence permit as on 1st January 2014 were 3,874,724. It goes further to show that since January 2014, 15,000 immigrants from Africa alone have been rescued while crossing the Mediterranean Sea, as confirmed by the Minister of Interior Affairs, Alfano Angelino (The Guardian, 9th April, 2014).

According to Carvalho (2014),

"...xenophobia and racism re-emerged in the 1980's and early 1990 are supported by changes in the composition of immigrant groups and by the increase of political refugees in the 80's".

Carvalho (2014) further argues that *"the absence of a comprehensive EU immigration policy has left so far sufficient discretionary powers to national governments to pursue their particular interests due to the slow shift from an intergovernmental to a supra-national approach"*. Giordano (2014) affirms that immigrants are often portrayed as a threat to national and supra-national identities, security, and cultural and religious values. This would mean, affirms Ranciere (1999), that recognition would call for a holistic approach to acknowledgement, where the difference introduces change in established discourses and thus discards the pre-existing categories.

Recognition presumes an object—the other—that can be known and translated into an identity category, while acknowledgement is not about knowing the other, but about the possible relations and encounters in which individuals and communities are blurred (Giordano, 2014).

Mazzucato and Schads (2011) emphasize the fact that transnational family arrangements are prevalent worldwide because of stringent migration policies in immigrant receiving countries that make it difficult for families to migrate together, families' attempts to escape violent conflict or persecution, or family members' preferences especially where child fostering is common practice (pg. 704).

Immigrants are often considered and portrayed as victims rather than agents, according to Benslama (2000). This implies that they are forced by circumstances to free from their country. As they arrive in their host country, they negotiate a process of acculturation and ask themselves: *"Who am I?"*, *"Where do I come from?"*, *"Where do I belong?"* When immigrants travel to their host country, according to Mazzucato and Schads (2011), family practices across borders are ignored or assumed to be unfeasible. Most women immigrants leave their family members behind, with the hope of reunification once they are settled.

Acculturation entails either assimilating or integrating into the new society (Wang and Freeland, 2004). In assimilation, *"individuals acquire a second culture while letting go of their original culture"*, while in integration, *"individuals can develop healthy identities and mutually positive intergroup attitudes in a multicultural, socio-political context"* (Wang and Freeland, 2004, pg. 165). Zhou (1997) however affirms that problems arise not from the process of acculturation, but from immigration itself, because, he claims, immigration disrupts normal familial relationships. As immigrants enter a new culture, transformations gradually take place in their lives (Baker, 2007). However, as Giordano (2014) affirms, immigrants often share fragments of their stories because they live in fear, and it takes them a long time to trust those who interview or interrogate them.

During the immigration process, children of immigrants may take significant roles in the life of the family. Most of these take the role of translating for their parents, hence the shaking of authority figures and the reversal of roles. Sometimes parents do not have any control of their children especially when the children show signs of settling before their parents. The living conditions for the immigrants are often times ghastly. They sacrifice themselves in order to send money over to the families they left behind (Reyneir, 2007). When immigrants arrive in their host countries, they may find themselves doing low level low-paying jobs to survive (Chien-Juh, 2012). For this reason, continues Chien-Juh (2012), women end up taking charge of providing for their family, something that does not happen in their own countries, thus gaining power in some areas and remaining powerless in others.

Sabates-Wheeler and Koettl (2010) argue that in order to ensure immigrants' access to social security, it is important to:

- Ensure basic human and social rights to all immigrants, independent of their status
- Support immigrant networks and associations

- Develop a migration policy framework
- Provide financial/technical support and training for assisting social security institutions.

The concept of immigration in Italy is a baffling reality and efforts are still being made to contain the large number of the influx. Challenges are numerous, as the government and the society struggle to come to terms with the changes that immigrants bring with them.

12. THE COUNSELLING PROFESSION IN ITALY

The context of Italian mental health counselling is complex and full of new and old premises, events, and arguments. Counselling is a profession whose need is being felt by the society as well as by the state. Farlex (2014) holds that the way counselling has developed and is perceived in Italy results from the intersection of old cultural legacies, such as Christianity, and new challenges, such as a multicultural and multiethnic society. This reality calls for a specific, focused, and oriented approach to the counselling needs of the Italian mixed society. Farlex (2014) goes on to argue that the development of mental health counselling in Italy is also the result of the encounter between the pragmatic, optimist US counselling and the phenomenological, hermeneutic traditions of European schools.

The onset of the counselling profession in Italy dates back to post-second world war era due to the many changes that characterised this period. In spite of these needs, it is only around the 1970's that psychotherapy and counselling achieved a significant scientific status (Farlex, 2014). However, Remley, Bacchini, and Krieg (2010) affirm that the counselling profession is still in its early developmental period. No university preparation programs exist and counsellors are not employed in schools. Counsellors maintain private practices, work in agencies, and are at times employed by the government. Remley, Bacchini, and Krieg (2010) go on to indicate that there are no university programs for counsellors in Italy; there exist counselling or counselling related classes in a few university programs in psychology and science of education programs, but there are no degrees in counselling. The university of Siena offers a Masters degree program in which relationship counselling (training on emotional-communication-relational skills) is taught, and this might be the only masters-level program in Italy that approximates counsellor education graduate programs in the United States of America (Remley, Bacchini, and Krieg, 2010).

Professional counsellor Associations in Italy offer counsellor preparation programs and issue certificates of completion. These associations have existed for not more than 10 years and they tend to be centred on theoretical orientations or models of counselling. For instance, in Trieste, the Gestalt Institute is the first and only institution that offers counselling based on the Gestalt theory, a 900-hour course that lasts three years, after which candidates go through a further 530 hours of internship and supervision of 70 hours (Istituto Gestalt Trieste, undated).

In fact, in the Italian language, the equivalent word for counselling does not exist, therefore the English term is used. Counselling got listed as an unregulated profession (Consiglio Nazionale dell'Economia e del lavoro, 2005), meaning that it is acknowledged by the government. In fact, psychologists in Italy are opposed to the recognition of or the regulation of counselling as a profession (Remley, Bacchinin, and Krieg, 2010). Lack of government regulation on counselling, note Remley, Bacchini, and Krieg, means that the different associations create their own standards regarding the preparation of counsellors and the practice of counselling. The social needs and the resulting development of counselling in Italy are profoundly influenced by location, history, people, religious heritage, culture, politics, and living conditions (Remley, Bacchini, and Krieg, 2010). Indeed, the individualistic attitude that characterises most Italians has given rise to several associations run differently and independently by different people.

According to Remley, Bacchini, and Krieg (2010), the major Italian Counselling Associations include, but are not limited to:

→ *SICO* (Società Italiana Counselling), with an approximately 700 members and 60 affiliated schools.

→ *FAIP* (Federazione delle Associazioni Italiane di Psicoterapia) with 550 members and 50 affiliated schools.

→ *CNCP* (Coordinamento Nazionale Counsellor Professionisti) with 70 counselling schools.

→ *REICO* (Registro Italiano di Counselling) with about 145 members.

→ *AICO* (Associazione Italiana Counselling), a Gestalt oriented group, established in 1993 and which changed its name to AICO Federazione Nazionale in 2007, has about 300 counsellors and about 20 counselling schools.

→ *ANCORE* (Associazione Nazionale Counsellor Relazionale).

→ *SICCOL* (Società Italiana Counsellor e Operatori Olisitici) with 300 members.

The Italian Psychological Society (Società Italiana di Psicologia, 2009), claims that only licensed psychologists have the necessary training and preparation to provide counselling services. Having been registered as an unregulated profession in Italy (CNEL, 2005), the Italian government does not define the requirements for practice and does not regulate access to the profession. In the regulated professions (medicine, law, engineering, architecture, psychotherapy...) the Italian government defines the requirements for practicing the profession, including the minimum required education, period of internships, and required state exams. Members of regulated professions are included in a government-published professional register, bar, or order (Remley, Bacchini, and Krieg, 2010).

Counsellors in Italy are generally self-employed. Most of them are psychologists and psychotherapists who are also counsellors. In Italy, there is a demand for professionals who do not focus on mental illness but provide services to people who want to be listened to, want to find their own way to change their lifestyle, or want to deal more effectively with their insecurities (Remley, Bacchini, and Krieg, 2010). Remley, Bacchini, and Krieg (2010) hold that the official number of counsellors in Italy is about 10,000.

The Italian National Council of Work and Economy (CNEL) has adopted the definition of a counsellor as *"a professional who, after a 3-year training program of a specific school of theoretical orientation, can help to solve some existential difficulty that does not need a deep reorganization of personality"* (CNEL, 2005, p. 93). Counsellors therefore provide a relationship of orientation and support that activates the inner resources of a client, making them aware of the possibilities available to them, to solve their own problems, and change the point of view of their clients through empathy, acceptance, and non-judgemental attitude. Following the guidelines of the Ministry of Health for Healthy Lifestyles, counsellors create programs and projects for the prevention of social problems and discomfort (Remley, Bacchini, and Krieg, 2010).

The philosophy of counselling in Italy is reflected partially in the job description of the social worker (assistente sociale) which is to help and assist people to develop and use their own personal skills in facing the challenges and problems in their environment (Remley, Bacchini, and Krieg, 2010). Indeed, the diagnostic category in Italy does not take into account the social, cultural, and historical contexts that are often at the root of patients' symptoms (Giordano, 2014).

13. IMMIGRANTS COUNSELLING

Immigrants have specific needs that require to be addressed in specific ways. Giordano (2014) notes that immigrant counselling's potential lies in the possibility of getting closer to the experience of the other, not only with the aim to *"understand"* the client, but to recognise their discourse. In order to listen to the complexity of an immigrant's experiences, it is essential to suspend the use of psychiatric diagnosis that are like other medical practices called traditional; they are products of a specific, historical, and cultural context (Giordano, 2014). Giordano further argues that these diagnoses translate suffering into medical codes that are believed to be universally true without paying attention to the larger cultural contexts in which the individual's experience is shaped. Emphasizing theory and practice as opposed to placing a greater emphasis on understanding the client's underlying philosophical assumptions and models which espouses a global view of mankind (Bauman, 1998) often leads to failed programs. Immigrants have had to face significantly serious life experiences and even trauma, and therefore counselling approaches need to be holistic and keep in perspective these experiences. Their healing can be enhanced through their background and cultural material. Multicultural counselling helps recover the lost culture and connectedness.

Culture is complex and can have an impact on multiple levels, thus, it is difficult to have a full grasp of every client's culture. Chung (2010) argues that valuing and respecting culture, being sensitive rather than judgemental, and having an openness to learn can benefit the client-therapist relationship. Every aspect of the therapeutic process including assessment, diagnosis, treatment goals and objectives, and interventions are influenced by culture (Chambers and Smith, undated). Christopher (2001) argues that all the aspects of counselling and psychotherapy, in addition to concepts of mental illness and psychological well-being theories of personality, and both normal and abnormal development, rely on presuppositions about the nature of what the person is and what the good or ideal person should be. Chambers and Smith (undated) maintain that one of the aims of counselling is differentiation, and changes in thinking lead to this differentiation.

Research suggests that immigrants would benefit greatly from mental health professionals who work at the community level (Callaghan, 1988, Tribe, 2002a, Miller & Rasco, 2004), who facilitate access to cultural practices (Eisenbruch, 1991), who understand and work from the immigrant's worldview (Loewy, Toliver, Williams, & Keleta, 2002), and who adapt their counselling practices to a multicultural perspective (Comant, 1999, Herr, 1991, Lee, 1991, Sue & Sue, 1990, Wren, 1985).

Giordano asserts that cultural identifications are considered tools to lessen pain, to lift the weight of suffering by activating a mechanism of healing that can only be triggered through certain words, allusions, and gestures (Giordano, 2014).

Intercultural counselling translates practices, experiences, ways of expressing suffering, rituals of cure, and symptoms into the language of the culture. The aim of counselling therefore is not only to reconnect patients to their cultural backgrounds, but also to produce the conditions for the subject to speak and find ways to be in the world (Giordano, 2014). Cultural influences may be quite pervasive, widespread, and powerful in forming the basis of *"being"* for ordinary people (Kitayama and Marcos, 2000).

ROLE OF COUNSELLING PROFESSIONALS

Baker emphasizes that counselling professionals have the ethical responsibility to examine the appropriateness of their counselling interventions with culturally diverse populations (Baker, 2007). Immigrants psychotherapy and counselling highlights the backgrounds and complex histories of their patients/clients, providing a different kind of listening that approaches differences as a distance that creates a relation, that binds by way of separation (Giordano, 2014). Giordano further argues that counselling seeks to provide an intermediate space—a space of mediation between therapists' theories and techniques and the patient's ways of expressing suffering in an attempt to avoid reducing symptoms to biomedical diagnostic criteria, as well as encouraging clients to maintain relations with their respective backgrounds in forms that range from being in contact with family members, performing rituals, or speaking in another tongue to attending groups of churches.

The American Counselling Association (ACA, 2005) code of ethics states that *"Counsellors should practice only within the boundaries of their competence based on their education, training, supervised experience, state and national professional credentials and appropriate professional experience*" (pg. 9). This presupposes the need to be trained in dealing with multicultural groups as well as groups with special needs.

Sue and Sue (2003) define a culturally competent helping professional as

One who is actively in the process of becoming aware of their own assumptions about human behaviour, values, biases, preconceived notions, and personal limitations, among others. One who actively attempts to understand the world view of their culturally different client. What are the client's values and assumptions about human behaviour, biases…? One who is in the process of actively developing and practicing appropriate, relevant, and sensitive intervention strategies and skills in working with his or her culturally different client" (pp. 17-18).

Pinderlughes (1995) also offers a list of abilities that mental health professionals are encouraged to develop as a means to expand their cultural competence and to challenge their personal assumptions, values, and biases namely:

1. The ability to respect and appreciate the values, beliefs, and practices of all clients, including those who are culturally different, and to perceive such individuals through their own cultural lens rather than that of the practitioner.
2. Knowledge of the specific values, beliefs, and cultural practices of clients.
3. The ability to be comfortable with difference in others and to avoid becoming trapped in anxious or defensive behaviour in response to differences.
4. The ability to change false beliefs, assumptions, and stereotypes.
5. The ability to think flexibly and to recognise that one's own way of thinking and behaving is not the only way to think and behave.
6. The ability to behave flexibly as demonstrated by the readiness to take the steps required to sort through general knowledge about a cultural group and to perceive the specific ways in which such knowledge applies or does not apply to a given client (p. 133).

Potocky-Tripodi (2002) affirms that in order to help immigrants effectively, one must be aware of one's own cultural and ethnic background, examine prejudices and stereotypes, value and respect other cultures and cultural differences, be knowledgeable about culture and characteristics of ethnic groups, and stand the influences that affect these groups. From this consideration, it takes time and effort to be an effective and efficient multiculturally competent health worker.

Immigrants' lives, stories, and histories are unknown, therefore professional health workers need to tread the ground carefully. Flexibility, creativity, openness, and self-awareness are prerogative in order to *"develop programs that meet the culture-specific needs"* (Wang and Freeland, 2004).

In Italy, culture oriented programs are lacking and cultural sensitivity is only now becoming a pertinent issue that calls for attention and change of direction in therapy.

It is, however, crucial for mental health workers to provide effective and culturally competent services to immigrants according to the National Child Traumatic Stress Network (2005). Cultural competence is being aware of cultural values and interventions used in planning and implementing services to the client (Fong, 2011).

Taking time to develop relationships and gain an understanding of the client's culture and values, making the effort to provide interpretative services, to examine reactions to cultural differences, and contextualizing services to assist the client in ways meaningful to them (Chung, 2010) is what any cultural mental health worker needs to build on. It is important to draw out clients' strengths, coping mechanisms, spirituality, social support, and other resources in order to assist them overcome and deal with present mental health challenges (Chung, 2010). In addition to needing a comprehensive understanding of the nature of culture and its relationship to the self, therapists must be able to think culturally (Chambers and Smith, u.d). Chambers and Smith (u.d.) further describe hermeneutics as a framework for thinking about the ways culture permeates every dimension of a client's world. Humans are expressions of culture long before they develop a sense of themselves as an *"I"* (Bruner, 1990). Humans can not detach themselves from culture—any distance one gets from their culture is always temporary and provisional (Chambers and Smith, u.d.). Guignon (1984) affirms that *"we can best know ourselves not by inward turning and introspection in the manner of Descartes, but by catching sight of ourselves as we are engaged and preoccupied in everyday contexts"* (pg. 232).

Culture may be determinant in how mental health issues are defined, for instance, *"going mad"*, meaning one is crazy or possessed by evil spirits, is the expression of mental illness in East Africa. As will be explained later in this literature review, this approach to mental illness affects the way immigrants view mental health services and their reactions to them.

Although each individual has a somewhat unique life history and a particular perspective within the culture, the individual's life history unfolds within the possibilities set forth by the shared background meanings that culture provides (Chambers and Smith, u.d.)

Different strategies of stories might be a defence/coping mechanism, telling stories to suit conditions, or represent multiple realities, ensuing from trauma, pointing towards dissociation. This will be explored further in this study under the chapter on some general common characteristics of the Eastern African culture. For instance, silence could be considered as conveying not the absence of speech or the vacuum of sense, but a narrative in itself. Furthermore, having to narrate life experiences to several people is considered a way leading to disintegration, hence the desire to avoid it as much as it is possible. This gives rise to the need for cultural negotiators whose aim is to facilitate people to express what they are experiencing so that the client can resort to different aetiologies and techniques of cure and borrow from both those of the host country as well as the home country. Cultural negotiators juggle words and become translators of concepts, adept enough at the task to make the words and concepts resonate and reverberate in the language of the other (Giordano, 2014).

Translation is a crucial process in counselling immigrants. According to Giordano (2014), the translators' task is principally to accept the difference and multiplicity of languages and find a *"somewhat provisional way of coming to terms with the foreignness of languages"*, which leads to the transformation of both languages.

Getting to know the immigrant's name and its significance is a way to create a relationship with the person. The name in the African context has a remarkable significance (Kenyatta, 1965). This will be detailed in the section on the general characteristics of the East African culture.

ETHNO-PSYCHIATRY

Giordano (2014) dedicates significant attention to ethno-psychiatry which she considers crucial in dealing with immigrants' issues. She says that ethno-psychiatry provides culturally sensitive therapeutic services to immigrants in addition to supervising the world of social workers, health practitioners, and other personnel who work with them. Here, difference is recognized and respected. Giordano further confirms that the client's symptoms are not to be translated into a diagnostic category. In this case, difference is reduced to the familiar—the diagnosis. In her research experience in group homes of immigrants in Italy, Giordano concluded that all agents involved in the integration of immigrants adopt a model of translation to be able to understand and relate to the other's differences.

Giordano (2014) affirms that ethno-psychiatry uses different mechanisms of translation to make sure that the foreigner's story and language is translated in its unique, singular difference. Ethno-psychiatry locates client's symptoms in larger political, cultural, and historical contexts of colonial and post-colonial domination.

In Italy, notes Giordano, Frantz Fanon, Franco Basaglia, Ernesto de Martino, and Tobie Nathan have all advocated for an acknowledgement of differences and ethno-psychiatry.

IMMIGRANTS' CONDITIONS

Immigrants oftentimes find themselves dealing with so many complexities and this does not make counselling or therapy easier. Giordano (2014) argues that it is easier to collect accounts of immigrants' lives in their host country than to find out about their lives before they migrated. When one tries to get to those stories, they are often impenetrable. This may be due to past experiences of violence or abuse, persecution, torture, war, fear, among other traumas. Stories about home often recall an inhospitable place, other times *"home"* is an opaque reality that has been overshadowed by the urge to assimilate, integrate, and become other in ways that live up to the receiving society's standards of behaviour and desire (Giordano, 2014). Immigrants need assurance and acceptance, to express themselves in their own terms, and confidence that their references are not foreign to the therapist.

Immigrants express a barrage of fears. In their research, Groleau and Kirmayer (2004) found out some of the fears immigrants experience, namely, fear of getting old or sick in a strange country, the loss of a sense of belonging and usefulness to the family and the society, the pain of losing membership in the extended family and their respective status within it, and the humiliation of depending on the government for food and lodging, and spending money.

Colangelo (2009) further differentiates between repression and dissociation. In repression, the memories are pushed down into the unconscious, whereas in dissociation, the memories are encoded but remain in an alter-nate stream of consciousness where retrieval is possible but only under certain circumstances or conditions (pg. 109).

Distrust leads to withholding information. People however find relief and therapeutic benefit in recounting their stories. Groleau and Kirmayer (2004) expound this concept by saying that narrating one's story *"moves the body through these spaces and times in ways that make sense of suffering while striving to protect the individual from further injury, leading to the organization of one's disarrayed traumatic events, creating a coherent sense of self"*.

Many Africans believe in personal karma. However, Maxwell (1993) found out that having a sense of personal responsibility for the experience of trauma may result in poor coping and psychological outcomes. Lee (2007) emphasizes this concept by saying that religious support can be a potential protective factor in mitigating depressive symptoms and enhancing life satisfaction.

Most immigrants are considered helpless and subjects in need of protection and guidance by their host country. This statement could be true to a certain extent, but they are people with a history, with a life, with aspirations, and with remarkable resilience. Hidden behind the protective shell is a person in need of understanding, acceptance, and unconditional support.

14. MENTAL HEALTH NEEDS OF IMMIGRANT WOMEN

Giordano (2014), after her research on immigration and psychiatry in Italy, concluded that the mental health of immigrants raises unresolved questions about psychiatry, a critical frame for exploring the legacies of colonial violence and post-colonial transition. Immigrants face a plethora of resettlement challenges including little choice and control of their own fate and their experiences with culture shock, homesickness, depression, distress, stress-related illnesses, post-traumatic stress disorder, exit and post-entry trauma, and acculturation stress (Khamphakdy-Brown et. al. 2006).

Gong-Guy et. al. (1991) and Musser-Granski and Carillo (1997) consider that some of the barriers to mental health services that immigrants face include:

- The lack of availability of counsellors who are trained cross-culturally
- A shortage in bi-lingual bi-cultural mental health personnel
- A lack of training in cross-cultural diagnostic skills

- A lack of training of clinicians on the use of interpreters in a clinical setting
- A lack of interpreters who have received formalized preparation.

The intricacies of translation complicate the real immigrants' story by revealing some facts and masking others. Written documents dispossess the subject of their stammering voice, fragmented memory, and opaque story (Giordano, 2014). Giordano goes further on to affirm that words are re-articulated, transformed, partly erased, partly produced, transmuted, and rendered by the cultural negotiator.

Mental health issues may not be typically of primary focus of immigrants on arrival in their host country (Baker, 2007). Psychological issues are rarely discussed unless a client shows visible symptoms; most common complaints are somatic in nature (Lin, 1986). Indeed, mental health assessment is rarely done when immigrants arrive in their host country, despite their background. Exploring and understanding the experiences of women can be helpful in developing and structuring counselling programs that can provide psychological assistance and social support (Baker, 2007). Weine et. al. (2004) note that, faced with a foreign environment with little or no emotional sources of support, immigrants are faced with loneliness, traumatic memories, depression, and anxiety. Often, as Tribe (2005) argues, immigrants do not access mental health services due to the stigma associated with being referred to a mental health professional.

Some of the symptoms that immigrants portray may be both an individual expression and a political and historical commentary on what crossing borders does to the psyche and the body (Giordano, 2014).

Italy uses cultural mediators that are fluent in the immigrant's language and are present during sessions to provide cultural and linguistic translation (Giordano, 2014), but often these cultural mediators are not trained in mental health issues and the mere fact that they speak the same language of the immigrant does not necessarily qualify them for the job. For this reason, there are risks of not communicating the real mental health situation of the immigrant.

This writer worked as a cultural negotiator for two years in Italy and it was evident that the need was purely linguistic. When immigrants presented some psychological or psychiatric problems, they were not well addressed or they merely were misunderstood, hence, erroneous diagnosis and incorrect treatment.

15. CROSS-CULTURAL COUNSELLING

Culture is a broad term that is becoming more and more relevant now as the world becomes a closely communicable global village. Culture impacts how people view the world around them, including values, belief systems, behaviours, customs, as well as one's view of life and society. Cross cultural counselling occurs whenever the cultural heritage of the therapist and the client differ (Mojab, C. G. 2006). Cultural differences need to be attended to if counsellor/client relationship is to be effectively therapeutic.

Cross-cultural psychology is the critical and comparative study of cultural effects on human psychology (Shiraev and Levy, 2004). A cross cultural approach not only considers human behaviour as a result or product of cultural influences, but it also considers people as free, active, and rational individuals who are capable of exercising their own will. This empowers people to take responsibility for their actions and thus creates the knowledge needed to carry this out.

Human motivation, emotion, thought, and reactions cannot be separated from human activity, which is determined by individual, socio-economic, environmental, political, and cultural conditions and also changes these conditions (Shiraev and Levy, 2004). In order to address the real needs of a client, it is necessary to have a holistic view of the person, since the person is an embodiment of all these characteristics—the whole person is not merely a sum total of the different parts, therefore disintegration is a disservice to the person.

Counsellors working with cross-cultural situations need to constantly be aware of their own world view and cultural heritage in order to be effective in their work. As global movement of the human race becomes more and more rampant, and the boundaries kept in place in the past gradually shrink, people's needs also take a different form, and addressing these needs not only efficiently but also effectively ensures growth and social change. Counsellors and therapists need to have a good understanding of the biases and prejudices that characterize people, even themselves, as well as be empathic with people who are different than themselves. There is also need to check out prejudices and biases that characterize counselling theories and concepts, as well as strive to see clients as individuals who come from a society that has its own characteristic heritage (Sue & Sue, 2003).

Hypso Risk Advisor Journal (2008) argues that lack of sensitivity to a client's unique background and experiences can result to miscommunication, a client's refusal to participate, and eventually an ineffective counselling relationship. Such relationships can also lead to resentments.

Language barriers are often the most complex challenges that such relationships experience. For instance, words may have different meanings, and the way a therapist perceives a word or phrase may be totally different than the way the client intends it. This has often been the cause of gross misunderstanding among professionals with their clients. It is important to seek to comprehend the different dynamics that characterize a person that may be different than us. Therapists need to understand not only the meaning of words or expressions, but the individual as a whole in order to be able to pull and pool all the aspects together and to make the therapeutic relationship effective. Effective counsellors need to constantly seek clarification of words used by clients in order to grasp what the intention of the client is, as opposed to trying to interpret clients' words in their own way (HYPSO Journal, 2008).

HYPSO Journal (2008) emphasizes that culturally competent counsellors invite open and honest dialogue about race and ethnicity in their therapeutic sessions and use professional resources and activities to develop their counselling skills with racially and ethnically diverse clients.

Becoming culturally competent in working with diverse populations is a complex interaction of many dimensions that involve broad theoretical, conceptual, research, and practice issues (Sue & Sue, 2012). Sue affirms that helping others requires understanding worldviews influenced by socio-economic status, race, and ethnicity, gender, among others, on both cognitive and emotional levels. People's unconscious social conditioning makes people associate differences with defiance, pathology, and lesser value in society. Stereotypes also harm racial minorities.

It is not possible to fully understand the psychology of a certain people without a complete understanding of the social, historic, political, ideological, and religious premises that have shaped the people of this group (Shiraev & Levy, 2004).

A holistic view of persons implies willingness to cross boundaries created by labels and categorization which includes beliefs, values, ritual, customs, and other types of behaviours (Van Beek, 1996). Van Beek goes on to affirm that counsellors need to be actively sensitive to the inter-related processes at work in the life of the client, the expectations of the counsellor in a particular encounter, the client's place on a gender role and identity awareness scale, the variations within cultural codes, the manifestation of class differences, the possibility of other different world views emerging in the interaction, the influence of inter-generational tensions as a result of cultural traditions, and the nature of culture as processes that provide meaning (1996).

According to Repetto (2002), cross cultural counselling is defined as psycho-pedagogical intervention based on metatheory which

- Recognizes that all counselling approaches and theories are developed in a specific inter-active context
- Refers to inter-action in which two or more participants come from different cultures
- Includes any combination of the techniques involved in a culture
- Is characterised by professional assistance with the knowledge, skills, and attitudes that are culturally appropriate
- Recognizes the use of western and non western approaches in assistance
- The changes involve not only the introduction of cross cultural counselling programs but also the inclusion of this approach in the curriculum and in all the dimensions of the educational system such as teaching techniques, motivation, grouping, student assessment, and teacher training.

CROSS CULTURAL COMPETENCIES

Humans without culture would be mere unworkable monstrosities. Human behaviour is a complex function of both biology and culture, and the boundaries between the two are uncertain, varying according to domain and context (Jahoda, 2002).

Cross-cultural counselling competency is seen as being the capacity to understand the cultural dynamics of clients and to respond to each of these cultural aspects in a way that facilitates its development (Sue, Arredondo, and McDavis, 1992). This looks at three dimensions, namely, the subject's attitudes and beliefs, knowledge, and skills.

The *subject's attitudes and beliefs* relate to the attitudes of the counsellor and their beliefs concerning race, culture, ethnic groups, gender, and sexual orientations; the need to assess prejudices and stereotypes and to develop counselling that is positive towards multiculturalism, and the way in which the values and thoughts of counsellors can affect the counselling and therapy (Repetto, 2001/2002). Therapists recognize the limits of their multicultural competency and expertise, as well as their sources of discomfort with differences that exist between themselves and clients in terms of race, ethnicity, and culture (Arredondo, et. al. 1996).

The second dimension relates to the *capacity of the therapist to know their own approach to the world and to become an expert in different cultures.* Knowledge and specific information on the cultures of the clients is not enough, a therapist needs to also understand socio-political influences. Therapists need to have knowledge about their social impact on others, communication style differences, how their style may clash with or foster the counselling process with persons from other cultures and how to anticipate the impact it may have on others (Arredondo, et. al. 1996). Therapists also need to learn from their clients. The client is the central point in therapy, therefore their situation should guide the therapist in the therapeutic relationship.

The third dimension relates to the *specific skills and capacities* (techniques for intervention and strategies) that are needed for working with groups in different cultures (Repetto, 2001/2002). Therapists seek out educational, consultative, and training experiences to improve their understanding and effectiveness in working with culturally different populations, in being able to recognize the limits of their competencies, seeking consultation, further training or education, referring out to more qualified individuals or resources, and engaging in a combination of these factors (Arredondo, et. al. 1996).

Applying counselling theory to cultures with different assumptions is likely to be problematic in that all the underlying theoretical assumptions stem from specific contexts that may not necessarily reflect the clientele at hand. However, the competent therapist is the one who provides an effective therapeutic relationship, irrespective of the client's background. Nevertheless, the ability to convey empathy in a culturally consistent and meaningful manner may be the crucial variable to engage the client (Patterson, 1996). Multicultural counselling and therapy promotes a mutual dialogue.

It essential for counsellors to understand the cultural dynamics of clients and to respond to each of these aspects in a way that facilitates its development (Sue, 2012). Counsellors' attitudes and beliefs concerning race, culture, ethnic groups, gender, and sexual orientations are important in cross cultural counselling. They also need to know their own approaches to the world and to become experts on different cultures.

Sue and co-workers (2012) list a few competencies namely:

- Knowing one's own theories, values, and prejudices

- Understanding clients' cultural differences
- Developing strategies for intervention and appropriate techniques
- Being able to define an organization that is efficient from a cross cultural point of view.

Lago (2006) also details some characteristic competencies in cross-cultural counselling including training, identity development and how it impacts on therapy, ethnic matching, and the use of interpreters, the implications of therapist identity, avoiding discriminatory behaviour, research findings, and culturally sensitive supervision.

ROLE OF THE CROSS-CULTURAL COUNSELLOR

Counsellors need to exercise the many skills required for becoming empathic supporters for their clients. The counsellor's approach is contextualized, in that behaviour can only be understood within the context in which it takes place (Repetto, 2002).

The APA (1993) holds that those who provide psychological services need knowledge and skills for evaluation and intervention. They must recognize that ethnicity and culture are significant parameters for understanding psychological processes. They should consider, when taking action, not only the results of differential diagnoses but also the beliefs and values of the client and of their community, and should familiarize themselves with the native practices and beliefs and respect them (pp. 45-47).

Counsellors working with cross cultural populations need to empower people to be their own experts on matters relating to them (Gilbert, 2001). The counsellor therefore is seen as a stepping stone towards the growth of the client, as opposed to a clutch to lean on.

THE IMPORTANCE OF LANGUAGE IN
CROSS CULTURAL COUNSELLING

Language is a very important and crucial aspect in cross cultural counselling. Words have different meanings to different people, and those words used by theorists may mean one thing to them and another to a different person. For instance, many common words in counselling such as *"stress"*, *"anxiety"* … have no direct equivalent translation in most African languages. Descriptions of emotions is also another factor. For instance, in most of East African languages, to *"feel"* does not have a direct equivalent, as it is referred to as to *"hear"*. The only other different way *"hearing"* is used is when one is ill.

Emotions are not openly talked about in most African cultures; therefore, it becomes difficult to put some aspects of the client into words, let alone suggesting different uses of words.

Individual approach to counselling could be a new concept for most of the African societies. For instance, people hardly talk in terms of *"I"* but *"we"*. In this way, it becomes difficult to express oneself freely, since the collective aspect of most Africans takes centre stage, and to talk about oneself is frowned upon and considered egocentric.

Counsellors therefore need to document sessions and note the steps they take in understanding the client's individual culture. They need to avoid making any assumptions on the client. For instance, eye contact is considered rude in some East African ethnic groups. In counselling, eye contact is an important communication aspect in the therapeutic relationship.

There is no better way to conclude this work than to mirror what Van Beek (1996) says about cross cultural counselling. This type of counselling, according to Van, aims at encouraging persons away from brokenness and toward wholeness in all areas of their life. Wholeness includes reconciliation and the restoration of communication in personal relations, acceptance of one's own talents and shortcomings, integration of one's value system-in-process, a harmonious experience of one's faith, as well as behaviour consistent with one's self-concept, values, faith, and the nature of one's relationships (Van Beek, 1996).

Almost all of the clients in this research have experienced some form of trauma, and there is a close connection between their culture and the way they live their traumatic experiences. Many of them may experience both physical as well as psychological trauma effects. An important aspect to consider in counselling is the fact that different cultures deal with trauma differently, and therefore therapists need to be conversant with the various ways clients have experienced and have dealt with trauma in their cultural context. Such groups may be used to alternative means of healing namely medicine men, traditional healers, culture specific rituals, conventional medical practices, and community based practices that offer forms of social and emotional support for the person suffering the trauma (Wilson & Tang, 2010) as well as prayers and religious rituals. This renders the therapeutic relationship quite complicated in that the counsellor needs to be well aware of these factors. Clients may at first be suspicious of the counsellor because they do not know what to expect. It is the counsellor's responsibility to help the clients experience trust in the relationship and consequently start to talk about their experiences.

16. MULTICULTURAL COUNSELLING AND THERAPY

Since its beginning with Freud, the field of therapy and counselling has changed significantly. For a significant amount of time, Freudian theory dominated most of therapy, and most of the therapists who were trained had to go through psychoanalysis. Later, cognitive-behavioural theory and existential-humanistic theory came into use. Roger's person-centred theory brought in a more humanistic view to the field of psychodynamic theories, along with Maslow, who both focused their attention on the importance of the person and relationship in therapy. These theories give minimal attention to the cultural base of helping.

Multicultural Counselling and Therapy (MCT) does not discount the importance of any theoretical orientation, rather, MCT recognizes, adapts, and supports all approaches to therapy (Ivey, et. al. 2002). Individuals present themselves with specific challenges within specific circumstances, and these need to be addressed as per need, tailor-making the treatment plan to fit every specific individual. Working with only one approach may not adequately address all problems, and an umbrella approach is bound to leave remarkable grey areas. A holistic approach is better placed to effect the desired outcome of treatment. Issues such as race, ethnicity, gender, age, socio-economic status, religion, lifestyle, and sexual orientation are crucial when establishing a therapeutic relationship with clients (Corey, 2001).

With the current globalization trend witnessed in the current world, diversification is happening at a fast rate, and clients' needs are becoming increasingly diverse, requiring a culture-centred metatheory. Understanding the cultural and socio-political context of a client's behaviour is essential to accurate assessment, interpretation, and treatment (Sue, et. al. 1996). However, each person has many different *"cultures"* or *"identities"*, with each identity becoming relevant at different times and places, therefore MCT emphasizes both the way people are different from and similar to other people (Pederson, 1994).

MCT recognizes the value of traditional methods of helping as long as they are employed in a culturally meaningful and culturally sensitive fashion (Ivey, et. al. 2002). MCT begins with the assessment of the client, family, and cultural experience. It seeks to find how the client constructs and makes meaning in the world, stressing an egalitarian, non-hierarchical therapist-client relationship. The main issue in MCT is to work with the client in a culturally sensitive way to find a technique, strategy, theory, or set of theories that meet the client's needs (Ivey, et. al. 2002).

MCT needs to include differences based on religion, sexual orientation, socio-economic factors, age, gender, physical handicaps, and levels of acculturation and assimilation (Sue, et. al. 1992).

Repetto (2001/2002) details five assumptions that can be identified in multiculturalism, namely:

→ Multiculturalism accepts the existence of many points of view, none of which are considered good or bad, correct or incorrect.

→ Multiculturalism involves social constructionism, in that people construct their world through social processes (historical, cultural, and social experiences) which contain cultural symbols and metaphors.

→ Multiculturalism is contextualistic in that conduct can only be understood within the context in which it takes place. This challenges the psychological and counselling theories that arise out of a specific cultural context.

→ Multiculturalism offers different approaches to the world because each perspective captures a different, valid approach.

→ Multiculturalism defends a relational sense for language rather than just a representational one, because language has a high correlation with culture and the perception of reality. The relational approach allows truths and realities to be seen beyond western scientific traditions.

→ Sue and co-workers summarise the characteristics of multiculturalism in ten ways namely:

→ It values cultural pluralism, teaching the value of diversity

→ It is a matter of social justice, cultural democracy, and equity

→ It helps people to acquire the attitudes, knowledge, and skills that are necessary for functioning efficiently in a democratic, pluralistic society, and for interacting, negotiating, and communicating with people from different backgrounds

→ It is more than just race, gender, class, and ethnicity, and includes diversity of religion, national origin, sexual orientation, skills and handicaps, age, geographic origin, among others

→ It welcomes contributions and achievements of one's own culture and that of others

→ It is an essential component of analytical thought

→ It respects and values other approaches, but is not neutral to values, thus implying a commitment towards changing social conditions

→ It brings change on an individual, organizational, and social levels

→ It implies tension, dissatisfaction, and a will to face matters with honesty

→ It means positive individual, community, and social attainments because it values inclusion, cooperation, and movement towards attainment of objectives.

These characteristics imply that since all counselling approaches and theories have been developed in specific contexts, they were originally adapted to the local cultural needs of the clientele in question. Multiculturalism seeks to be inclusive, and deals with each person in relation to their cultural context.

The American Psychology Association (APA, 1993) states that those who provide psychological services need knowledge and skills for evaluation and intervention, must recognize that ethnicity and culture are significant parameters for understanding psychological processes, should consider, when taking action, not only the results of differential diagnoses, but also the beliefs and values of the client and of their community, and should familiarize themselves with the native practices and beliefs and respect them (pgs. 45—47).

RELATIVITY
Although people belong to the same world, each person makes different sense of what they see. Each person constructs meaning in a unique way. It is essential for therapists to understand the challenges and problems the clients face, the sources of strength that help sustain them through difficult times (Ivey, et. al. 2002). Maintaining a flexible and open-minded attitude by the therapist is paramount in working towards the attainment of the objectives in a therapeutic relationship.

Ivey et. al (2002) notes that when therapists embrace the notion of relativity in their work, they acknowledge that:

• Clients' stories represent different ways of constructing meaning about their lives and the challenges they are experiencing

- The theories that therapists have historically used when working with clients reflect a host of cultural biases, values, and beliefs about mental health and do not represent universal truths about psychological wellness
- There are numerous approaches to helping persons who are experiencing personal distress in their lives.

It is essential to enter into contact with a client's world for a time and join them on their journey, which leads to new understanding and respect for how their worlds differ from the therapist's own.

MULTICULTURAL INTENTIONALITY

Intentional individuals can be described as having a sense of capability (Ivey, et. al. 2002). People who act with intentionality are able to generate alternative behaviours in a given situation and approach a problem from different vantage points. Such people respond to situations in a dynamic way and work towards long term goals in a therapeutic relationship. Intentional living occurs in a cultural context. Ivey et. al. (2002) describe three major abilities through which cultural expertise and intentionality are experienced:

- The ability to generate a maximum number of thoughts, words, and behaviours to communicate with self and others within a given culture: Immobility is the inability to act intentionally and resolve problems—feeling fixated in one place. In this approach, a multiculturally oriented therapist examines a client's historical, cultural, and social contexts, giving special attention to the different modes of being that exist among different cultural groups. The aim of this approach is to increase response capacity and the ability to generate or create new behaviours and thoughts.
- The ability to generate thoughts, words, and behaviours necessary to communicate with a variety of diverse groups and individuals. Both the therapist and the client need to communicate within their own culture and learn to understand other cultures. Some theories may not be effective in some cultural settings. The goals and the process, style, and techniques of traditional helping may be inappropriate for those of minority cultures. It is advantageous to be prepared in many theories in order to address the client's needs effectively depending on the need at hand.

- The ability to formulate plans, act on many possibilities existing in a culture, and reflect on these actions. Generating new behaviours is necessary, but as important is action oriented towards change.

MCT is concerned with counselling and psychotherapy as liberation, thus, the viewing of self in relation to others and to social and cultural contexts (Ivey, et. al. 2002).

GOALS OF MCT

The main goal of multicultural counselling therapy is to be intentionally cultural, thus, the ability of the therapist to create options with the client, formulate plans, and act on many possibilities existing in a culture and reflect on these actions. MCT also identifies frameworks and concrete helping skills and strategies that are culturally sensitive. MCT is more of a method than a theory, and begins with the awareness of self and the pervasiveness of culture throughout the therapeutic process (Seah, 2007). MCT aims at freeing the individuals, families, groups, and organizations so that they can generate new ways of thinking feeling, and acting, and thereby live intentionally (Ivey, et. al. 2002).

ROLE OF THE THERAPIST

According to Ivey, et. al. (2002), therapists and counsellors need to be highly competent in traditional theories, need to have developed an understanding of MCT metatheory, and over time develop an understanding of the specific needs, wishes, and developmental histories of many highly diverse multicultural groups (pg. 360). The therapist also needs to understand the impact of religion on the client, and how this is usually used in coping with difficult situations. This means a high degree of openness and readiness to venture into specific areas of the life of the client in order to be able to better empathize with the client. The multiculturally competent therapist needs to be able to accurately assess and use interventions that are consistent with the racial identity development of the client (Roysircar, & Gard, in press).

SUMMARY OF MCT

While emphasizing the importance of multicultural approach to therapy, it may be essential to recognize that universal human themes unite people in spite of whatever factors separate them. Irrespective of one's culture, everyone needs to receive and give love, to makes sense of their psychological pain, and to make significant connections with others. It is important however, to explore any difference that has the capacity to create a gap in understanding namely age, gender, lifestyle, socio-economic status, religion, and sexual orientation (Corey, 2001).

MCT focuses on the individual in a familial and cultural context (Ivey, et. al. 2002). This seeks to show clients how their difficulties may be tied to societal and social justice issues concerning race or ethnicity, gender, or socio-economic status.

MCT is a practical approach to therapy, as it forces therapists to deal with realities of difference. The very complexity and high demands of MCT are simultaneously its strength and weakness, providing challenges and opportunities (Ivey, et. al. 2002).

Multicultural counselling needs to consider the client's context (family and society), cultural beliefs and practices, communication, and the entire *"way of doing things"* in order to address real needs.

Richard Nelson-Jones (2002), in his article Diverse Goals for Multicultural Counselling and Therapy, details the twelve goals for multicultural counselling and therapy namely:

- → Reconciliation
- → Support
- → Coping with post-traumatic stress
- → Assisting acculturation and assimilation
- → Avoiding further marginalization
- → Addressing racial and cultural discrimination
- → Assisting clients to manage close cross-cultural relationships
- → Assisting clients to manage inter-generational conflict
- → Assisting long stay transients and expatriates
- → Assisting with gender roles and equality issues
- → Attaining higher levels of development
- → The formation of the good society.

MCT therefore aims at improving the client's life, inspiring them to change and become better people, and improve their relationships.

17. TRAUMA HEALING AND RECOVERY

The past I need to amend.
All traumas that had preceded.

In the hopes to transcend -
It first needs to be conceded.

In order for me to properly heal -
I need to acknowledge past pain.
Such is this life, not always ideal.
Still, I think there is much to regain.

I try my best not to be bitter.
There's so much to uphold.
They won't call me a quitter!!
The future can not be foretold.

So I'll face the past in the present.
Then I shall leave it far behind
No longer will it rot or ferment!
For once it shall not be confined!
Sandra Wyllie

According to Peter Levine (2006), trauma is a basic rupture, a loss of connection to ourselves, to our families, and to the world. The loss, although enormous, is difficult to appreciate because it happens gradually. People adjust to these small changes, sometimes oblivious of their presence. Trauma is not an ailment or a disease, but the by product of an instinctively instigated, altered state of consciousness, where a person enters into the survival mode when they perceive a threat to their life (Levine, 2006). People get stuck in this survival mode if they feel overwhelmed by the threat and are unable to defend themselves. If this state is left untreated, it begins to form the symptoms of trauma, which can invade every aspect of a person's life. Trauma repeats itself in symptoms and regressions, punctuated by multiple temporalities and interruptions that resist direct access. Giordano (2014) posits that one characteristic of trauma is that a person ignores the existence of a past traumatic event in the sense that they don't hold a distinct rational memory of it. However, this memory makes itself visible in repetitions in acting out old patterns of behaviours, and it operates despite the subject being unaware of it. A client, notes Beneduce (2010), is possessed by this memory; it has a life of its own, and cannot be reduced to a single narrative, and there is no coherence of facts.

Michenbaum (1997) defines a traumatic event as *"so extreme or severe, so powerful, harmful, and/or threatening that it demands extraordinary coping efforts"* (pg.17). Another definition by Briere and Scott (2006) see psychological trauma as something that is extremely upsetting and at least temporarily overwhelms the individual's internal resources.

DSM-IV-TR (2000) indicates that experiencing threat of death or serious injury to self, witnessing death, injury or threat of another person, and learning about an unexpected or violent death, serious harm, or threat of death or injury of a family member or a close person, are considered traumatic events.

Trauma is a reality in life. Many people have experienced one form of trauma or the other. In trauma, the mind becomes profoundly altered (Levine, 1997). The initial reaction to trauma is to protect the mind from emotional reaction through dissociation and denial, which allows a person to go through the situation without crushing under its weight. At the same time, one prepares themselves to fight or take flight, the body tenses, is characterised by fear, and can freeze. When everything goes back to normal, the body relaxes and the mind allows itself to go through the motions of the trauma. If this relaxation is thwarted, trauma's effects become fixated and the subject becomes traumatised. The instinctive reaction to trauma is to banish it from consciousness. Some experiences are too terrible to verbalize, and people tend to bury them and continue living as if they had not occurred. It is also difficult for people to put their traumatic experiences into words, and often tend to see just one aspect of the traumatic experiences at a time.

Spinoza (1632—1677) noted:

Whatever increases, decreases, limits, or extends the body's power of action, increases, decreases, limits, and extends the mind's power of action. And whatever increases, decreases, limits, and extends the mind's power of action, increases, decreases, limits, and extends the body's power of action.

Trauma generates pervasive fear and feelings of helplessness. Unfortunately, trauma is on the increase in most parts of the world, both in the so called developing as well as developed world. Cohen Martin (2000), in his article *Ten Steps to Healing from Trauma*, argues that trauma victims may go through persistent re-experience of the event in the form of nightmares, flashbacks etc., avoidance of people or events that remind them of the trauma, and hyper-arousal, thus jumpiness, feeling on edge, and irritability, among others. This is referred to as Post Traumatic Stress Disorder.

Trauma disrupts the body's natural equilibrium, freezing one in a state of hyper-arousal and fear (Robinson, et. al. 2013). One's nervous system gets stuck in high gear while trying to protect themselves from collapsing. Some of the ladies interviewed had experienced deep trauma and at one point, one lady froze while recounting her experiences in the dingy which brought her to Italy. She started shaking and requested to postpone the session in order for her to compose herself.

Trauma is both objective (exposure to a traumatizing event) and subjective (personal response through feelings of fear, helplessness, and horror) (Allen, 2005). The interference of the past to the present is one of the main problems traumatized people experience, like the lady cited above. The effects of trauma are not necessarily all psychiatric. It is possible to find traumatized people who are cynical, suspicious, bitter, vengeful, and with no hope or faith.

EMOTIONAL AND PSYCHOLOGICAL TRAUMA

Extraordinarily stressful experiences that shatter one's sense of security, making one feel helpless and vulnerable; can lead to emotional and psychological trauma. However, any situation that leaves one feeling overwhelmed and alone can be traumatic, albeit not involving any physical harm (Robinson et. al, 2013). Robinson et. al. (2013) go on to affirm that it is not the objective facts that determine whether an event is traumatic, but one's subjective emotional experience of the event. The more frightened and helpless one feels, the more likely they are to be traumatised. One lady actually shared about how her father used to beat her when she was growing up. She lived this experience in a traumatic way and had problems relating with men in her entire life. She confirmed that her failure to get married is due to her experience of horror under the tyranny of her father.

Emotional and psychological trauma can be caused by single-blow, one-time event such as a horrible accident, a natural disaster, or a violent attack, while at the same time trauma can also stem from ongoing, relentless stress (Robinson, et. al. 2013). Not all potentially traumatic events lead to lasting emotional or psychological damage. It is possible for some people to rebound quickly from traumatic experiences, as it is also possible for some others to be devastated by experiences that may appear less upsetting. Usually, people are more susceptible to trauma if they are already under duress and have recently suffered a series of stressful experiences. Two ladies shared how the uncertainty of the basic needs while in Italy caused reactions similar to those they experienced when they were being physically abused by their father, especially when he used to come home drunk and violent. They appeared susceptible to further experiences of uncertainty because they were still very fragile.

The ordinary human response to danger is a complex, integrated system of reactions, encompassing both body and mind. Threat initially arouses the sympathetic nervous system, causing the person in danger to feel an adrenalin rush or go into a state of alert (Herman, 1997). This propels one to take action, either fight or take flight. These changes in arousal, attention, perception, and emotion are normal, adaptive reactions. Traumatic reactions occur when action is of no avail (Herman, 1997). This causes the human mind to become overwhelmed and disorganized. Herman (1997) goes on to affirm that traumatic events produce profound and lasting changes in physiological arousal, emotion, cognition, and memory. Traumatic events may also alter the good communication between these faculties, throwing the person into disarray. This may lead one to become disconnected and experience a sense of distance. Herman concludes that trauma tears apart the complex system of self-protection that people have, and may lead to post traumatic stress disorder. Most traumatised people may act as if their nervous systems have been disconnected from their present life.

EMOTIONAL AND PSYCHOLOGICAL SYMPTOMS OF TRAUMA

Different people react differently to different forms of trauma. There is no universal way of experiencing trauma, but some characteristics are common. Dass-Brailsford (2007) lists some of these characteristics namely shock, denial, disbelief, anger, irritability, guilt, shame, self-blame, sadness, hopelessness, confusion and difficulty to concentrate, anxiety and fear, withdrawing from others, a sense of disconnection and numbness, among others. All these are defence mechanisms that the brain takes on in order to protect itself from crushing. Different trauma levels differ with different people and the type of trauma experienced. One's psychological and emotional state during the traumatic event may also influence the way the person lives the consequences of the trauma.

Kastrup (1995) posits that people also experience physical symptoms of trauma namely fatigue, muscle tension, elevated heartbeat, insomnia, body aches and pains, among others. In this case too, experiences vary with persons. These symptoms may last from few days to months, depending on the person's ability to process the traumatic experience. It is common to see people having episodes that give the evidence of a traumatic experience, even after years. It is often recommended to seek professional help when one continues to experience traumatic flashbacks even after the traumatic experience is long past. Vesti and Kastrup (1995) list some psychological symptoms of trauma namely avoidance, numbing, recurrent nightmares, and flashbacks. Physical symptoms, namely poor appetite, dizziness, asthma, gastritis, body pains, liver and heart problems (Eisenman, 2007) and other psychosomatic symptoms could also be experienced, while psychological symptoms such as fear and anxiety, sleeplessness, shame, shattered assumptions, cognitive impairment, somatic reactions, feelings of helplessness, shame, anger, denial, grief, sensitivity to injustice, and survivor guilt (Dass-Brailsford, 2007) may be experienced. Two ladies manifested several psychological symptoms mainly fear and anxiety, sensitivity to injustice, and survivor guilt.

TREATMENT FOR PSYCHOLOGICAL AND EMOTIONAL TRAUMA

Allen (2005) holds that it is paramount for a trauma victim to face their feelings and memories, otherwise these feelings and memories are likely to keep recurring time and again. Coping with trauma entails separating the past from the present and gaining control over both the painful emotions and the self-protective defences erected against them. Robinson et. al. (2013) affirms that trauma treatment involves the following:

- Processing trauma-related memories and feelings
- Discharging pent up fight or flight energy
- Learning how to regulate strong emotions
- Building or re-building the ability to trust other people.

According to Herman (1997), the fundamental stages of recovery are establishing safety, reconstructing the trauma story, and restoring the connection between survivors and their community.

HEALING TRAUMA

Successful trauma healing needs to address the body's and mind's imbalance and re-establish one's physical sense of safety. A traumatised person needs to understand themselves and the ways they react to situations, and accept themselves without blaming themselves for having gone through the trauma. The goal of trauma healing is to relieve suffering, not to intensify it (Rothschild, 2000).

Herman (1997) identifies three stages that trauma victims go through as part of the healing process namely: safety, acknowledgement, and reconnection. Providing a safe place for the victim is the first step. Feeling safe will encourage the traumatised person to open up and reveal details of their ordeal. This is done only in so far as it helps the traumatised person in their healing process. When the experience is shared with another person, it can lead to acknowledgement, apology, forgiveness, and reconnection. Establishing a positive relationship with the therapist offers good ground for healing.

Cohen (2000) details 10 steps towards healing:

→ Recognizing that one's symptoms are normal reactions to abnormal circumstances—one is likely to be experiencing post traumatic stress symptoms.

→ Talking about one's experience with people one trusts—as much as possible, until one feels they no longer need to talk about the traumatic events.

→ Doing whatever it takes to create an environment of safety and tranquillity.

→ As soon as possible, resuming one's daily routines and responsibilities. Traumatic events can throw one's life into disarray, and it is essential for one to return to their previous life structure in order to feel secure.

→ Giving oneself proper rest, nutrition, and exercises.

→ Taking affirmative actions on one's behalf. This means even going legal if need be. When a trauma perpetrator is taken to book, the victim feels better.

→ Becoming aware of one's emotional triggers and learning to cope with them. Flashbacks are normal after a traumatic event especially when one goes back to the place of trauma, sees something related to the event, among other factors. One way to cope is to recognise that one is experiencing an emotional trigger and they need to engage themselves into positive self-talk, reassuring themselves that they are now safe even if the triggers are frightening.

→ Trying to find deeper meaning in what happened. Despite having been a trauma victim, one can become a thriving survivor. It is possible to learn from the experience and grow strong.

→ Seeking therapy. In most cases, therapy is essential after a traumatic experience.

→ Being patient with oneself as healing takes a long time. Recovery usually has its ups and downs, and it is prerogative for one to know that they need to be patient and consistent in their efforts to get better.

Mindfulness is another way of coping with traumatic experiences.

An understanding of psychological trauma begins with rediscovering history (Herman, 1997). Through trauma healing, a transformation can take place and lead to improvement of one's life. A person needs to accept that they may have been traumatised, but they can choose their attitude towards life, because they have the power and the capacity to do so. Everyone has the potential to grow and become better and stronger.

Herman (1997) notes that some trauma victims may end up numb, unable to feel. This does not mean that the person is not living the after effects of trauma. Many people, especially children, blame themselves for whatever may have happened to them, and this self-guilt does not make things easier.

Levine, in his book *Waking the Tiger: Healing Trauma*, notes that traumatic symptoms are not caused by the *"triggering"* event itself but from the frozen residue of energy that has not been resolved and discharged. This residue remains trapped in the nervous system where it can wreak havoc to our bodies and spirits (Levine, 1997).

Robinson, et. al. (2013) describe three therapies that are used in trauma healing. These are:

Somatic experience: This approach takes advantage of the body's unique ability to heal itself. The focus of therapy is on bodily sensations. When one concentrates on their body, they gradually get in touch with the energy and tension related to the trauma. From here, one's natural survival instincts take over, releasing the pent up energy through shaking, crying, and other forms of physical release.

EMDR (Eye Movement Desensitization and Reprocessing). This incorporates elements of cognitive-behavioural therapy with eye movements or other rhythmic, left-right stimulation. These back and forth eye movements are thought to work by *"unfreezing"* traumatic memories, allowing one to resolve them.

Cognitive-Behavioural Therapy: This helps one to process and evaluate one's thoughts and feelings about a trauma. For good results, CBT is combined with another form of therapy like EMDR or somatic experience.

As noted earlier, many of the immigrants have experienced one form or the other of traumatic experiences, and, depending on the circumstances, the perpetrator, personal experience, the facts, and the reasons, they may be going through very varied experiences and therefore need a tailor made approach to healing. Most traumatised women do not consider themselves as traumatised. They may base their feelings on what other people say about them (interview responses by one of the ladies). Some ladies expressed feelings of sadness, depression, and emptiness. Due to their lethargy, some consider themselves incompetent, eventually rating themselves as failures. Most of them also compare themselves with other women who appear *"normal"* and able to run their lives without much struggle. This can drift to despair and a feeling that life is not worth living (Harris, 1998). Some other women talked of being thought of as bad, and were angry, and easily provoked. Some expressed having experimented with self-destructive behaviours such as using alcohol or drugs to soothe themselves, falling into different forms of addiction, or getting into obsessive behaviours (Giordano, 2014). They may also be involved in crime, because their self-esteem may be so low that they may consider themselves as deserving punishment. Many of these women may also suffer several psychosomatic illnesses.

Immigrant counselling, according to Chung (2010), needs to take into account that immigrants experience pre-migration, transit, and post-migration stages and they encounter different types of traumatic experiences in these stages which can have an impact on their psychological health.

In their research, Schweitzer, Melville, Steel, and Lacherez (2006) found out that Sudanese refugees experienced pre-migration trauma in form of separation from their families, violence, social isolation, rape, brainwashing, being kidnapped, and isolated from others, witnessing murder, deprivation of basic needs, and loss of significant loved ones during migration. During the migration stage, immigrants may face dangerous conditions and physical deprivation such as starvation, risk of death through drowning, separation from family members, and may even witness death (Potocky-Tripod, 2002), threats and dangers due to illegal travel, threat of discovery, compulsory prostitution, and abandonment (Drozdek and Wilson, 2004). These traumatic experiences have a strong effect on how individuals deal with their current stressors or resettlement, which can affect mental health status (Nicholson, 1997). One lady shared with this interviewer how she was forced into prostitution by her own dad, and she was very bitter about it. She claimed to have lost trust in men and wondered if she would ever get married.

During the post-migration stage, notes Potocky-Tripodi (2002), immigrants may be dealing with multiple losses: family, friends, possessions, familiar surroundings, and status. Chung (2010) emphasises the fact that immigrants may arrive in their host country thinking they will have a chance for a better future, only to find out that they cannot find a job. They may not have legal status, further compounding the challenges they may be facing, and are in constant fear of deportation. The ladies interviewed in this study experienced the problems of lack of jobs and discrimination, and they claimed to continue having these feelings even if some of them have found some kind of casual employment. They are disappointed because their expectations when they were coming to Italy were not fulfilled, and they live with a strong sense of defeat.

B. H. Ellis, MacDonald, Lincoln, and Cabral (2008) carried out a research among Somali refugee adolescents and found out that post-traumatic stress disorder (PTSD) and depression are prevalent in immigrant populations. Cumulative trauma was related to PTSD and depression symptoms. Post-settlement stressors, acculturative stressors, and perceived discrimination were associated with greater PTSD symptoms and depression.

Harris (1998) lists four core assumptions in trauma treatment approach namely:

- Some current dysfunctional behaviours or symptoms may have originated as legitimate coping responses to trauma
- Women who experienced repeated trauma in childhood were deprived of the opportunity to develop certain skills necessary for adult coping
- Trauma severs core connections to one's family, community, and ultimately to self
- Women who have been abused repeatedly feel powerless and unable to advocate for themselves.

CHILDHOOD TRAUMA

Children who have experienced trauma often see the world as a frightening and dangerous place. If these children are not helped to deal with the symptoms they experience, they are likely to carry these experiences into adulthood, setting the stage for further trauma (Robinson, et. al. 2013). Childhood trauma results from whatever disrupts a child's sense of security and safety including violence, all sorts of abuse (physical, sexual, psychological, among others), serious illness, separation from a parent or both parents, bullying, among others. Children then develop fear and have problems trusting other people. A traumatized child may experience memories of the trauma. The child is unable to control these memories, and these memories may intrude into a child's day to day life. The child may also experience nightmares as well as recollections of the traumatic event (AACAP, 2010). Since the child cannot give a logical explanation to the trauma, they often tend to find answers to the many questions they may have, as well as imagine ways in which the trauma could have been prevented. Since the child may not understand these events, they may become insecure and suspicious about whatever happens around them, be hyper or hypo alert, which may spill over to experiences of lack of purpose in life. It is also common for children to experience numbness especially after repeated traumatic experiences, appearing detached and not portraying any feelings of any kind (Robinson et. al. 2013).

After a traumatic experience, a child may experience denial and eventually emotional numbness, in an attempt to try to stop thinking about the traumatic experience. They therefore develop psychological coping mechanisms. Dissociation is one of the most common mechanisms, that is, a kind of self-hypnosis that enables the child to deaden, at least in their mind (AACAP, 2010). Children are also likely to have anger bouts and violent behaviours, towards themselves and towards others. They may identify with the aggressor by turning their rage towards other children. On the flip side, other children may experience aggression as dangerous; therefore, they become highly reserved and passive, at the cost of being taken advantage of. They may resort to psychic numbing which protects them from experiencing pain, as well as associate the trauma to specific situations or things. In situations of physical disfigurement, children may experience guilt, shame, self-revulsion, or other forms of rage. Such children may experience suicidal attempts or self-mutilating behaviour (Robinson, et. al. 2013). One of the ladies interviewed shared about her childhood trauma in the hands of her paternal uncle. Even after moving to Italy, she attempted suicide once. It was her way of coping with problems of having been abandoned by her boyfriend.

POST-TRAUMATIC STRESS DISORDER (PTSD).

DSM-IV-TR defines traumatic events as those experiences that involve experiencing or observing actual or threatened death, physical injury, or threat to physical integrity (APA, 2000) and that result in feelings of terror, horror, or helplessness. PTSD is a form of psychosis and different people experience it differently (Joseph, Williams, and Yule, 1997).

According to Herman (1997), the many faces of PTSD fall into three categories namely *hyper-arousal* (persistent expectation of danger), *intrusion* (indelible imprint of the traumatic moment), and *constriction* (numbing response of surrender). However, avoidance characterises many a traumatized person. This is because thinking about the trauma, or facing it, brings one back to *"relive"*, as it were, the traumatic experience. It is not uncommon to find traumatized people experiencing high levels of frustrations with themselves, being extremely critical of themselves, adding insults to their injuries (Allen, 2005).

HYPER-AROUSAL

After a traumatic event, the human system of self-preservation appears to be on constant alert, as if anticipating the danger at any moment. A person suffering from PTSD startles easily, reacts irritably to small provocations, and may have poor sleeping patterns. They may find it hard to fall asleep, awaken often, and be very sensitive to noise. Thus, traumatic events appear to re-condition the human nervous system (Herman, 1997). As reported in one interview, a lady shared about being persecuted by others, and she portrayed a strong sense of paranoia. Every time she got onto a bus, she felt all the eyes of the passengers fixed on her, and, according to her, they were all talking ill of her and pointing accusatory fingers on her. She said she could not hear exactly what they were saying, because they were talking in low tones, but one thing she was sure about was that they were talking negatively in her regard. She was totally convinced about this. She reported to have experienced severe suffering under the father as well as hostility from neighbours.

INTRUSION

Even after the traumatic event is past, many people with PTSD tend to live the reality of the trauma in their current life. The trauma disturbs them so much so that they are unable to reconstruct their normal life. Flashbacks when one is awake and traumatic nightmares when one is asleep becomes the way through which the trauma is encoded into the person's consciousness. For this reason, even normally safe environments may feel dangerous, since the person can not be reassured that the event will not repeat itself (Herman, 1997).

Traumatic memories lack verbal narrative and context; rather, they are encoded in the form of vivid sensations and images (Herman, 1997). However, reliving a traumatic event in whatever form carries with it the emotional intensity of the original event. These emotions are intensive, and are far from normal emotions of fear or range, and are overwhelming. This explains why most traumatised people avoid facing their trauma. According to Herman (1997), the effort to ward off intrusive symptoms, though self-protective in intent, further aggravates the post-traumatic syndrome, for the attempt to avoid reliving the trauma too often results in a narrowing of consciousness, a withdrawal from engagement with others, and an impoverished life.

CONSTRICTION

Herman (1997) holds that when a person experiences total powerlessness, and any effort to resist is deemed futile, they often go into a state of total surrender. The otherwise active system of defence shuts down, and alters their state of consciousness as an escape from their situation. People often freeze, therefore numbing themselves against feeling the pain. This is called constriction. It is as if one becomes anaesthetized. Some people may experience the event happening in slow motion, while others see it as a movie, happening outside of themselves. These perceptual changes combine with a feeling of indifference, emotional detachment, and profound passivity in which the person relinquishes all initiative and struggle (Herman, 1997). These detached states of consciousness are similar to hypnotic trance state. They resemble the features of voluntary surrender, suspension of initiative and critical judgement, subjective detachment or calm, enhanced perception of imagery, altered sensation, including numbness and analgesia, and distortion of reality, including depersonalization, derealisation, and change in the sense of time (Herman, 1997).

Constriction symptoms usually interfere with anticipation and planning. These also narrow and deplete the quality of life and ultimately perpetuates the effects of the traumatic event.

A person suffering from PTSD oscillates between the extremes of intrusion and constriction.

While specific trauma related symptoms may seem to fade over time, they can be revived, even years after the event, by reminders of the original trauma (Herman, 1997). Numbing and constriction symptoms dominate as intrusive symptoms diminish. People with unrecognized PTSD live a diminished, less than fulfilling life, and are tormented by memory while experiencing helplessness. It is not uncommon to see many profoundly traumatized people wish they were dead, because in any case, part of them dies with the trauma. Traumatised people have difficulty modulating intense anger, and they oscillate between uncontrolled expressions of rage and intolerance of aggression in any form (Herman, 1997). The lady cited above talked about experiencing uncontrolled rage especially when things do not go her way. She takes it out with her adoptive parents, friends, teachers, among others. She talked of experiencing a strong force within which tells her to attack whoever it is she is dissatisfied with. In turn, any form of aggression towards her is lived with extreme intensity and a sense of injustice, and therefore calls for revenge, and the vicious circle continuous.

Another characteristic of PTSD sufferers is the way they handle relationships and intimacy. Due to the fact of losing their trust in people, themselves, or even God, the feelings of shame and guilt, and the need to avoid any small reminders of the traumatic experience, they may withdraw from close relationships (Herman, 1997). At the same time, the terror of the traumatic event may intensify the need for protective attachments. This leads to alternation between isolation and anxious clinging onto others. The above named lady shared about feeling strongly the need to own people, to control them, but at the same time, she did not want them to get too close. She feels threatened by the closeness of people; therefore, she tries to avoid entering into intimate relationships. However, any time someone goes away from her life, she experiences great sense of loss.

Four major types of symptoms namely *re-experiencing, avoidance, numbing,* and *arousal* are all tied to an overwhelming experience as detailed by Curren (2010). When someone experiences powerlessness and a sense of defeat in the face of an event, and their physical and psychological resources are insufficient for effective coping, they are likely to experience the symptoms related to trauma. Individuals suffering from PTSD are missing the explicit information necessary to make sense of their distressing somatic symptoms—body sensations—many of which are implicit memories of trauma (Rothschild, 2000).

DISSOCIATION

Dissociation refers to splitting in awareness (Rothschild, 2000). Splitting may involve forgetting simple things at best and dissociative identity disorder at worst. According to Rothschild, the most severe consequences of PTSD result from dissociation. Trauma victims often use dissociation unconsciously during the time of their trauma in order to get away from overwhelming feelings of hopelessness and terror, therefore dissociation provides an emotional departure which acts like the steam release valve on a pressure cooker (Valenti, 2010). People suffering from dissociation experience remarkable fragmentation especially when under stress. Valenti goes on to say that there is no internal connection with the self, therefore it becomes impossible to make healthy connections with other people. This is usually a coping mechanism that protects the traumatised person from the horror and terror of their trauma.

ROLE OF THERAPIST

As seen in earlier sections, trauma therapists need to have experience in treating trauma in order to avoid re-traumatisation of the client. They should be welcoming and accommodating, keeping in mind that the client may find it hard to trust them due to their past experience. Trauma therapists need to take the client's experiences seriously and show the same to the client. They need to demonstrate compassion and respect, and be trustworthy.

Benanno (2005) holds that a trauma therapist needs to be patient and understanding, offer practical support by being present and listen to the client, or suggest activities that the client could be involved in, in order to face their trauma, not insist that the client talks when they do not feel like doing so, offer tips on how one can socialize and avoid isolation, and not take the client's trauma personally.

Therapists also need to take care of themselves, since the experiences of their clients can also take its toll on therapists. Doing so helps avoid secondary or vicarious trauma. They need to take care of their own needs possibly through supervision and work directed to themselves.

Benanno (2005) holds that the therapist needs to give ample time to stabilizing work, where the client is helped to feel safe. It is essential not to expect much more than a client is ready to share, therefore the therapist goes at the client's pace, not their own. If the client is not ready to do some particular task, the therapist needs to be patient and support them in their difficulties. The therapist keeps the objectives and goals constantly in mind and walks with the client keeping in mind these goals and objectives.

Dealing with dissociation is essential in the client-therapist relationship (Valenti, 2010). The therapist needs to assure and reassure the client of their safety and help them take control of their life, as opposed to allowing the trauma to dictate the way they live their life.

Every client is unique, therefore, a tailor made approach needs to be embraced, as opposed to a blanket approach. If a therapist finds themselves unable to help a client, it is best to refer the client to another therapist. This will put the client's interests before those of the therapist. Therapists need to take their clients' fears seriously and not dismiss them as mere beliefs. They need to stand by the client's defence against damaging forces that could bring about illness, madness, or danger. Growth, therefore, comes when normal functioning can be regained with possible subsequent personal growth (Benanno, 2005).

Trauma can procure both physical as well as psychological lasting effects. As noted earlier, it is essential for one to identify their trauma, face it, and share it with someone they can trust. Social network is important for healing. Attachment trauma prevents many people from dealing with their subjective experience of trauma. According to Brahm (2004), trauma can have a range of effects on one namely: *cognitive* (this includes memory difficulties, lack of concentration, poor judgement, inability to discriminate, and inability to make choices), *emotional* (depression, withdrawal, flashbacks, intense fear, helplessness, loss of control, loss of connection and meaning, generalized anxiety, and specific fears), *physical* (stomach pains, tightness of the chest, headaches, perspiration, and psychosomatic complaints), and *behavioural* (irritability, startling easily, hyper-alertness, insomnia, communication difficulties, and substance abuse). Some ladies interviewed reported experiencing a series of symptoms, and therefore, as far as this researcher is concerned, they need to go through tailor-made therapy which keeps in mind the multicultural aspects of healing.

Traumatic events are unforgettable (McNally, 2005), and the fact that these events are not in the consciousness does not mean that they have been wiped out and can not recur. Failure to think about the trauma is not the same as amnesia or an inability to remember them, but it could most likely be a coping mechanism in order not to feel crushed by the traumatic experience.

People who have experienced devastation and trauma not only have to rebuild their lives, but they also have to deal with anger, anxiety, panic attacks, flashbacks, claustrophobia, insomnia, nightmares, rage, depression, fatigue, obsessive thoughts, guilt, and a number of issues related to PTSD (Volkman, 2005). Trauma is a psychophysical phenomenon, even when the traumatic event causes no bodily harm.

Looking at immigrant women's plight, it is important to assess whether they have experienced traumatic events and how these have affected them. By so doing, it becomes much more effective to assist them in their integration process by addressing their real issues and empowering them to live better lives.

18. RATIONAL EMOTIVE BEHAVIOUR THERAPY (REBT)

Rational emotive behaviour therapy (REBT) is a comprehensive approach to psychological treatment that deals not only with the emotional and behavioural aspects of human disturbance, but places a great deal of stress on its thinking component (Abrahams, undated). Human beings are highly complex, and there is no one single way that can effectively deal with the disturbances that characterize humanity. Albert Ellis, the founder of REBT, holds that psychological disturbances arise from misconceptions and mistaken cognitions about their perceptions, from emotional under-reactions or over-reactions to whatever stimuli they face, and from habitually dysfunctional behaviour patterns, which enable them to keep choosing and repeating unhealthy responses despite their failure to work (1962).

REBT is based on the assumption that how we label our emotional reactions is largely caused by our conscious and unconscious evaluations, interpretations, and philosophies (Abrahams, undated). This means that we feel angry because we strongly convince ourselves that we are being treated unjustly and that the other person has something against us. We feel hostile because we believe that people who act against us should not act the way they do therefore their behaviour in our regard is unjustified (Ellis, 1962, revised in 2011). REBT focuses on uncovering irrational beliefs which may lead to unhealthy negative emotions and replacing them with more productive rational alternatives (Mulhauser, 2013). It aims at reducing emotional pain and helping clients make healthy choices. REBT is based on the idea that it is not external circumstances that make a person happy or unhappy, but internal thoughts about events, others, or self. Thinking, feeling, and behaviour are seen as linked and influencing one another (Ellis, 2011). REBT therefore focuses on changing one's thinking. REBT also emphasizes the importance of preferences in life when processing thoughts versus the flexibility of absolute thinking with respect to the outcome of events (Greenfeld, 2011). Preferences lead to individuals attaining their goals. In contrast, irrational beliefs tend to inhibit achievement of their goals. This theory emphasizes that each person is responsible for changing their own beliefs and that changing their own thoughts and feelings is within their control.

REBT is holistic in its approach, in that it teaches many types of thinking, feeling, and behavioural techniques to identify, investigate, and change dysfunctional behaviours. It encourages insight, realistic perspective, reasoning, and logic, but holds that these rational elements alone, without strong emotion, motivation, and action, are not enough for lasting change (Ellis, 2006). REBT is a style of therapy that is active, directive, and individualized to each client (Greenfeld, 2011). It attends directly to the individual belief patterns of clients (Ellis, 1962) and how individuals change their thinking.

Abraham (undated) posits that REBT is the founding cognitive, multimodal, and integrative therapy approach, although it differs from other cognitive behaviour therapies in that it has a strong philosophical emphasis. It emphasizes the importance of unconditional acceptance.

Ellis (2011) argues that much of what is called emotion is nothing more or less than a certain kind—a biased, prejudiced, or strongly evaluative kind—of thought.

BIOLOGICAL TENDENCIES

According to Ellis (1993b), there are two opposing innate creative tendencies. People have the tendency to create, develop, and actualize themselves as healthy goal attaining human beings. This implies that human beings possess a great potential to be rational and pleasure-producing. On the flip side, people have tendencies to create, develop, and implement irrational cognitions, inappropriate emotions and dysfunctional behaviours (Jones, 1995). The innate tendency towards dysfunctional thinking and behaviour is manifested in people's failure to accept reality. Ellis believed that certain severe mental disturbances are partly inherited and have strong biological components (Ellis, 1962). For instance, schizophrenia is seen as illustrative of biological limitations that inhibit thinking clearly and logically (Sharf, 2012).

SOCIAL FACTORS

REBT holds that people also possess the tendency to choose how much they allow themselves to be influenced by external forces, to help or damage themselves. First, they can choose to think differently and more effectively about what is happening, and second, because they possess the capacity to think about how they think, they can choose to acquire and maintain the cognitive skills for containing and counteracting their tendencies to irrationality (Jones, 1995). People are likely to define themselves as good or worthwhile depending on how they see others reacting to them (Sharf, 2012). Individuals who constantly receive criticism from those around them are likely to view themselves as bad and worthless. Individuals are faced with the reality of dealing with the *"musts"* and *"shoulds"* that they achieved from interacting with others.

THE GOAL OF HAPPINESS

REBT views human beings as responsibly hedonistic in that they strive to remain alive and to achieve some degree of happiness (Mulhauser, 2013). However, Ellis advocates responsible hedonism, which seeks to focus on long-range rather than short-range hedonism (Sharf, 2012). Individuals with a responsible attitude towards hedonism think through the consequences of their behaviour on others as well as on themselves.

According to REBT, all people want to be happy, whether alone or in company. People seek to have fulfilling relationships, and get along well with others (Ellis, 1992). People desire the best in life, they want to be educated, well informed, and at the top of things. People want a good job, a good remuneration, and the ability to enjoy their leisure time without being conditioned by other factors. When people want to survive and be happy, they have several desires to perform important tasks well, to relate successfully to others, and to do what it takes to help them reach their goals (Ellis, 2011). This is the ideal situation, but concrete life shows that people hardly get all they want, and instead, are thwarted by the *"slings and arrows of outrageous fortune"* (Ross, 2006). When people's goal to be happy is blocked, they may respond in ways that are healthy and constructively happy, or in unhealthy and unhelpful ways. These reactions are determined by people's beliefs. These beliefs trigger people's emotional and behavioural responses. People's irrational beliefs and behaviours often take the form of extreme or dogmatic 'musts', 'shoulds', or 'oughts', contrasting with the rational and flexible desires, wishes, preferences, and wants (Mulhauser, 2013). REBT holds that people have it within their power to profoundly change their beliefs and philosophies, and therefore to radically change their state of psychological health.

CONSTRUCTIVISM

Constructivism holds that people have considerable power to construct self-helping thoughts, feelings, and actions, as well as to construct self-defeating behaviours (Ellis, 2011). Despite some biological and societal limitations, to some degree, people generally have a choice in how they conduct their lives, and therefore with some effort, they can become what they want to be. People can motivate and force themselves to change. Having highly developed language skills, they can think, think about their thinking, and think about thinking about thinking (Ellis, 2005). Thinking, feeling, and acting influence and interact with each other, hence, when people think, they also feel and act; when they feel, they also think and act, and when they act, they also feel and think.

THE ABC MODEL

REBT employs the ABC framework to clarify the relationship between activating events—the actual event and a person's immediate interpretation of the event (A); our beliefs about them—evaluations that may be rational or irrational (B); and the cognitive, emotional, or behavioural consequences of our beliefs—emotions, behaviours, and other thoughts (C) (Mulhauser, 2013). Ellis (1988) added D (disputing irrational beliefs) and E (effective new philosophy of life) to cover change and the desirable result of change. The letter G (goals) can be placed at the beginning to provide a context for people's ABC's (Jones, 1995). Disputation refers to detecting irrational beliefs, discriminating irrational from rational beliefs, and debating irrational beliefs (Sharf, 2012). It's only when beliefs have been disputed that one can experience E—a new effect, a logical philosophy and a new level of affect appropriate to the problem (Sharf, 2012).

The aim of ABC is to clarify the role of mental activities or predispositions in mediating between experiences and emotional responses. When a person experiences a negative event, and they respond to it through rational belief, the consequence is healthy negative emotions. If a person experiences a negative event, and they respond in an irrational belief, the consequence is unhealthy negative emotions. Individuals have goals that may be supported or thwarted by activating events. Based on their beliefs, people usually experience behavioural consequences according to these beliefs (Ellis, 2011).

Mulhauser (2013) offers three other insights on the ABC framework:

→ While external events are of undoubted influence, psychological disturbance is largely a matter of personal choice in the sense that individuals consciously or unconsciously select both rational and irrational beliefs at B when negative events occur at A.

→ Past history and present life conditions strongly affect the person, but they do not, in and of themselves, disturb the person; rather, it is the individual's response which disturbs them, and it is again a matter of individual choice whether to maintain the philosophies at B which cause disturbance.

→ Modifying the philosophies at B requires persistence and hard work, but it can be done.

A—the activating event can be divided into two: what actually happened, and what the client perceived happened. It is important to get a clear picture of the activating event, watching out whether a previous behavioural consequence itself becomes an activating event (Sharf, 2012).

Ellis divides belief systems into two basic categories: rational beliefs (rB) and irrational beliefs (iB). Ellis (1988), proposes that neurotic problems can be grouped in two main headings according to the three main musturbatory (based on 'must') beliefs discussed above and their derivatives namely: *Ego disturbance* (self-damaging), and *low frustration tolerance* or discomfort disturbance. Ego disturbance arises from the belief that *"I must do well and win the approval for all my performances..."* This leads to one thinking and feeling inadequate and undeserving when they do not do as well as they believe they must. Here, one demands that they be special, perfect, outstanding, superhuman, and hence godlike (Jones, 1995). In discomfort and ego anxiety, individuals have a belief that if they don't get or do what they want, the results will be awful or catastrophic (Sharf, 2012).

Low frustration tolerance springs from the ego disturbance belief that people think they are special and perfect. This progresses to *"Others must treat me considerately and kindly..." "Conditions under which I live must be arranged so that I get practically everything I want comfortably, quickly, and easily..."* (Sharf, 2012). Ego disturbance and low frustration tolerance leads to beliefs such as *"I must have an easy life, I must be perfect, and people and conditions should always cater to me, me, me, and me!"* (Ellis, 1988). The ABC theory of personality is also the central focus for personality change (Sharf, 2012). This theory is the core of assessment in REBT.

THERAPEUTIC APPROACH OF REBT

The main aim of REBT is to help clients replace their absolutist philosophies with more flexible ones, which includes learning to accept that all human beings, including themselves, are fallible, and learning to increase their level of tolerance to frustration while aiming to accomplish their goals. Ellis' emphasis in therapy is more on how people sustain their irrationality than on how they initially acquired it: the past cannot be undone and it is counterproductive to focus excessively on how people feel about the past (Ellis, 1991b).

In REBT, the client acknowledges the existence of a problem and identifies any form of 'meta-disturbances' about the problem (problems about the problem, for instance, feeling guilty about being depressed) (Mulhauser, 2013). The client goes on to identify the underlying irrational belief that caused the original problem and comes to understand why it is irrational, and why a rational belief would be a healthy alternative. The client therefore challenges this irrational belief system and adapts a range of cognitive, behavioural, emotive, and imagery techniques to strengthen their conviction in a rational alternative. Rational emotive imagery (REI) helps clients to practice changing unhealthy negative emotions into healthy ones at C, while imagining the negative event at A, as a way of changing their underlying philosophy at B, helping clients move from an intellectual insight about which of their beliefs are rational and which are irrational, identifying impediments to progress and overcoming them, as they work continuously to consolidate their gains and to prevent relapse (Mulhauser, 2013).

THE THREE BASIC 'MUSTS'

According to REBT, despite the difference in expression that characterizes people, the beliefs that upset people are variations of three common irrational beliefs, each of which contains a command. Ross (2006) lists these irrational beliefs in the following way:

- → I must do well and win the approval of others for my performances or else I am no good at all. This belief often leads to anxiety, depression, shame, and guilt.
- → Other people must treat me considerately, fairly, and kindly, and in exactly the way I want them to treat me. If they don't, they are no good and they deserve to be condemned and punished. This belief often leads to rage, passive-aggression, and acts of violence.

→ I must get what I want, when I want it, and I must not get what I don't want. It's terrible if I don't get what I want, and I can't stand it (Ross, 2006). This belief often leads to self-pity and procrastination.

The demanding nature of the beliefs causes the problem, therefore less demanding, more flexible beliefs lead to healthy emotions and productive behaviours.

REINFORCING CONSEQUENCES

People can emotionally, cognitively, and behaviourally reinforce their irrational beliefs (Jones, 1995). Emotionally, musturbatory beliefs lead to negative emotions (anger, depression …) that make them seem true. Cognitively and behaviourally, people who seek social approval may avoid taking social risks, and by so doing, convince themselves that it would be too difficult and dangerous to do otherwise. While avoiding such risks, they may experience a form of emotional relief, therefore the combination of emotional, cognitive, and behavioural reactions makes them more rather than less socially anxious (Jones, 1995). Jones (1995) further notes that people who get extremely angry exaggerate the negative qualities of their enemies thus justifying and reinforcing the original self-disturbing beliefs. Their behaviour may create hostile reactions in others which then gives their beliefs validity and turns them into self-fulfilling prophecies. Once the self-disturbing and re-disturbing processes occur over a period of time, and people vainly try to correct their emotional disturbances, often they conclude it is not worth trying any more. This is what Ellis (1987) called the unkindest cut of all—people give in to their emotional disturbances.

GOALS OF REBT.

The main goal of REBT is to empower clients to internalize healthy and un-defeating philosophies and meanings and quickly react sensibly and fulfillingly to unfortunate life events, hence minimising emotional disturbances, decreasing self-defeating self-behaviours, and becoming more self-actualized so that they can lead a happier existence (Ellis, 2005). Rationality in this context is seen as the use of reason in pursuit of chosen short-range and long-range hedonism (Jones, 1996). Not only should a client remove symptoms of disturbing behaviour in their life, but they also need to develop what Ellis (1980) calls disturbability. One develops new philosophies and internalizes them, choosing to think in flexible and preferential rather than rigid and musturbatory ways. People with effective philosophies keep working on disciplined, goal-oriented reactions to everyday obnoxious activating events (A's) so that such reactions become somewhat automatic; they also think scientifically and fight and act against narrow-mindedness and arbitrary intellectual-emotional-behavioural restriction (Ellis, 1991b, pg. 166).

Sub-goals of REBT include helping the individual think more clearly and rationally, feel more appropriately, and act more efficiently and effectively in achieving goals of living happily (Sharf, 2012).

ROLE OF THERAPIST

The therapist in REBT works towards helping a client change their irrational beliefs into rational ones. The therapist disputes these irrational beliefs. Disputing is considered the D in the ABC model (Ross, 2006). The therapist asks the client why they must win another person's approval, why other people must treat them fairly, why they must have all that they want, among other questions. By answering these questions, the client understands that it is irrational to expect this of other people. The therapy works towards helping the client to reduce the frequency, duration, and the intensity of irrational beliefs by developing some insights, namely that one does not get upset, but they upset themselves by holding onto irrational beliefs, that no matter when and how one starts upsetting themselves, they continue to feel upset because they cling to their irrational beliefs, and the only way to get better is to work hard at changing their beliefs. This calls for constant practice.

According to Ross (2006), REBT therapists seek to help clients develop three types of acceptance:

Unconditional self-acceptance: I am a fallible human being; I have both my good and bad points. There is no reason why I should be flawless, and despite my good and bad points, I am no more worthy and no less worthy than any other human being.

Unconditional other acceptance: Other people will treat me unfairly from time to time. There is no reason why they must treat me fairly, and the people who treat me unfairly are no more worthy and no less worthy than any other human being.

Unconditional life acceptance: Life doesn't always work out the way I would like it to. There is no reason why life must go the way I want it to, and life is not necessarily pleasant but it is never awful and it is nearly always bearable.

The therapist teaches the client to understand exactly how they create their own emotional reactions by telling themselves certain things, and how they can create different emotional reactions by telling themselves other things (Ellis, 2011). This presupposes that emotional disturbance essentially arises when individuals tell themselves negative, unrealistic, illogical self-defeating sentences. In most cases, disturbed individuals may not be aware that they are talking to themselves illogically. The role of the therapist is to make these individuals aware of their inner verbalizations.

The therapist employs the usual expressive-emotive, supportive, relationship, and insight-interpretive techniques, making a forthright, unequivocal attack on the client's general and specific irrational ideas and to try to induce them to adopt a more rational one in their place (Ellis, 2011).

THERAPIST-CLIENT RELATIONSHIP.
The main role of the therapist is that of a teacher who strives to impart to clients self-helping skills conducive to thinking rationally, feeling appropriately and behaving effectively so that they can attain their goals (Jones, 1995). Empathic listening from the part of the therapist is essential for building a rapport with the client and promotes growth. Therapists refrain from showing undue warmth to their clients, in order to avoid collusion with the client's dire needs for approval. Therapists are however committed to clients' welfare and therefore the client perceives this as warmth and care. Therapists freely share their opinions and self-disclose, as long as this is not detrimental to clients (Jones, 1995). Homework is part of therapy, because clients need to repeatedly challenge their irrational beliefs and to practice their disputing skills both to learn them and also to reinforce their new rational philosophies (Jones, 1995). Homework can be in form of self-help forms where a client disputes their irrational beliefs, reminder cards, listing disadvantages of keeping to certain behaviours, visualizing themselves competently performing situations that they currently fear, (Jones, 1995) among others. Both the therapist and the client need to rate or criticize their deeds, acts, or performances but not their essence or themselves (Sharf, 2012).

Ellis believed that the best way to develop a therapeutic relationship is to help solve the client's immediate problem (Ellis, 2004). After asking the client what they wish to discuss, the therapist then identifies the activating events, irrational beliefs, and emotional and behaviour consequences (Sharf, 2012). Clients then experience empathy through this process.

SUMMARY OF REBT

There are some factors that affect the development of irrational cognitions and musturbatory beliefs namely biology, social learning, and choosing irrational cognitions. In all these, a person has the capacity to choose how to react to situations and to change their belief systems. However, humans mostly embrace short-range hedonism, preferring the pleasures of the moment, hence, the main source of resistance to change (Ellis, 2011). People maintain their emotional disturbances by looking for causes in the past (Jones, 1995). Focusing on the past interferes with people focusing on the present in which they still may be upsetting themselves with the same irrational beliefs with which they upset themselves in their pasts. Focusing on the past emphasizes on other people's behaviour rather than one's own, hence depriving one of their responsibility for their own cognitions, emotions, and behaviour.

People often reinforce their beliefs through unwillingness to change their cognitions, emotions, and behaviour. Jones (1995) lists some reasons why people fail to change their beliefs namely:

→ Some people may lack insight into their irrational beliefs, their derivatives, and their emotional and behavioural consequences
→ People resist the risk and effort involved in taking action
→ Some may not be clear about what to do
→ Others may know what to do but lack the skills, confidence, and support to do it
→ Some people change their actions but lack the staying power to maintain them, especially when faced with difficulties and setbacks (pg. 275).

REBT can be used with most kinds of clients: those who are mildly disturbed, juvenile delinquents, borderline personality disorders, psychotics (when they have some contact with reality) among others. REBT's therapists are tolerant to their clients and fully accept them; it is their behaviour that they dispute by challenging, confronting, and convincing the clients to practice activities in and out of therapy that will lead to constructive changes in thinking, feeling, and behaving (Sharf, 2012). Therapists offer insights about irrational beliefs and about becoming aware of how individuals harm themselves through absolutist beliefs and then the client uses these insights to make constructive changes in their lives (Sharf, 2012). Working with immigrants using REBT is detailed in a later chapter.

LITERATURE REVIEW CHAPTER CONCLUSION

THE FUTURE OF COUNSELLING IN ITALY

The wave of change in the Italian territory calls for a more specific approach to the new needs arising from these changes. The pressures of an unstable political climate and the transition of the country from a homogeneous state to multiculturalism call for counselling services (Remley, Bacchini, and Krieg, 2010). The rapidly increasing and significant diversity of the population brings into question what it means to be Italian.

The people of Italy are challenged with many societal pressures that are in conflict with life as they have known it in the past generations (Remley, Bacchini, and Krieg, 2010). These include the development of a more mobile society in which children are drawn to urban centres and away from their families of origin (Cardamone, 1990), a changing role of women from housekeeping and mothering to working outside the home (BBC News, 2006), an increasing divorce rate (Povoledo, 2003), an influx of immigrants (Hamilton, 2003), an increase in the alcohol and drug consumption (Poldrugo and Patussi, 1996), and movement away from the Catholic Church, yielding a more secularized society that has brought with it a higher rate of divorce and abortion (Thavis, 2004).

Immigrant integration is not easy, and the intrinsic value of multiculturalism has to be learned and appreciated, and people must be equipped to dialogue with each other and co-exist (Remley, Bacchini, and Krieg, 2010). Immigration in Italy has resulted in Italians coming into contact with persons of different values and habits, thus challenging the status quo of what was once a relatively homogeneous society, bringing discomfort and confusing the cultural identity of many Italians, affirm Remley, Bacchini, and Krieg (2010).

Schools in Italy particularly need counsellors and the counselling approach to help students make career decisions to prevent violence and adolescent gangs, and to teach students how to mediate in order to solve interpersonal problems in the relationships between teachers and students, teachers and parents, and children and parents (Remley, Bacchini, and Krieg, 2010).

Anticipated reform in Italian laws could result in counselling being recognized as a profession in Italy, with counsellors being licensed and therefore eligible for positions in schools and government agencies (Remley, Bacchini, and Krieg, 2010).

One's way of life is prior to self-consciousness and it is not easy to alter cherished beliefs and deeply ingrained social practices (Chambers and Smith, 2006). Growth is a process with significant intricacies, and immigrants often find themselves groping with many realities and trying to keep afloat. Migration stories emphasize individualised self-realization narratives of the decision to migrate (Benson and O'Relly, 2009). Benson and O'Reilly (2009) expound this concept by affirming that migration is represented as a way of overcoming some form of trauma, of taking control of one's life, or releasing one from ties and enabling one to live a life more true to oneself. Life after migration is thus presented as an antithesis of life before migration, not only generally, but also on a more personal level. What happens in between is what calls for notable efforts.

The fundamental features of the different lifestyle sought by immigrants include the good life, escape from past individuals and community histories, and the opportunity for self-realization, strategies, post migration often include the renegotiation of the work-life balance, maintaining quality of life, and freedom from prior constraints (Benson and O'Reilly, 2009).

By detaching oneself from the community, it is evident that some values are no longer considered fundamental, therefore the immigrant favours a sense of self-fulfilment over life in the community. As Giddens (1994) notes, the lifestyle choices that individuals make thus *"give material form to a particular narrative of self-identity"*.

Immigration is not necessarily a break from one's past, previously envisioned (Benson, 2007, O'Reilly, 2007a). Immigrants bring with them their identity, skills, expectations, and aspirations (Benson and O'Reilly, 2009).

It is important to consider that the interviews, evidence in the testimonies, are simply words, so that all the information is filtered through memory and speech, but the words do convey a range of meanings. They can tell about consciousness, feelings, and identity, at the same time about things that happened and that people did (Bauer and Thompson, 2004).

As a way of conclusion, Bauer and Thompson (2004) affirm that

> *Narrated life stories always refer to the present coping with the past, and also to the experiencing of these past events at the time. If we wish to avoid interpretative fallacies, we are required to reconstruct both levels—the 'experienced life history' and the 'narrated life story'—irrespective of whether we are interested first and foremost in the history of a life, in the experience of specific historical epochs, or in the recon-*

> *struction of the present meanings of experiences … Only the contrasting of experienced and narrated life stories constitutes the historical, thematic and biographical context necessary for a critical interpretation of sources in which the respective statements are comprehensible and analysable.*

The potential for migrants' capacity to relocate to new contexts, to be wanderers between cultures and nations, is evidence of the capacities of migrants to reach across national and linguistic borders to establish a wide network of relationships, and to show a considerable amount of cross-cultural sensitivity (Ekue, 2009). Ekue goes on to say that migration is a transitional phase in which people experience both vulnerability and strength.

All human behaviour is constrained to some extent. Choices are never unlimited because we live in groups and our behaviour reflects our need to remain part of the group (Chatty, 2013). Therefore, our decisions are determined by forces which hold the society together, known as the structuration process (Richmond, 1994). Transnational families are those that live some or most of the time separated from each other, yet hold together and create something that can be seen as a feeling of collective welfare and unity, namely, *"familyhood"*, even across national borders (Bryceson and Vuorela, 2002).

CHAPTER TWO

RESEARCH METHODOLOGY

2 1. PROJECT INSPIRATION

This project is a result of a series of experiences that the writer has had. Hiles (2001) holds that research is an addition of knowledge, and people undertake research because they care and want to make a difference. This is exactly what inspired the writer to embark onto the long process of a doctorate research degree. Over and above all, being an immigrant, albeit one who freely chose to relocate from Kenya to Italy in June 2006, has had its impact in deciding which topic to research on. Whether one immigrates by choice or not, there are some common experiences that most immigrants go through, namely, leaving one's familiar shores to venture into the unknown, change of several basic, apparently banal things that one hardly thinks about in normal life namely food, the way of dressing, relating with people, among others. Language is one of the major significant barriers that immigrants experience, having to learn a new language, or not understanding the local language altogether affects everyone's integration process considerably. The experience of leaving one's homeland is in itself traumatic for some people; one feels deracinated from their own security. One needs to adapt to the local life including food, seasons, customs, traditions, lifestyles, among others. The integration process is usually a painstaking process, especially in a country like Italy which is conservative in nature, where immigrants are often viewed with some underlying hostility, and therefore having to deal with this hostility may cause stress which is likely to further complicate the integration process. This writer has met a good number of Africans who have been in Italy for a long period of time yet still feel foreign and unable to participate fully in the life of the community. The mental dynamics tend to be much more complicated than the external factors; therefore, these mental schemes may need to be addressed in order to empower those women who have difficulties in settling.

There is a constant influx of immigrants coming into Italy and the issue can not be swept under the carpet, immigration is a reality and immigrants are here to stay, therefore facilitating their integration process is in itself a crucial process in creating and maintaining a cohesive community.

This writer worked as a cultural negotiator for two years upon arrival in Italy. She had the advantage of having learned the Italian language prior to arriving in Italy, therefore she was in contact with immigrants who needed mediation on a daily basis. This is where the need to design a counselling approach suitable for the needs of immigrants arose from. Through cultural negotiation, immigrants' difficulties in expressing themselves were identified. In this process, the cultural negotiator worked with hospitals, mental health centres, police stations, and the procure. Incompetence and lack of preparedness of the health care workers and local police was also an important factor in deciding what to research on. Most operators found it hard to deal with immigrants' issues, and often, there was misinterpretation of data and/or non-verbal language.

The fact that counselling is a fast growing profession in Italy adds to the reasons why this research was considered important. This experience suggested the need for a multicultural counselling approach in the Italian context.

2 2. RESEARCH TEAM

This research involves people with significant roles. The principle investigator (PI) is the author of this dissertation, who is an immigrant herself and a doctorate student with Intercultural Open University Foundation.

The supervisor, by the name Dr. Ambra Cusin, is a psychoanalyst/psychotherapist, member of the Italian Association of Psychoanalysts, practicing in Trieste, Italy. She has been extremely instrumental in this research, offering her critics, views, expertise, and guidance. Having worked with several immigrants, she is well equipped to address issues pertaining to their psychological wellbeing and having authored books and several articles on issues concerning immigration, being open-minded and multicultural in her approach, and conducting seminars, conferences, and workshops for various groups, she best suits the role of supervisor.

The doctorate committee, comprising of Dr. Sandra Hurlong and Dr. John Toothman, has been instrumental in helping to design the research process, supervising, giving advice and critics whenever necessary. They have been great sources of encouragement even when the going seemed tough, and their constant affirmation has been priceless. Their availability and professionalism has demonstrated and reflected the strong aspects of IOUF as a higher learning Institution, and restored faith in the abilities of this writer.

2 3. PROCEDURES

After the approval of the research proposal by the doctoral committee, this writer laid down the research procedure. Between the months of April and August, several people were approached in order to be able to select those specific ladies that were needed and suitable for the interviews using the random method. Associations such as Caritas, Italian Consortium of Solidarity (ICS), Interethnos, Association of Women of Africa, the department of mental health, and acquaintances, were involved in identifying the suitable participants for the interviews. Caritas support was remarkable, since they directed the writer to 3 of the 6 ladies that were interviewed. Several ladies met with the PI, but many of them did not meet the criteria of being from Eastern Africa (Kenya, Uganda, Tanzania, Somalia, Ethiopia, and Eritrea), having been in Italy for less than 6 years, and fitting the age-group 18-45. These ladies also had to be English speakers. Two of the ladies identified could not complete the interviews because of issues related to their traumatic experiences. Participants withdrawing or outrightly refusing to participate speaks volumes about how their background, the immigration process, and their settlement process affect them.

These ladies immigrated to Italy in search of a better life. Each one used a different means of transport. Three out of the six ladies travelled by plane, while three came by dilapidated, risky, dinghies. The circumstances of their departure and arrival differed, as will be seen in the narratives.

2 4. PARTICIPANTS.

This is the identification and selection of persons whose lives involve a revelatory relationship with the subject matter under investigation (Wertz, 2005); people whose experience most fully and authentically manifests or makes accessible what the researcher is interested in.

In this research, a group of about 10 ladies were approached. These are East African English speaking immigrant women who have been in Trieste for not more than 6 years, aged between 18 and 45. The number 10 target was arrived at considering drop out and the unwillingness of some participants to share as fully as the research requires. The author worked on making the experience as interesting as possible, by speaking in these ladies' language, working in the open, taking a walk, and creating a peaceful environment and offering coffee as well. The subjects were assured of confidentiality and anonymity, and in deed, they were informed that only codes would be used for the research purposes. This helped in keeping them going and playing their part actively in the research.

An explicit timetable for the research was formulated, which contained all the intermediate staging posts and their deadlines, when the data collection would begin and end, when the explication of data would be conducted, when the writing up of the research would take place (Breakwell, 1995), among others. A period of three months was considered sufficient for the interviews, then another 2-4 months for the compilation of data.

Some of the ladies approached were too scared to participate in the interviews. Indeed, most of them were very suspicious of the motives of the research, despite the writer explaining it to them continuously. Some of these ladies feared to be deported should any information they divulge leak out to the authorities. It was only after constant reassurance that those who decided to participate gave their consent, availability, and willingness to take part in the research. There were times when this researcher felt as if she would not get enough number of participants because the efforts put in finding and selecting were at times overwhelming, and at one point, she was somewhat discouraged. Thanks to the professional intervention of Dr. Hurlong, the process did not stall.

Interviews were then conducted between May and August. The venue of the interviews was predominantly the offices of Caritas, where the interviewer was given the possibility of using their premises. The interviews took between 60 to 90 minutes. The interviews were face to face, one on one, as well as leisure walks alongside the participants as the interview process continued. Respondents spoke freely because there was no group pressure. There were guiding questions, but the interviewer avoided being restricted to a series of questions and allowed the narratives to flow. Once the participants were confident enough that whatever they shared would be kept confidential, they spoke freely and the interviewer organized that information into categories. The fact that the interviews were open ended and not restricted to answering a series of questions helped the flow. In most East African communities, asking direct questions is considered rude and intrusive, therefore this fact was to the advantage of the interview process. Direct questions were only asked when taking the demographic information, as well as when the participant appeared stuck.

The use of a small sample of single cases helped understand the background and experiences of the ladies interviewed and whether they may need counselling to help them integrate and how REBT could be applied.

2 5. LIMITATIONS OF STUDY

All the participants in the study were volunteers who could withdraw from the study at any time if they so wished. The participants finishing the study might not, therefore, be truly representative of the population (Ellis & Levy, 2009). Most of the participants might hold back information due to fear of being victimized. Others were likely to share just what they thought the interviewer wanted to hear.

The study is limited to East African ladies who have been in Italy for not more than 6 years. It was very difficult to find and identify these ladies, as most of the immigrants who have recently arrived in Italy come from French speaking Africa. Most of those interviewed still get some form of support from the local city council, and so they did not feel free enough to say anything negative about the situation they are living in.

The interviews were time consuming, and involved a small number of participants who may not necessarily represent East Africans adequately. Views can hardly be generalised due to the diversity of East Africans and their particular needs. It is usually not easy to analyse qualitative research method, and this may be one of the limitations in this study.

Most of these ladies have gone through traumatic experiences and their emotional distress was evident. Seeing as the interviews were purely for research purpose, the emotional distress of the ladies could not be addressed, and this created a difficult situation both for the researcher and the participants. Some wounds were opened but not helped to heal. Again, some ladies would have liked to continue talking in order to feel better, but this was not the aim of the interviews and this was felt by both the participant and the interviewer.

2 6. DELIMITATIONS

This research does not address the needs of those women who have been in Italy for more than 6 years. It also does not target minors or people aged over 50. The research does not target French speaking Africans albeit coming from Eastern Africa. It is exclusively for women immigrants.

2 7. THE RESEARCH PROCESS

The scientific method of research is the procedure by which researchers collect information and draw conclusions about their disciplines. Observations are made systematically and objectively, in order for the results to be meaningful (Schweigert, 1992). In this research, effort is made to determine the effect of some factor on some type of behaviour—thus, if a change in the independent variable will cause a change in the dependent variable. The research question in this research is: Could Rational Emotive Behaviour Therapy be used as a counselling tool with East African women in their settling process? Precision and concreteness are two important characteristics that the researcher sought to uphold in this research in order to be able to foresee pitfalls, ambiguity, and confounds that could make the results void of meaning. In this particular research, it was found prerogative to define all the important concepts to avoid confounds and ambiguity. For this reason, operational definitions suffice for the sake of the research at hand. The working definition of terms is detailed earlier in this study.

HYPOTHESES

The hypothesis in this study attempts to answer the questions *"How?"* and *"Why?"* (Shaughnessy and Zechmeister, 1997). The hypothesis is tested in order for it to be valuable to science through the interviews and explication of data. The hypothesis in this study is derived from a theory. In this research, the hypothesis is: *Culturally oriented counselling using Rational Emotive Behaviour Therapy will improve cultural integration of East African Immigrant Women in Trieste, Italy.*

This hypothesis is a good ground to start with, but it opens up several areas of study regarding the area of counselling in Italy, as is seen in the chapter on reflections. It is a starting point that is likely to pose several other questions which may warrant further research. The findings may lead to curiosity to find other findings. This is because behaviour is complex, and there are no clear cut answers to the hypotheses, and also the fact that human beings are complex and dynamic makes it necessary to delve further into more research as new questions arise.

2 8. CONDUCTING RESEARCH

In order to know whether a research topic is feasible, it is necessary to state exactly what it is that the researcher wants to find out about the topic. For the sake of this research, the question is: Is Rational Emotive Behaviour Therapy (REBT) an effective counselling tool with East African immigrant women in their integration process in Trieste? The researcher qualifies the research question further by stipulating the appropriate contexts which are of interest (Breakwell, 1995), thus, movement from a developing world to a developed one, the difference in culture and traditions, the existing counselling tools used in the developing world, and other factors affecting both the origin and the host countries. The data collected, in form of interviews and personal narratives, as well as the researcher's own process, is aimed at answering this question as fully as possible, in spite of the small number of interview representation.

In the chapter on the literature review, this author attempted to offer a critical and comprehensive review of related research and information about the above named research topic. Jackson and Taylor (2007) argue that literature review needs to be analytical, and not merely a retelling or listing of the cited studies or information. In this literature review, three concerns were addressed namely

a) **Evidence that the study in question is needed:** Through working with immigrants, several of their unfulfilled needs were identified by the author, these needs called for attention, and seeing as the author herself is an immigrant, who underwent culture shock and all that it encompasses, she felt the need to have someone accompany her in her journey, but this help was not forthcoming. This is the advent of this research. The researcher's prior and current experiences are not only equally emphasized, but are an actual measuring research instrument for this study.

b) **Evidence that the methodology used is most appropriate for the research questions and hypotheses:** Personal experiences, participant interviews, observations, and descriptive narratives were used in a blended research method combining heuristic and phenomenological approaches. The process and the reasons behind the choice of method are described below.

c) **Documentation of prior research on the research topic or related research topics.** This is detailed earlier in the literature review.

INDEPENDENT VARIABLES

In this research, the researcher is interested in the effect that cultural based Rational Emotive Behaviour Therapy could have on the East African immigrant women in their settling process in Trieste. This is the presumed cause, the antecedent. It was measured, manipulated, and selected by the researcher to determine its relationship to an observed phenomenon (Hiray, 2008), through the interviews and the research on REBT.

DEPENDENT VARIABLES

In this research, the researcher wants to see if the participants' performance on this variable is dependent on the condition of the independent variable assigned—whether it causes a change in the dependent variable. This can be referred to as the presumed effect, the consequence. For the sake of this study, the improved settling process and a sense of self-fulfilment are the dependent variables. This is considered the effect of using Rational Emotive Behaviour Therapy as a counselling tool for the immigrant women.

PARTICIPANT PROTECTION.

Participants in this study are protected in that anonymity is respected. They are informed about their rights and given the freedom to withdraw from the study should they deem fit—without any obligations or consequences whatsoever. The informed consent form is clearly explained to them, and they are given a chance to express any concerns, fears, or apprehensions that they may have. Results of the study will be available to them should they desire to have a copy. Data that will have been collected will be stored with the researcher until it is analysed, and then disposed of through burning after the final report has been made.

2 9. STEPS FOLLOWED IN CONDUCTING THIS RESEARCH (SCHWEIGERT, 1992)

This research followed the following steps:

Step 1: Identifying a topic to be studied. After a long period of reflection, the topic identified for this study is: *The use of Rational Emotive Behaviour Therapy (REBT) with East African Immigrant Women in Trieste, Italy.*

Step 2: Learning about what has been done in the area: A detailed literature review has been done on this topic and the results documented in the chapter on literature review.

Step 3: Focus on a specific research question and form a hypothesis. At the beginning of this research, the author had several doubts on the many topics to research on. After a series of consultation with the doctoral committee, the author was able to narrow focus from a general area of research to a specific question that she sought to answer. The predicted answer to the research question is the hypothesis. This hypothesis was derived from a personal experience which inspired the research topic. The research question and the hypothesis guided how the study was designed. The research question in this study is: *Is Rational Emotive Behaviour Therapy an effective counselling technique with East African Immigrant women in their integration process in Trieste?* while the research problem is: *East African immigrant women have difficulty in integration into the Italian society despite current counselling techniques.*

Step 4: Designing the study so that the results would either support or refute the hypothesis. In this step, the author decided on interviewing a small sample as a basis to understand whether Rational Emotive Behaviour Therapy could be used as a counselling tool with East African immigrant women. At this step, specific decisions about the study were made namely

- The participants in the research study had to be East African women settling in Trieste
- The number would range from 6—10 ladies,
- One on one interviews would be conducted, in the most relaxing and reassuring way possible
- The researcher interacted freely with the participants
- The researcher recorded her own experience as she carried out the interviews
- Interviews were held within the Caritas premises. The time was agreed upon by the researcher and the participant.
- The interviews, as mentioned earlier, would take between 60—90 minutes, with a possibility of continuing into another session if need arose
- Some participants mentioned that they would appreciate to have the results of the interviews and they were assured that once the whole work is complete, they will be given a copy of the results.

Step 5: Make personal observations and collect data according to the procedures prescribed in the research design. The researcher paid close attention to whatever was happening, the different forms of verbal and non verbal language, the condition of the participants, what was happening within the researcher as the participants shared their difficult and sometimes traumatic experiences, among others. Procedures however remained in order not to disrupt the whole process. For instance, the author noticed that she was going through counter-transference and she had to be extremely careful not to influence the process. At this point, the weekly supervision was really helpful.

Step 6: The data that have been collected are summarized and explicated to determine whether the results support the hypothesis. Explication of participants' responses is made. Word explication replaces *"analysis"* because analysis *"has dangerous connotations as it means breaking of the whole phenomenon"* (Hycher, 1999). Explication implies an *"investigation of the constituents of a phenomenon while keeping the context of the whole"* (ibid, p. 161). Narratives are given and detailed. Use of direct quotes from participants' whole attitudes, beliefs, experiences, and thoughts are revealed in the interviews. Some common themes and patterns that arise from the interviews are important and recorded down. This is done in a later chapter. This explication will determine whether it is likely or unlikely that the results will answer the research questions and recommendations given.

Step 7: Interpreting the results of the statistical explication and drawing conclusions about the hypothesis. At a later chapter, implications of these results in relation to the topic in focus are assessed and documented.

Step 8: Communicate research results to others. This will possibly be done through conference presentations and probable publications. When the article is published, experienced researchers are likely to give their critic to the work done and thus offer opportunities for growth.

This research provides the author with new information, new insights, or new questions, which is a challenge for an open mind to new research in the new area.

When a study is designed well, so as to provide reliable and valid data for which there is only one explanation, then the study is said to have good internal validity, which is not threatened by confounds such as experimenter effects of demand characteristics. If the results may be generalized beyond the original set of participants, it is said to have strong external validity (Schweigert, 1992). To increase external validity, random selection of participants was made in this study, since it represents the general population much more than when a limited group is selected. Ladies from the wider East African community offer a broader range of information, considering, however, the common cultural characteristics as lived out within Eastern Africa.

2 10. APPROACH METHODS IN RESEARCH

The researcher prefers to engage in research where the data are subjective and wants to have a close affiliation with the research participants, thus, the choice of qualitative research, as opposed to engaging in research where the data are standardized or objective, with a detached relationship with the research participants, which is quantitative (Jackson and Taylor, 2007). Given the limited number of participants in this research, quantitative method could not be applied. In this study, this researcher is part and parcel of the whole process, and whatever happens challenges her status quo and her general world overview, and stirs up her curiosity and desire to learn. This researcher, as reported earlier, went through deep feelings during the interviews, especially when two ladies shared about their traumatic experiences while crossing through the desert, and the hardships of suffering hunger and thirst, to the point of drinking their own urine. These experiences triggered very strong feelings in the researcher and she had to interrupt the session and talk to her supervisor. This process brought growth for the researcher and the resolve to dedicate time and efforts to assist the less fortunate.

A mixed qualitative method was used in this study, with the aim of attaining the most through understanding of the phenomenon being studied with the goal of personal as well as social transformation. Personal experiences, participant interviews, observations, and descriptive narratives were used in a blended research method combining heuristic and phenomenological approaches.

THE QUALITATIVE APPROACH
The qualitative method of research used in this study involves an unstructured and flexible approach to interviewing that explore immigrant women's views, behaviours, perceptions, and motives in more depth (Jackson, 2007). It is directed to grasp the underlying causes, the rationale behind issues, and

their relative importance. This method of research looks at human experience as opposed to the quantitative method which is prevalently numerical.

The collection of data was used to provide narrative descriptions of phenomenon. The inductive method—thinking from the specific to the general, is used. The researcher's observations and findings formulate the rationale for the procedures and conclusions. This approach is naturalistic, where the research participants' setting was not controlled (Jackson and Taylor, 2007). The human behaviours and experiences are described with words and reported in narratives. This approach is open ended, in that measurements emerge throughout the course of the research, while avoiding bias as much as it is humanly possible. It is value laden, and addressed a small, non representative sample. The researcher's skills are intimately involved and they freely interact with what is being studied and the research participants. This method is comfortable with lack of specific rules and procedures, and has a high tolerance for ambiguity. The immigrant women needed reassurance and bringing in strict rules and regulations could have served to put them off, hence, interfering with the research process.

This research process is designed to reveal participants' behaviours, and the perceptions that influence them with reference to social and cultural issues (Jackson and Taylor, 2007). This approach generated a remarkable quantity of data for the researcher to organize, explicate, and interpret. A small number of participants is studied in this approach because the researcher seeks to discover as much information as possible regarding the participants or experiments in question.

This research is interested in presenting the participant's story, as in a singular, coherent whole. This research process is from the ground up, sometimes questions posed to the participants change in order to by and large answer the research question (Creswell, 2005), as well as to avoid deviating from the objectives of the research. Since the availability of participants is also limited, a small group of ladies is interviewed in depth.

In this study, the immigrant women are encouraged to talk about their own experiences. Open ended guiding questions which allow the women to go deep down beyond the surface are asked. One on one interviews favour the ladies in that there is no group pressure, thus, they tend to open up without fear of being influenced by what others think and say.

The researcher does not draw her own conclusions while interviewing the women. She also refrains from imposing her own framework or meanings, avoiding seeking to understand the perspective of the people being studied and the meanings they attach to their words and actions (Maxwell, 2004). The researcher also had to deal with issues of bias, seeing as her origins are East African, and she herself is an immigrant.

PHENOMENOLOGICAL APPROACH

The phenomenological tradition allows meanings and explanations to emerge from the words and constructs of the participants rather than from the investigator (Creswell, 1998; Strauss & Corbin, 1990). In this research, the researcher describes the phenomenon, refraining from any pre-given framework, but remaining true to the facts (Groenewald, 2004). The researcher is interested in the participants' as well as her own experience, process, freedom, as well as the relationship between the researcher and the participants. She seeks to view the client's problems from her own perspective (Halling and Nill, 1995). This approach allowed the researcher to embark on clearing off bias and pre-conceived ideas, leading to the researcher's recollection of her own experiences and empathically entering and reflecting on the lived world of other persons in order to apprehend the meanings of the world as they are given in the first person point of view (Wertz, 2005).

This phenomenological approach was chosen because it helped the researcher strive to leave her own world behind and enter fully, through the written description, into the situation of the participant. This set the basis for reflection on meanings and experiential processes—free from value judgements, from an external frame of reference and instead focus on the meaning of the situation purely as it is given in the participant's own experience. This approach requires an outstanding amount of self-awareness which the researcher had to exercise. After every interview, the researcher went through the process of debriefing with her supervisor. This approach aided the researcher, participant, and the object or phenomenon on the path to discover universal themes.

Moustakas (1994) defines the aim of phenomenology as *"to determine what an experience means for the persons who have had the experience and are able to provide a comprehensive description of it"* (pg. 13). Each of the interview participants, for instance, lived trauma in a completely unique way, and each interpreted their experiences in their own ways as will be seen in the narratives.

HEURISTIC APPROACH.

The heuristic approach was chosen because it facilitated the reconciliation of experiences, feelings, and knowledge for both the interviewer and the participant.

In order to participate in heuristic self inquiry, the researcher experienced and practiced inner dialogue, used feeling to enter the tacit dimension, and allowed intuition to make connections in the structures of tacit knowledge (Patton, 2004). This researcher uses meditation as a form of heuristic self-inquiry, and this was found to be useful in the entire study process, and more specifically during the interviews. There was so much that the researcher learned from the participants, especially their resilience and determination to make life better despite all odds.

Since the goal of heuristic self research is to come to a deeper understanding of whatever is calling out from the inside of the self to be understood, the researcher thought it would be beneficial both for her and for the participants. Moustakas (2001) posits that in every learner, in every person, there are creative sources of energy and meaning that are often tacit, hidden, or denied. This infers the involvement of the researcher, to the extent that the lived experience of the researcher becomes the main focus of the research (Hiles, 2001). Being an immigrant herself, the researcher was motivated by this fact, which propelled her to think and decide on this particular research topic. While carrying out the interviews, this researcher came face to face with some of the issues she had not dealt with that were triggered during her early immigration experience, especially anger towards the system and more specifically the local culture for appearing so insensitive to the plight of immigrants, and the supervisor came in handy to support this process.

In this research, it was not at all clear from the beginning what needed to be done, but the researcher knew that there is a need that calls to be addressed, and this need would be discovered with time. Seeing so many immigrants suffering and feeling lost definitely triggered the research process. It was however not clear how best to help them, so, as a starting point, counselling was seen as prerogative, and specifically, a culturally oriented counselling approach.

Hiles (2001) argues that in heuristic research, immersion requires the whole self to be engaged in the focus of the research by surrendering to it in such a way that the research unfolds, rather than an observing self attempting to control and direct the process to assure that it moves in the right direction. The research process itself set the direction of this study, as needs were being addressed as they arose. This called for openness on the part of the researcher. The researcher also considered it prerogative to get personally involved in the entire process, putting herself in a learning mode, and focusing on the transformative effect of the inquiry through discernment.

It was clear from the beginning that the researcher was seeking to find inner meaning and transformation, make a difference in her own life, as well as impact the society.

According to Moustakas (1990), and from the experience of the researcher, the heuristic experience showed the presence of the researcher throughout the whole process, and while understanding the phenomenon with increasing depth, the researcher also experienced growing self-awareness and self-knowledge. This approach involved self-search, self-dialogue, and self-discovery. Personal discovery came as a result of the personal involvement experienced.

Contact with the ladies offered several challenges to the interviewer. The interviewer had to postpone an interview because some of the issues that were raised were extremely intense. The interviewer decided to take some time off to process this information and talk with the supervisor. The traumatic experience of the lady interviewed triggered feelings of helplessness in the interviewer. The trauma was so deep and raw that as the lady recounted it, she broke down more than a few times.

The researcher clearly explained to the participants that even if the interviews were a requirement for the doctoral degree the researcher was pursuing, their experiences were very important to the researcher and each and every single aspect that they shared was valued and taken seriously. The interviewer was not just a reporter jotting down everything that the interviewees said in a hurry, but was an active participant in the entire process. The interviewer experienced intense feelings due to the fact that the raw issues experienced by the immigrant women brought the interviewer face to face with trauma and abuse, especially mental and physical abuse of a father to a daughter, issues that the interviewer finds abhorrent.

2 11. DATA SOURCES

In this study, interviews are used in order to explore responses to items and to adequately measure the content validity in order to provide consistent information. An interview survey was developed based on the knowledge of the topic at hand and subsequent readings.

DEMOGRAPHIC SURVEYS

This has been used to gather demographic data about the contextual information regarding research participants through interviews. Background information about participants relating to the study, namely age, ethnicity, gender, educational level, language spoken, marital status, and nucleus family, among others, are explored. This is explained to the participants, and this demographic data gathered towards the end of the interview, when the participant is at ease and has shared personal information. This is so that they don't get overwhelmed by the questions posed, since most of them may still be going through uncertainty and fear.

PARTNER INSTITUTIONS.

Frequent recourse was made to Caritas, a Catholic organization in Italy that is involved in research, studies, and publications concerning immigration. Caritas offers humanitarian services to most of the homeless immigrants, and keeps an updated record of immigrants in conjunction with the prefecture.

Italian Consortium of Solidarity (ICS) is a lay and private organization that works for refugees and high risk persons, and reference was made to them for information, as well as for practicum purposes.

ACTIVITIES

- → Reading books on social data analysis and research methods. Research journals are crucial and essential, as they are constantly updated and offer current information.
- → Implementing the above tools to gather information on whether Rational Emotive Behaviour Therapy could be useful as a counselling tool with women immigrants.
- → Working with Caritas Italia and ICS quoted above.
- → Frequent recourse to the doctoral committee on the progress of the PDE, and insights sought.
- → Literature review is core, and some of the books used in Research Skills and Statistics also apply here as per the selected bibliography.
- → Constant feedback from the supervisor.

ASSUMPTIONS

In every study, there are assumptions that may be both expressed and otherwise. In this study, the following assumptions are made:

- The immigrant women approached will be willing to participate in the study, and they are likely to do their best in being active participants, sharing their experiences without fear since they will be reassured, and the sessions will be on a one on one level.
- Immigrant women are available on scheduled meeting days and times.
- This study offers the required basic information needed to assess whether REBT can be a useful tool in counselling East African immigrant women in their integration process in Trieste, Italy.
- Local authorities will be willing to collaborate and consider the results of the study
- The researcher is as free from bias as possible
- The researcher will become a more critical thinker
- ICS and Caritas Italia will be willing to collaborate, and offer a room where interviews can take place.

According to Thompson (1999), research is driven by theories and hypothesis (basic research), and practical real world problems (applied research). Critical thinking was considered crucial to this research because it provides an informed judgement of the value of research. This research sought to be as unbiased as it was humanly possible, and when this happened, the researcher made the effort to be aware of it through supervision as well as meditation and reflection.

In this study, some aspect of behaviour (dependent variable) was observed—the immigrants' integration process, while some aspect of the environment (independent variable) was manipulated—in this case, the way the immigrants settle within the Italian soil, while considering other possible influences of behaviour (control variables), thus, Rational Emotive Behaviour Therapy. In order to conduct a good research, it was deemed imperative to develop a testable hypothesis that stated the relationship between the two variables and specified how these variables were to be measured, as indicated earlier.

2 12. INTERVIEW PROCESS

As described above, phenomenological and heuristic approaches were used. These are useful to study the lives of a culturally diverse population, with symbolic verbal and non verbal language, allowing meanings and explanations to emerge from words and constructs of the participants rather than from the researcher herself (Creswell, 1998). This researcher sought to describe, not judge, what the ladies narrated, yet remained loyal to the facts (Groenewald, 2004, p. 5) as they shared them. Each and every word shared was pregnant with meaning.

After the initial preparations, this writer made several telephone calls to Caritas and other offices dealing with immigrants including associations of cultural negotiators and the procure in order to schedule appointments whereby the researcher explained what she was aiming at doing. This is also the time when this researcher identified a supervisor and scheduled an appointment with her. With the help of all these people, ladies were identified and approached. Several ladies were not willing to participate and only 10 were available. However, 4 of the ladies were too wary to participate in the study and they took leave. The researcher therefore scheduled appointments with the remaining 6 ladies at Caritas premises. After introducing herself, the researcher explained verbally about the project and what she was looking for. Then she explained the informed consent/confidentiality form. After the ladies understood what the project entailed, they were invited to sign this form and the interview began. As noted earlier, some ladies, after hearing about the project, were reluctant to participate and the researcher made them understand that they were free not to participate and there were no constraints. At the end, only 6 ladies completed the interviews. According to this writer, there were several reasons why some ladies were reluctant to participate. Some of these include fearing to be deported should their information get to the authority's ears, anxiety about getting the relevant documents necessary to stay in Italy, the culture of silent as explained under the chapter on some characteristics of East African culture, the fact of talking to a stranger about their personal lives, and other cultural convictions.

As noted earlier, asking too many questions is considered rude in most African societies, therefore the interviewer invited the participants to tell their stories the way they wanted to. Most of them started narrating about their childhood. The researcher used open ended questions whenever necessary. The researcher took very few notes because some participants were uncomfortable with note taking. After each interview, the interviewer took time to reflect on what was shared, before transcribing the narratives. This was necessary because it made it possible for the interviewer to deepen her understanding of what was shared before putting it on paper, as well as deal with her own reactions to what was shared. However, transcribing was done on the very day of the interview or at most the following day, in order to avoid forgetting important information. The interviewer had the time to reflect on the narratives since the interviews were performed apart. There was one interview every two weeks.

After this, files were created which contained the signed informed consent/confidentiality form, field notes taken during the interviews, the interview questions, the demographic information, and transcribed narratives.

After all the interviews were conducted, the phenomenological approach requires the extraction of meaning and identification of common themes (Byrne, 2005) through reading and rereading transcripts several times, which was done by the interviewer, and these themes were placed into categories. Interviews were transformed into narratives from the first to the last participant. There was no logical reason for choice of who was first, but participants were interviewed as they came.

Data explication was done. After consultation with this researcher's mentor, the word *"analysis"* was replaced with *"explication"* because analysis refers to breaking into parts (Hycner, 1999, pg. 161), while explication implies an *"investigation"* of the constituents of a phenomenon while keeping the context of the whole (ibid). Direct quotes from the participants' narratives were used, whose attitudes, beliefs, experiences, and thoughts were revealed in the interviews (Baker, 2007).

This involved determining what an experience means for the person who lived the experience (Moustakas, 1994, p. 13).

2 13. ETHICS IN RESEARCH

Psychology is a discipline based on research, and it requires awareness and consideration of some ethical concerns. Ethical guidelines are stipulated by the American Psychological Association (APA). There are two major areas of ethical consideration in research namely the treatment of participants while conducting research, and the use of research results (Schweigert, 1998). Scientific integrity is prerogative in research. A variety of activities constitute violations of scientific integrity namely data fabrication, plagiarism, selective reporting of research findings, failure to acknowledge individuals who made significant contributions to the research, misuse of research funds, and unethical treatment of humans and animals (Shaughnessy and Zechmeister, 1992). This research sought to be as ethical as possible and when doubts arose, reference to the supervisor was made.

ETHICAL TREATMENT OF RESEARCH PARTICIPANTS

The ethical treatment of participants is the primary responsibility of the researcher. It is the researcher who decided on how to conduct the research, what and what not to do. The anonymity of the participants was considered crucial. The informed consent form was issued to each participant prior to participation in the project, whereby information about the purpose of the study and what the participant was asked to do was explained. The researcher and the participant entered into a social contract. Any known risks or benefits related to the study were made clear to the participant. Both the researcher and the participant are held responsible by ethics in such a way as to honour their respective parts. Despite signing the consent form, the participants were informed that they were always free to interrupt participation at any point during the project if they so decided, and it is clearly stated in the consent form. The informed consent form called for accuracy, was easy to understand, and was clearly written (Schweigert, 1992). The written consent form was however not enough in explaining the role of the participant, therefore the researcher took the time to describe the project orally and give participants a chance to ask questions. Participants needed to make informed decisions; therefore, the researcher facilitated this. The consent form simply documents that the participant has understood and accepted to participate in the project. Nothing in the research was left to chance. Ethical issues were however addressed throughout the project life. This researcher often took recourse to her supervisor in case of any doubts. Thankfully, ethical issues did not arise and therefore the process went on smoothly.

In this research, there was no recognized risk, therefore participants were not exposed to any kind of risk, and this made it easier for the project to move on.

Participants were never coerced to take part in the project, and as much information as possible was communicated to them in order to help them make a free consent.

All the information collected in the course of the project is confidential —thus, this information will not be shared with anyone outside the research project. Participants participated more willingly and effectively because they were reassured that the information they shared would be safeguarded. The researcher reassured the participants that confidentiality was highly upheld, and this would go on till the completing of the study, after which all the information gathered and the consent forms would be destroyed by fire.

The narrative report would use codes in order to protect the anonymity of the participants.

In this research, participants were reassured that they could have access to the results of the research when it is complete and feasible, if they so desired.

Participants were assured of the fact that they could withdraw from the research at any point, and any data pertaining to themselves would be destroyed once they withdrew and were no longer part of the research process (Breakwell, 1995).

In this research, a small sample was used which could be representative of a larger population. It is impossible to test a whole population, so only a sample of the members can be tested. Statistics therefore help to determine how confident one can be that a characteristic of the sample can be generalized to the population. In this research, a mixed qualitative approach was employed. The number of participants was also low owing to the fact that the East African population is not highly represented here; therefore, the information gathered from the ladies could be used as a foundation for future research.

CHAPTER CONCLUSION

The aim of all research is to use research skills to extend knowledge for the sake of ultimate human betterment (APA, 1982). The researcher in this study, to the best of her capacity, planned her research thoroughly, sought to be responsible, complied with laws and standards, had the institutional approval required to carry out her research, had very clear research responsibilities, and obtained informed consent to research (Schweigert, 1992) from IOUF. To the best of the researcher's capacity, participants were thoroughly informed about the study in order for them to make a conscious free decision to participate in the study or not. Participants were also exhorted to maintain respect and honour their commitments, and be true to their words.

The scientific research method in psychology requires researchers to identify a problem and formulate a hypothesis, design experiments using dependent and independent variables, perform the experiment using experimental and control groups, evaluate the hypothesis, and communicate results. All this was exercised in this research to the best of the researcher's capacity. This is an involving process which calls for clear ideas and methods. The researcher invested remarkably in this research, and is always ready to be challenged on her findings. Research provokes more research, because questions can generate further questions, and thus the process continues as the complexity of human life becomes more and more evident. As noted in the recommendations for future research, this research is just a starting point. It opened up very many other areas that could be used for future research.

CHAPTER THREE

PARTICIPANTS' PERSONAL NARRATIVES AND THE INTEGRATION OF REBT WITHIN THE COMMON THEMES AND PATTERNS

INTRODUCTION

A group of six participants willingly accepted to participate in this study. It was not easy to find ladies from Eastern Africa who had immigrated to Italy within the last six years, who were English speaking, and who felt safe enough to take part in the interviews. The original intention was to interview women from Kenya only, but it was impossible to find more than three. This number was not sufficient for the purposes of this study. Several people were approached and requested to help identify prospective participants and these requests were turned down by some entities. Reasons that were given included privacy policy, fear, or outright lack of collaboration due to lack of faith in the research work. It was necessary to get in touch with different organizations in order to identify the required ladies who met the criteria indicated above. There was a strong resistance by most of these people, but the author did not get discouraged. She went on looking for the ladies and was able to identify, at first, three willing ones. After an intensive period, others were suggested by Caritas Italia, and this was a real help in jump-starting the process.

These ladies were interviewed at different times, within the Caritas venue. In some cases, the interviewer had to make a remarkable number of telephone calls in order to get appointments. Detailed interviews can be found in the appendix. Part of each lady's experiences is documented in this chapter. For the purpose of this study, common themes are identified, and a synthesis made on how Rational Emotive Behaviour Therapy could or could not be used in counselling based on the experiences and exigencies of these ladies. This synthesis is given within each common theme.

Culturally, East Africans approach most issues holistically. The whole is much more important than the sum total of the parts. Everything is inter-connected, starting from persons (I am because we are). Dissecting reality is considered unacceptable. This concept inspired the organization of this chapter, where the themes were integrated with REBT as opposed to the description of themes with a separate depiction of how REBT works. For this reason, the integration serves to view the larger picture, holistically.

There will be a separate chapter later in this work addressing the use of REBT vis-à-vis other psychological approaches, and what makes REBT more suitable than other approaches in this contest. A summary of other theories will be given, and the reasons why REBT works better explained.

Doan (2011) argues that narratives are a form of qualitative research which helps dig deeply into the human nature. Doan further holds that narratives must contribute to our knowledge and understanding of human beings and the world by promoting insight into and interpretation of life experiences. They must contain an honest, personal reflection of life events, convey genuine emotions, beliefs, and values, illuminating one's true identity in the process of developing character through dramatic action... Narratives have the ability to explain social phenomena such as resiliency in humans and our aptitude in piecing together one's fragmented self. These ideas are reflected in the women's narratives.

The experiences of each woman are presented in a narrative form (in the appendix) in order to truly understand their realities, and how their settlement experiences affect their daily life. The purpose of this study, therefore, is to create a general explanation from individualized experiences (Yin, 2009).

Codes were used in order to protect the participants' privacy and anonymity. The study is descriptive in that it provides a detailed description of the depth and breadth of data that emerge from interviews with the immigrant women. In this chapter, only the recurring themes will however be considered.

The descriptive narratives are the researcher's rendering of meaning, insights, and feelings of self and the participant. Each descriptive narrative is the researcher's attempt to capture the essence and characteristic qualities of each individual research session. Those words or phrases that reflected meaning for the researcher were sorted and eventually grouped into themes or clusters of words that were repeated, stood out, or felt meaningful.

The data explication took this form: Interviews=>Common Themes and Categories=>Consolidated themes=>Consolidated themes generated an understanding of using REBT as a counselling tool for East African women in their integration process in Trieste (Greenfeld, 2011). Common themes are important in highlighting participants' experiences to assess the common or uncommon beliefs that influence their integration process.

After some common themes, the writer gives her own personal experience in the first person singular for ease of information flow. The participants' excerpts are written in Italics in order to highlight them and to avoid confusion. The chapter is organized in such a way that the themes are stated first, then the writer's personal experience, followed by relevance of REBT intervention. As indicated in the chapter on methodology, this chapter follows the steps outlined and is consistent with the research methods the writer chose for the sake of this research.

3 1. SOME GENERAL CHARACTERISTICS OF EAST AFRICAN CULTURE.

East Africa is a place of great diversities in terms of ethnicity, languages, cultures, religions, and political contexts (Ekue, 2009). For this reason, it is impossible to generalise and talk about the East African culture. However, there are some characteristics that are common, and that were confirmed by all the women interviewed for this research. Some of these common characteristics will be expounded, since they may relate to finding out whether REBT as a theory could be used in counselling East African women immigrants in Trieste.

NAMES:
Traditional African names often reflect the circumstances surrounding birth. Choosing a name in the African context is a very important process and is done meticulously. It is believed that the actual choice of a name can influence the life of both the child and the family (African Fathers Initiative, u.d). An overly ambitious name could have significant repercussions whereas a simple name may not carry such high expectations.

Names have a religious connotation and are chosen and given during particular rituals, hence their importance. Naming is often the climax and conclusion of a ritual event (Ejizu, u.d.).

Names within the East African context reflect their user's hopes, dreams, and aspirations. They may reflect their user's geographical environment, their fears, their religious beliefs and ideas, and their philosophy of life and death (African Fathers Initiative, u.d.). One's name shows to which tribe, clan, or group one belongs. Since East Africa has significantly large ethnic groups, one's name defines one's identity. This explains the reason why being called by one's name is considered extremely important and helps to create rapport.

Most of the ethnic groups in Eastern Africa give hereditary names, this is a way of keeping the family genealogy alive. For instance, this writer's name Wanjiku (pronounced Wahn-gee-koh) was the name held by her paternal third born aunt who is said to hold significance physiological and behavioural resemblance. This enhanced the aunt's *"responsibility"* over this writer, and the aunt had to make sure that this writer grew up well within the Kikuyu traditions. Wanjiku was one of the nine daughters of Gikuyu and Mumbi—the couple believed to have founded the Kikuyu tribe, the major tribe in Kenya. Consequently, these nine daughters formed the nine Kikuyu clans. This name can not be confounded with any other tribe's names; it is uniquely Kikuyu. Wanjiku signifies dignity, and this conditioned the growing up of this writer in a significant way. The name was a constant reminder that this writer had to be of good moral standing. The name was associated with good behaviour, sensitivity to others, peace keeping, among other values. Not only was there this association, but it became an expectation from everyone else. This, needless to say, conditioned this writer in a considerable way. This will be elaborated further in the section on the personal experience of the writer and how REBT helped her to deal with her primary conditionings.

It is impossible to relate with an East African without knowing their names, therefore counsellors and therapists need to know and remember the names of their clients because this is where relationship begins. One takes great offence if they are called by a name that is not theirs, and some people have been known to hold resentments for a long time because someone mistook their name.

SENSE OF COMMUNITY

Africans make frequent use of the term *"we"* and *"us"* in everyday speech (Ejizu, u.d). Ejizu goes further on to say that an individual *"owes"* their existence to other people, including those of the past generations as well as contemporaries. Whatever happens to the individual happens to the whole community, and whatever happens to the group happens to the individual. The *"harambee"* spirit, meaning literally *pulling together*, coined by the first president of the republic of Kenya, Jomo Kenyatta, characterises the communal essence of Africans (Kenyatta, 1965).

The terms *"mother"*, *"father"*, *"brother"*, *"sister"*, *"uncle"*, and *"aunt"*, define far more for Africans than the average European or North American (Ejizu, u.d.). Ejizu goes on to ratify that normally, a child would refer to any of his uncles and aunts as their father or mother, and their nephews, nieces, and cousins as their brothers and sisters. Children are hardly referred to with their names but as a son or daughter of so and so. This means that one's significance is only as important as the relationships one has. Invisible members, especially ancestors, spiritual beings, and the dead, are far more superior to the living beings. Their legacy is seen through naming of the current children (Ejizu, u.d.).

In his research, Ejizu (u.d.) affirms that everything is interconnected. The worldview is fundamentally holistic, sacred, and highly integrated, therefore whatever happens is explained from the contexts' perspective. The belief in ancestors and the supernatural order, in addition to its inherent religious import, provides traditional African groups with a useful over-arching system that helps people organize reality and impose divine authority and sanction to their life (Ejizu, u.d.).

FAMILY

The African concept and experience of family is quite different from the experience of the average Western individual. Gashaw-Gant (2004) affirms that the African family is hierarchical with an extended family orientation. Authority therefore rests with the males, elders, and parents. Sue and Sue (1990) describe this traditional orientation succinctly as follows:

> *Within the family, the father assumes the role of the primary authority figure. Children are seen as a source of pride. They are expected to be obedient, and are usually not consulted on family decisions. The sexual behaviour of adolescent females is severely restricted and sexual topics are rarely discussed with the children. Children are expected to contribute financially to the family when possible. Parents reciprocate by providing for them through young adulthood and even after marriage (pp. 232-233).*

Older children are expected to take care of their younger siblings and to tend to household chores, such as cooking and cleaning (Baker, 2007). Gashaw-Gant (2004) describes the hierarchical structure of the East African family that provides structure and sources of support during times of adversity, with special attention given to the elders, who are a source of wisdom for the families.

The extended family raises and supports the family (Onyango, 1984). Onyango further lists some characteristics of the traditional African family namely:

- The importance of the extended family beyond the nuclear family
- Lack of public display of affection
- Care and respect for the elderly
- Polygamy as a desired measure of social success and status
- Less prominence of romance in courtship and marriage
- Constrained communication between parents and their children.

Onyango (1984) expounds his points as follows:

"It is the responsibility of the family members to take care of their sick or old members, and therefore it goes without saying that those who have money support those in need as their primary responsibility. Failure to do this is considered rude, and renegation of family responsibility. One gives back what they have received".

The family is to be protected at all times. One does not paint a negative picture of their family, no matter what they have done. Talking about one's family's problems is considered a betrayal because family problems should be solved within the secrecy and the intimacy of the family. This explains why most Africans maintain silence when faced with situations where they have to say something unpleasant about their family. In this case, therefore, silence is used as a way of protecting one's own family. This poses a problem in therapy because one may not be free and willing to talk about how their family influenced their growth and their current situation. It takes notable trust for one to be fully open.

RELIGION

East Africans are radically religious. The presence of a higher power constantly accompanies them in their daily life. Religion makes sense of intolerable situations and helps deal with frustrations—a strategy to answer to the disappointment one goes through. Spiritual and religious beliefs are important in maintaining good health and are sources of strength and hope (O'Mahony and Donnelly, 2007), as well as providing meaning and hope when encountering loss and trauma (Boehnlein, 2006).

Religious beliefs emphasize the importance of helping and mercy. Helping demonstrates a fulfilment of moral obligation (Baker, 2007). Everyone gets together to help whoever is in need. Adversity is viewed as a spiritual problem. Bishaw (1991) affirms that illness is considered a punishment for sin or inflicted through witchcraft and mental illness may indicate being possessed by the devil. This separates phenomena outside oneself, leading to seeking spiritual avenues to resolve illness (Bakeer, 2007) and any other kind of problems.

Nudelman (1993) describes this perspective as follows

The interpretation of emotional illness or distress has its own cultural context: it has a meaning within its specific culture that's unavailable to Western diagnostic technique. The aetiology of illness is usually considered to be due to external sources. These may be natural ones, such as a person with an evil eye, or supernatural sources including various types of spirits and demons (p. 223).

Religion, according to Ejizu (u.d.), is the belief in the visible and the invisible world. Religion gives value to life. It is central in inculcating the promotion and realization of harmonious inter-relationship among individuals and the community. Ejizu further argues that religion pervades and permeates all aspects of life and infuses the social, economic, political dimensions of Africans with meaning and significance. It is transmitted through initiation practices, ritual activities, sacred symbol forms, and vital public institutions (Ejizu, u.d.).

Ejizu concludes by saying that the African is psychologically fully equipped and motivated to promote the delicate balance and equilibrium believed to exist in the universe through ensuring harmony in their relationship with the invisible world and among members of the community.

Immigrants continuously construct their religious identities in the context of the other, the local believers, and the way they perceive their religious articulations (Ekue, 2009). In fact, immigrants have survived incredible challenges and often possess many strengths and resources. Existence is actually articulated in many different forms (Binswanger and Foucault, 1986). These forms include physical, spiritual, dreams, fantasies, and divine.

Rituals, mainly religious, have powerful meanings and spirits can speak and be spoken to.

Most Africans are very religious. There is no single one God, but people can believe in diverse deities. Everyone professes some form of religion. It is part and parcel of one's existence. Spirituality contributes to resiliency. Most East Africans have strong religious beliefs that help them transmit their cultural heritage, cope with stress or powerlessness, gain spiritual fulfilment, and is a source of emotional and social support (McGoldrick, Giordano, and Garcia-Preto, 2005). Resiliency, according to Chung (2010), can be a protective barrier against mental illness. In this study, some of the women interviewed possess qualities such as self-determination, optimism, inner strength, and hope, and the ability to bounce back despite challenges.

Dreams are also part of East African spirituality. They are an instrument of the present, an experience that provides memories from the past and reworks them in the light of the present. Dead people are not memories or dreams, they are real (Giordano, 2014). Indeed, one's death is real only in the waking life, but present in dreams.

HEALING IN THE EAST AFRICAN CULTURE

In the East African context, disease is viewed from a religious point of view (Eisenhauer et. al. 2012). As noted earlier in the introduction, whatever happens in one's life is viewed from the spiritual perspective. Kirmayer, et. al. (1994), in their research, concluded that mental illness or psychiatric disorders are often attributed to demonic possession. A person's sudden changes in demeanour, unusually bizarre behaviour, or speaking in a different voice, are associated with demon possession. Bishaw (1991) affirms that traditional healers provide treatment in a holistic manner and provide means to deal with illness and personal misfortunes through physical and spiritual strategies.

Religious healing rituals are seen as a means of establishing a relationship with the spirit world, and resolving complex occurrences (Gashaw-Gant, 2004). Traditional healers possess healing powers for the community. They tend to take a holistic approach as they deal with disease physically, spiritually, and psychosocially. In this regard, as Baker (2007) notes, dream analysis, projective techniques, trances, hypnotic states, and words of wisdom are employed, which bear a strong resemblance to Western psychoanalysis.

In his research, Pretorius (1993) describes the traditional healer as follows:

> *The traditional healer is defined as someone who is recognized by the community in which he or she lives as competent to provide healthcare. The healer employs treatment methods based on the individual's social, cultural, and religious backgrounds; causes of disease, and disability in the community. The traditional diagnostic process seeks answers not only to the question of how the disease originated (immediate causes) but also to who or what caused the disease (efficient cause), and why it has affected this person at this time (pp. 1-8).*

The family, religious beliefs, healing rituals, and traditional healers are all part of the healing and coping system of East Africans. When immigrants experience wars or other disasters, not only do they experience trauma such as being exposed to war, losing family members, and enduring persecution, imprisonment, or torture, but they also may lose connection with their community and their source of healing and coping (Tribe, 2002a). This lack of connection with their cultural traditions may make their adjustment much more difficult, because they experience a sense of identity loss.

Mental illness, therefore, is a sign of something that has occurred or someone that wants to punish another one. Several ways are employed to deal with mental illness, including fasting, among many East Africans as a means to be strengthened physically and spiritually (Gashaw-Gant, 2004).

Religion, therefore, is seen as the judge—the ultimate supernatural power—and authority that sanctions and reinforces public morality. Success in life, therefore, is based on one's merit being rewarded by ancestors, spirits, or spiritual beings (Ejizu, u.d.). Baker (1991) affirms that illness is seen as a punishment for sins inflicted through witchcraft and mental illness may indicate being possessed by the devil. Disease causation is also ascribed to divine providence (Calestro, 1972).

Baker (1991) concludes that these perspectives on physical and mental illness, which separate phenomena outside oneself, lead to the seeking of spiritual avenues to resolve illness.

NORMS AND TABOOS

Every African community has its norms and accepted behaviour, which promote harmonious living. Everything is geared towards promoting life. Anything that alienates a person from the community is avoided, and if one commits a crime to this effect, they are ostracised—the most severe punishment one can receive (Ejizu, u.d.). Being ostracised is equivalent to death, and therefore everyone avoids a possibility of it happening to them. This shows the tremendous power of the community over the individual (Ejizu, u.d.).

When a grave offense is committed, moral pollution has to be cleansed and special rituals performed to appease the spiritual beings that might have been offended, and until it is done, the entire community stands a serious danger of experiencing calamities (Ejizu, u.d.). This explains why every calamity, natural or otherwise, is interpreted through the actions of individuals or the community.

Ejizu goes on to affirm that the breach of the peace and harmony destabilises the fundamental balance of the community and it is likely to receive severe sanctions from the supernatural *"custodians and guarantors of morality"*.

HOSPITALITY

Hospitality, warmth, building rapport through small talk, and asking about the family is appropriate in East African culture. When one meets another person, the first question is how they are doing, how their family is fairing, if there have been any problems, and how they have been able to handle them. Before one addresses the aim of the meeting, small talk is necessary to break the ice, to make the person feel at home and accepted, and only then can serious matters be discussed.

The guest, in the East African context, is considered a river. The river flows, bringing and leaving blessings as it moves along. It is never stagnant, therefore a guest is supposed to be treated with all possible respect and hospitality. As this writer was growing up, she was taught by her parents and community to respect guests. They could come in at any time, unannounced, and be welcomed without any problems. Whatever one was caught doing when a guest arrived was considered secondary, welcoming the guest was primary. In the house, there were special cups, plates, and cutlery for guests, which were always kept beyond the children's reach, and only the mother or father could access them and get them whenever a guest, whatever kind of guest, arrived.

Hospitality is defined as the extension of generosity, given freely, without strings attached; the unconditional readiness to share (Echema, 1995), carrying one another's burden without expecting anything in return. Olikenyi (2001) argues that African hospitality, which is a vital aspect of existence among the community, is one of the few facets of ancient African culture that is still intact and strongly practiced today by most Africans, no matter where they are. It is a way of life, it is part and parcel of the African lifestyle. Even those Africans in diasporas seek to form groups that help them to feel a sense of belonging, and they tend to be very hospitable to one another and even to those that do not belong to their circles.

Moila (2002a), defines African hospitality as follows:

Each member of the same family group is bound to offer food and shelter to any member of his or her group who needs it. However, it is also an African custom to offer hospitality even to strangers. Hospitality is perceived and practiced by Africans as open handed, instinctive, and the most natural thing in the world (p. 2).

Bishop Tutu (1989) notes:

Africans believe in something that is difficult to render in English. We call it ubuntu, botho. It means the essence of being human. You know when it is there and when it is absent. It speaks about humaneness, gentleness, and hospitality, putting yourself on behalf of others, being vulnerable. It embraces compassion and toughness. It recognises that my humanity is bound up in yours, for we can only be human together (p. 69).

Hospitality is extended to the ancestors—pouring a little drink on the ground or leaving some bits of food on the plate, as a way of seeking blessings from the ancestors, thereby appeasing them (Gathogo, u.d.). It creates a harmonious relationship between the living and the dead.

Some parts of East Africa believe that ancestors are incarnated in strangers, so they should be treated well (Olikenyi, 2001), and in some other communities, handicapped people, orphans, beggars, and lepers are treated with dignity because they are the manifestation of the reincarnation of the ancestors (Olikenyi, 2001).

Hospitality is also shown through social life, uniting the community. Community activities such as singing and dancing are perceived as hospitable activities that bind the community together (Moila, 2002a). Dancing celebrates joy, grief, love, hate, among others, while singing enables one to minimise tensions within the community (Thorpe, 1991. Idowu (1973) affirms that *"songs constitute a rich heritage for the whole of Africa. For Africans are always singing and in their singing and poetry, they express themselves. In this way, all joys and sorrows, their hopes and fears about the future, find an outlet. Singing is always a vehicle conveying certain sentiments or truths. When songs are connected with rituals, they convey the faith of worshippers from the heart—faith in the Deity, belief in and about divinities, assurance, and hopes about the present and with regard to the hereafter"* (p. 84).

Songs therefore express a mood and the meaning of a given situation. Dance, combined with songs, becomes a manifestation of the feeling of the individual, or a group, communicating their inner sentiments, expectations, and aspirations (Gathogo, u.d.). Hospitality eradicates loneliness (Moila, 2002a). Individuals can not exist alone: *"They are because they belong"* (Thorpe, 1991).

African hospitality has a lot to do with material support on occasions such as betrothals, marriages, initiations, fund-raising, mourning the dead, burials, education of children, and social gatherings (Gathogo, u.d.). One person's happiness is everyone's happiness, whereas one person's sorrow is everyone's sorrow. Hospitality, therefore, as Mbithi (1969) confirms, signifies that no one is an island in themselves, rather, each is part of a whole: *"I am because we are, and since we are, I am"*.

SILENCE

Silence is a very delicate concept in the East African culture. It is also an integrative part of the communication process in the African culture (Oyinkan, 2009). It is sometimes used to indicate, more than words can, the real attitude of the speaker, and meaningfully punctuates information units (Oyinkan, 2009). The African silence is different than the *"Western"* silence, because non-verbal language has different connotations.

Silence is often used as a communication tool when one is angry. Not uttering a word in itself is loud enough to send the right message. A person prefers to keep silence to uttering words that could be regretted later. Silence therefore becomes some form of damage control.

In the presence of elders, it is usually considered polite to keep silence. Even if a question is asked, one's silence is not interpreted as bad etiquette, but it is respected and the elder needs to interpret the silence within the context in which this occurs.

Women usually maintain silence as a sign of respect (Oyinkan, 2009). It may be an expression of compliance as most are subordinate to the male figures in the family, mainly the husband or any male in a leadership position. Men can maintain silence as a sign of disinterestedness in what the woman is up to, as well as a way of denying the woman whatever she may be asking. People learn not to talk unless talked to, and therefore maintaining silence is a sign of good grooming.

Silence therefore communicates cultural values that express a way of interpreting the external world through the various contexts which exemplify them (Oyinkan, 2009). In therapy, when one keeps silence, it is a sign that they may not be in concurrence with what is being said. Since expressing oneself is a new phenomenon, the person prefers to go along with what is being said in order not to rock the boat. This could be misinterpreted by therapists who may not be aware of what the silence may signify.

The words of Leonard (1968) forms a succinct conclusion of what African culture could imply:

They (Africans) are, in the strict and natural sense of the word, a truly, deeply, religious people, of whom it can be said, as it has been said of the Hindus: "They eat religiously, drink religiously, bathe religiously, dress religiously, and sin religiously". In a few words, the religion of these natives, as I have endeavoured to point out, is their existence, and their existence is their religion. (pg. 409).

Though there are many changes in the modern African society due to the influence of the West, civilization, and technology, most of these values still remain fundamental for most East Africans.

3 2. INTERVIEWS

During the interviews, participants were offered a chance to express themselves without interruption. When deemed fit, they would keep moments of silence, and it was acceptable. Silence as explained above, is a precious aspect among East Africans, as is further explained under the common themes. When one is narrating something important, moments of silence once in a while are in order. Participants chose their own words to express themselves and describe their experiences. The author did not interrupt them, she only intervened when it was deemed necessary. The questions found in the questionnaire were not used chronologically, because the flow of information was important, and posing questions would interfere with the flow. This experience was confirmed especially with one lady who seemed uncomfortable with direct questions, and every time a question was posed, she showed signs of discomfort and confusion. For this reason, the writer decided to let the ladies talk uninterrupted. It was only when the participant needed prompting that the researcher posed specific, open ended questions which then led to a smooth flow of information. Non verbal behaviour was noted as well as the author's own feelings and thoughts during the interviews. The researcher's own process before, during, and after the interviews is recorded. As will be seen, qualitative research *"provides perspective rather than truth, empirical assessment of local decision makers' theories of action rather than generation and verification of universal theories, and context bound extrapolations rather than generalizations"* (Patton, 1990, pg. 14).

Interviews were conducted in English, Italian, Swahili, and Kikuyu languages. The writer translated those interviews in Italian, Swahili, and Kikuyu into English while keying in data into the computer. The keying in was made soon after the interviews in order to avoid forgetting important information or mixing up data. This method was found useful because the writer relived the interview experience while transferring information into the computer.

Later, after consultation with this writer's mentor, it was considered significant to interview an Italian psychotherapist who has been working in the territory within the public service and has had a direct contact with some immigrant women. The aim of this particular interview was to learn whether any counselling skills have been used, and if so, whether they proved useful to these ladies or not.

The interview is recorded right before the common themes and patterns. This is because her ideas were considered important, despite not very detailed. Culturally, people in authority are given their due respect. What they say and do is taken very seriously, and, since they are considered *"God sent"*, they are always given the first place as they are seen to pave way for the necessary directions. For this reason, the interview with the psychologist is given its due importance by being placed before the ladies' interviews. This is in tune with East African accepted and approved cultural traits

INTERVIEW WITH AN ITALIAN PROFESSIONAL PSYCHOLOGIST
Dr. C. A. has been in contact with immigrants who have been referred to her for assessment and administration of various tests in her career in the public

service. The writer used just a handful of questions to set the ball rolling. These are written in italics for ease of understanding.

Doctor C. A.

What do you think is the role of counselling here in Italy?
Counselling is a relatively new discipline in Italy and it is slowly taking root. However, people are much more familiar with psychotherapy or psycho-analysis, and they don't seem to understand what counselling is all about. In fact, in our training, little emphasis is made to counselling and the various counselling approaches. However, seeing as counselling is a widely known and accepted discipline in Africa, Asia, and America and the rest of Europe, it is essential in Italy too, as the country opens its doors to foreigners and immigrants.

In your experience as a psychologist, which approaches do you use in working with immigrants?
Most of my work involves tests and evaluation. These tests have been formulated in Europe and America, therefore they are not culturally oriented. I have tried to establish a structured programme for these clients but I have not been successful. This is because these immigrants get referred to other districts, or they find it very difficult to open up and therefore lack of progress makes it difficult to continue.

Why does this happen?
In most cases, these immigrants did not choose to come to me. They were constrained by one circumstance or the other. Most of these are under the care of the social services, so they are referred to me when a need is perceived. Opening up has been very difficult and I have had the impression that they are very suspicious of our motives as the service in charge of taking care of their psychological needs. I also consider it cultural for them not to want to talk about their problems with someone who is supposed to have a say in whether they get their permit of stay or not.

Which are some of the major blocks you encountered with these immigrants?
In most cases, the problem of language has been a major one. Most of these immigrants come to us without knowing any Italian at all, and in most cases, cultural negotiators come along with them. This further compounds the problem of opening up because a trio is involved. Sometimes what they say in their own language may have a completely different connotation in Ital-

ian, therefore misunderstandings may occur. Sometimes the translation may be scanty, and this distorts the meanings they may want to give to situations. Culture is also very different, and what we consider acceptable here may not necessarily be acceptable in their own countries and vice versa. Silence has also been a stumbling block. When someone keeps silence, we may not understand what that silence means, and therefore it becomes difficult to help them, because we interpret the silence as a negative way of communicating.

What do you see as the future of counselling of immigrants here in Italy?
I consider it important to draw a multicultural counselling approach that would encompass all the needs of these people, which may be very different than our own approaches. I think it would help to form professional immigrants who would in turn empower their people for a better society. The number of immigrants is increasing and we can no longer hide our head in the sand. It is time to act and to act in the right way if there is to be an integration of cultures.

Which counselling theories would work best with immigrants?
As I mentioned, counselling theories are little known here in Italy. However, I think a theory that keeps in mind the cultural background of a client, that is open to adapt to the needs of the client, that has a multicultural approach, and that is flexible enough could help immigrants in their integration process. Maybe the best approach would be to have theories originating from other parts of the world apart from Europe and America, so that they can encompass a larger community.

3 3. COMMON THEMES AND PATTERNS

The ladies interviewed, as noted earlier, all hail from Eastern Africa (Kenya, Ethiopia, Eritrea, and Somalia). They are all Anglophones who have migrated to Italy in search for a better life. Some common themes were deduced from the interviews held and some of these are listed below. These themes were used to help understand how REBT could or could not be used in therapy for these ladies.

COMPLIANCE—EARLY CONDITIONING
All these ladies report extreme early discipline: they were taught, through discipline, that actions led to consequences. Each of them reports avoiding doing certain things due to fear of punishment—their behaviour was condi-

tioned by compliance—doing things in order to avoid punishment or to gain a reward. One lady notes: *"In fact, discipline at home was very strict. If we misbehaved, we were thoroughly beaten—my mother would use any means to hit us and teach us that some things were better watched from afar than done. We grew up knowing clearly the difference between right and wrong. We acted right because we really feared the beating, and when we acted right, we could occasionally receive praise."* They suffered silently, taking the blame despite sometimes being innocent. It seems as if their voices were unheard, they wanted to express themselves but no one listened. They also report having spent very little time with their parent/parents or guardians, but they knew exactly what was expected of them and they lived up to it. There was hardly any close relationship with parents. All but one of the ladies' reports being abandoned by one or both of their parents. They experienced anxiety and fear due to the abandonment experienced. As they narrate their experiences, the majority of these ladies became downcast, and regret could be read in their eyes.

Mulhausser (2013), explaining REBT, argues that past history and present life conditions strongly affect the person, but they do not, in and of themselves, disturb the person; rather, it is the individual's response which disturbs them, and it is a matter of individual choice whether to maintain the philosophies at B which cause disturbance. It is likely that this behaviour has become so part of the ladies that they are unconscious of the choices they make, but the fact is that they choose to act the way they do based on the feelings they experience when a negative event takes place. This is not easy to internalize for a person who believes that *"I am because we are"*. Besides, they may need education on how their earlier conditioning affects their current life. REBT would come in very handy here as a theory that educates a person on how their irrational thoughts and responses entirely depend on themselves and not on what happens around them.

Personal experience of the Interviewer: I was also brought up with serious discipline. I had 6 siblings senior to me, and my mom was very busy. She had no time to entertain any nonsense. My dad used to work far from home, and only came home twice a week. When he did, he expected to find everything perfectly at its place, and there was no room for ambiguity, he left no doubts about what was expected of us. For this reason, we grew up in fear of my dad, it was very difficult to relate with him, and the distance between us made me learn coping mechanisms, pleasing my dad under all circumstances in order to receive a reward or to avoid punishment. His return home was awaited with anxiety and trepidation because it was hard to predict what mood he would be in and how he would react to us. If I did not score good grades in school, he used to be very tough on me, so my motivation was fear rather than working hard for its own sake. I did comply because there were consequences to the contrary. It is only when I went through therapy myself that these issues came up, I had not grasped the relationship between what happened in my earlier childhood and the way I was living out my current life. I developed a people pleasing attitude—this is what I learned as I was growing up. If I did not please people, I feared they would reject me, and I loathed being rejected and abandoned in any way.

LIVING UP TO FAMILY'S EXPECTATIONS

The ladies experienced a rather stifling life prior to migrating, where they were constantly living in poverty and the level of anxiety was high because some of them did not know where their next meal would come from. Their migration was in search for a better life, and the family, relatives, and friends back home expect money and any other kind of help because the women are considered lucky to be living abroad. *"I came to Italy not by choice, but due to poverty. I needed to help my family, especially my mom and my son, so I left my son there with my mom, and came over alone."* They continue to experience high levels of stress due to these expectations, and also worry over those left behind, hence they suffer survivor guilt. They feel obliged to support their families back home, and when they can't, they go through remarkable levels of stress. *"I learned from my mom to sacrifice myself for others, as she constantly gave up her own needs and showed that they did not matter. In fact, I am the one who has to provide for my mom, my son, my uncle, my grandmother, my aunt, and my cousins. I send them money constantly and if I fail to do so, they have serious problems."* Each of them feels dissatisfied with the family's demands, and would like to free themselves of this burden, but they do not know how. However, they experience a sense of guilt for thinking and feeling this way, since they consider it their duty and obligation to provide for the people they left back in their countries. They feel trapped in a vicious circle and are resentful. However, they do not seem to find ways to get out of this vicious circle.

Albert Ellis affirms that the innate tendency towards dysfunctional thinking and behaviour is manifested in people's failure to accept reality. Ellis believed that certain severe mental disturbances are partly inherited and have strong biological components (Ellis, 1962). There is a tendency in these ladies to suffer from somatic problems which they are unable to explain. Through REBT, they may be able to grasp the relationship between their problems and their emotional states.

"Even after I got a job, I was still living under stress because I had to sustain my family back home. I was struggling to get somewhere to stay, at the same time I was under pressure from home. I felt a lot of discrimination in Italy, and just the fact that I am black made it difficult for me to get a job easily. Having no college degree also contributed to lack of proper jobs. I regretted why I did not pursue higher education." The underlying condition of this lady could be addressed using the ABC model. The lady strongly believed that other people had the power to decide how she lives her life. The ABC framework clarifies the relationship between activating events—the actual event and a person's immediate interpretation of the event (A)—*mother taught her to sacrifice herself for others*; our beliefs about them—evaluations that may be rational or irrational (B)—*she should, under all circumstances, give up her own needs for others, self-sacrifice is the greatest virtue and the way to be accepted by others*; and the cognitive, emotional, or behavioural consequences of our beliefs—emotions, behaviours, and other thoughts (C)—*feeling distressed if she is not able to live up to the expectations of others, and at times angry with herself for not fulfilling others' desires, as well as with others for expecting too much from her, a vicious circle*, (Mulhauser, 2013). In order to come out of this entanglement, this lady may need to do some inner work.

Ellis (1988) added D (disputing irrational beliefs) and E (effective new philosophy of life) to cover change and the desirable result of change (Jones, 1995). Disputation refers to detecting irrational beliefs, discriminating irrational from rational beliefs, and debating irrational beliefs (Sharf, 2012). This approach might be useful in the inner process as these ladies seek to come to terms with themselves and the internal dynamics that characterise their everyday life, and that makes their life difficult. It is only when beliefs have been disputed that one can experience E—a new effect, a logical philosophy and a new level of affect appropriate to the problem (Sharf, 2012).

The aim of ABC is to clarify the role of mental activities or predispositions in mediating between experiences and emotional responses. When a person experiences a negative event, and they respond to it through rational belief, the consequence is healthy negative emotions. If a person experiences a negative event, and they respond in an irrational belief, the consequence is unhealthy negative emotions. Individuals have goals that may be supported or thwarted by activating events. Based on their beliefs, people usually experience behavioural consequences according to these beliefs. This process could be painstaking for the ladies seeing as they have always had these beliefs and the consequences have always been the same. This approach may be very difficult for them to internalize, but chances are that it may produce positive results if they choose to work on themselves. Some of these ladies have taken everything as normal and the way it should. This may pose a problem for them to recognize the stifling irrational beliefs; therefore, the application of REBT could have either positive or negative results, depending on each individual lady.

"I was not very close to my mother, I never used to confide in her, and, although it was not verbalized, my siblings and I felt that we had to deal with our problems on our own without resorting to our parents, except when the situation was critical. My mother was too busy taking care of many other issues to listen to our menial problems. I grew up knowing and believing that I had to solve my problems by myself, I could not just talk about them to other people. In fact, we were taught that you don't wash your family dirty laundry in public, so we never used to discuss problematic situations."

This particular lady felt obliged to make some decisions based on other people's expectations of her. REBT holds that people possess the tendency to choose how much they allow themselves to be influenced by external forces, to help or damage themselves. It appears that this lady could not exercise this choice right from the beginning. The cultural reality reinforced this situation. REBT emphasizes that people can choose to think differently and more effectively about what is happening, and since they possess the capacity to think about how they think, they can choose to acquire and maintain the cognitive skills for containing and counteracting their tendencies to irrationality (Jones, 1995). People are likely to define themselves as good or worthwhile depending on how they see others reacting to them (Sharf, 2012). This was expressed severally by the lady, explicitly and implicitly. Individuals who constantly receive criticism from those around them are likely to view themselves as bad and worthless. Individuals are faced with the reality of dealing with the *"musts"* and *"shoulds"* that they achieved from interacting with others. Almost all of the ladies interviewed hold that they feared what others would think or say about them if they did not live up to the set standards and expectations.

RELIGIOUS ATTITUDE

The ladies report that religion takes a very central part of their entire life, as it was transmitted by the parents or guardians. God is very important in the lives of each and every lady that was interviewed, and they report this being the trend in their entire family. They all profess different faiths, but the faith they have is deeply rooted. God is associated with everything that happens, hence giving meaning to the events of life. They accepted religious beliefs without questioning them, simply because they were passed down to them by the family and society. They felt that they could not act differently, otherwise they would be considered outcasts. There was therefore no internalizing of religion.

One lady reports: *"religion is a very crucial aspect of my family's life. Everything is explained with the optic of religion. Religion is considered a way of life, and it offers one the basic principles of life. Those who do not profess any religion are considered outlandish. It moulds one to become a better person, and to have meaning in life. God is mentioned in every conversation. Suffering is also explained through the eyes of faith. Whatever one goes through is meant to purify them and make them better people. This explains why even when one is dying, they are serene."*

Another lady says: *"My mother was a very religious woman, and we used to sit together every evening to pray. My mother taught us that there is nothing impossible before God, and we lived in this perspective."*

Another lady recounts: *"Illness in the family is considered some form of punishment from God. If someone falls sick, they need to do an exam of consciousness to understand where they have gone wrong. They need to purify themselves and go through a cleansing rite in order to get their health back. God communicates with us through illness. If God has a reason to keep one alive, no matter how serious one's illness is, they will recover, so I learned to accept illness the way it comes and wait on the Lord. Illness is therefore taken as a personal issue—one feels responsible for being ill. Some illnesses are treated in hospitals, while others are treated traditionally. It depends on the kind of illness and its duration. When one has a simple cold, they can not waste time in bed, they need to be strong and face the daily activities without retreating. If someone has malaria, some evil spirits might be involved, so some cleansing is required."*

Using REBT in this issue might be tricky, in that all responsibility is placed on God and not on the individual. It is difficult for these ladies to change their mind about this issue, as there is great fear involved—they believe that by doing so they risk calling a curse on themselves and this is uncalled for. REBT therefore might not be applicable in this issue, and the therapist might need to employ other strategies to help the client internalize faith and find their own role in living out their faith without blindly complying to what has been inculcated and indoctrinated into their minds.

Interviewer's personal experience: My mother taught me that nothing has meaning without God. Being religious was not a choice—it was part of my family's life. Whatever happened was interpreted in the eyes of faith. My mom used to be very active in church, she was the point of reference and a leader, and everyone respected her. We learned that life is meaningless without God, and whatever happens possesses a divine interpretation. We learned that nothing exists outside God, therefore whatever happens in life has a divine connotation. We could not question that. God rewards those who are faithful to him and punishes those who choose wayward ways. We were implicitly taught that we have to please God constantly in our life and seek to fulfil His will in all ways to avoid unnecessary illnesses or bad omen for that matter. However, this teaching was disputed when I underwent my own therapeutic process. I came to understand and accept the fact that God is not like a policeman who is conditioned by my actions in order to love me or otherwise. I experience God's love as unconditional. I came to the understanding that I can't be passive when it comes to matters of faith, but I determine my own relationship with God, since God's faithfulness is not dependent on my behaviour, otherwise He would be a conditional God.

SILENCE

As noted earlier, silence is an acceptable aspect of East African people's traditions. One lady reports: *"In my family, silence is common. When we get angry, we prefer to keep silent. I don't talk to the person I am angry at for some time until the anger eases. Sometimes I also refuse to talk to other people, I prefer to keep things to myself and deal with them. It is not easy for me to let go of grudges. I cling to them because I think people are unfair to me. I feel as if people are out there to hurt me. Sometimes I prefer to close myself into my own world and ignore the rest of reality. I often do this through withdrawing and keeping silent. Even when people ask me what is happening, I don't tell them because I know that they will just continue judging me. I'd rather deal with my problems by myself. When the going gets very tough, I call my mom and she helps me deal with the situation."*

Silence is lived both constructively and destructively. When people keep silent in order to get deep into themselves and get in touch with inner feelings, it is constructive. Instead, when people keep silent because they are hurt or angry at someone without telling the other person, it can have a negative impact. It could help this lady if she would see that despite this earlier conditioning, she still can change her attitude towards herself and towards others. She may need to create coping statements that help her to dispute her irrational beliefs. This aims at helping her understand how important her thoughts are in the process of change.

Allowing others to determine whether she gets angry or not is something that can be addressed through REBT. The activating belief needs to be disputed.

When one is going through some difficult times, it is not uncommon to find them withdrawing and keeping to themselves. This is culturally acceptable, and people are left alone for as long as they need. This period is taken as a time to reflect and mentally organize oneself for decision making. People are able to interpret silence, and can distinguish between healthy and unhealthy silence. In most cases, however, issues are just let go of and life resumes as if nothing happened.

This could become a stumbling block in therapy using REBT because REBT holds that it is important for one to recognize their issues in order to start the process of change. When one is in this condition, it becomes very difficult to work with them.

DIFFICULTIES LIVING WITH THE PAST

Most of these ladies seem to struggle with their own past. Most of them do not have the courage to address their past issues since they claim that it is better not to open those closets. One lady retorts:

"I experience deep anger, anger towards my mother, my father, my step mother, my foster parents, and all those who have tried to help me in various ways, but I don't think I want to deal with that..."

This lady shared how hard it is to free herself from the ferocious anger that she holds against all those people in her life that she considers culprits for her current situation. She believes that she was unjustly treated, that she has always been the victim of circumstances. She talks about people going out of their way to hurt her. REBT talks about the reinforcing consequences. People can emotionally, cognitively, and behaviourally reinforce their irrational beliefs (Jones, 1995). Emotionally, musturbatory beliefs lead to negative emotions (anger, depression...) that make them seem true. Cognitively and behaviourally, people who seek social approval may avoid taking social risks, and by so doing, convince themselves that it would be too difficult and dangerous to do otherwise. While avoiding such risks, they may experience a form of emotional relief, therefore the combination of emotional, cognitive, and behavioural reactions makes them more rather than less socially anxious (Jones, 1995). Jones (1995) further notes that people who get extremely angry exaggerate the negative qualities of their enemies thus justifying and reinforcing the original self-disturbing beliefs. Their behaviour may create hostile reactions in others which then gives their beliefs validity and turns them into self-fulfilling prophecies. Once the self-disturbing and re-disturbing processes occur over a period of time, and people vainly try to correct their emotional disturbances, often they conclude it is not worth trying any more. This is what Ellis (1987) called the unkindest cut of all—people give in to their emotional disturbances. The lady quoted above appears to be entangled in this web.

The main goal of REBT is to empower clients to internalize healthy and undefeating philosophies and meanings and quickly react sensibly and in a fulfilling way to unfortunate life events, hence minimising emotional disturbances, decreasing self-defeating self-behaviours, and becoming more self-actualized so that they can lead a happier existence (Ellis, 2005). Rationality in this context is seen as the use of reason in pursuit of chosen short-range and long-range hedonism (Jones, 1996). Not only should a client remove symptoms of disturbing behaviour in their life, but they also need to develop what Ellis (1980) calls disturbability. One develops new philosophies and internalizes them, choosing to think in flexible and preferential rather than rigid and musturbatory ways. People with effective philosophies keep working on disciplined, goal-oriented reactions to everyday obnoxious activating events (A's) so that such reactions become somewhat automatic; they also think scientifically and fight and act against narrow-mindedness and arbitrary intellectual-emotional-behavioural restriction (Ellis, 1991b, pg. 166).

Interviewer's Personal Experience: Fortunately, I did not have a big problem living with my past, except the stifling anger towards my father which I dealt with when I went through therapy. Were it not for therapy, I think I would not have processed my issues. I consider it prerogative to process the inner struggles in order to come to terms with one's reality, and to live the here and now as opposed to the past or the future. My own experience shows me that therapy is important.

RELATIONSHIPS WITH MEN.

The ladies report difficulties relating with men, and most of them report having issues with their father figure in the family. One lady reports: *"I was brought up by my mother, who was a Muslim, I never met my dad as they both separated soon after I was born. According to my mom, my dad was a mean person and so my mom left him as soon as I was born. My mom openly talked about him to me. She never permitted him to even come closer to me, and even when he wanted to get involved in caring for me my mom distanced him completely. He used to attempt to visit me at school, he would wait at the school entrance, just to have a glimpse of me, but he would not talk to me or give me anything, because if my mom came to know that he came to visit me at school, he would face serious consequences."*

The relationship with the father figure in this narrative is a difficult one. The lady feels conditioned by the mother on what to think about the father. Anything related to the father was termed negative, therefore, as the lady reports: *"Every time I thought of my father, or my mother talked about him to me, I felt angry and even sad"*; this means that the lady's feelings in regard to her father were influenced by the information received from the mother. The mother always portrayed the father as an unjust person who caused tremendous suffering to the family through his behaviour. Both the lady and her mother felt that they did not deserve the treatment they got from the most important man in the family. As far as this kind of thought pattern is concerned, REBT aims at uncovering irrational beliefs which may lead to unhealthy negative emotions and replacing them with more productive rational alternatives (Mulhauser, 2013). In this case, REBT would be useful in that it would help the client to reduce emotional pain and make healthy choices. REBT is based on the idea that it is not external circumstances that make a person happy or unhappy, but internal thoughts about events, others, or self. Thinking, feeling, and behaviour are seen as linked and influencing one another (Ellis, 2011).

Another lady shares about her relationship with the father figure in the family: *"When I was 4, my mom left us, and we were taken to my paternal grandmother who took care of us while my dad worked in Nairobi. My dad had a good job, but he had a problem with alcohol. He used to spend all his money on alcohol, so we lived in extreme poverty. We feared our father because he used to come home drunk. The activating event in this situation was the father coming home drunk."* The children were conditioned by this behaviour so much so that their relationship with men has been influenced by their experience of their father. The lady reports that this event has caused her to distrust men and therefore she finds it hard to have any healthy heterosexual relationship. The main aim of REBT is to help clients replace their absolutist philosophies with more flexible ones, which includes learning to accept that all human beings, including themselves, are fallible, and learning to increase their level of tolerance to frustration while aiming to accomplish their goals. Ellis' emphasis in therapy is more on how people sustain their irrationality than on how they initially acquired it: the past cannot be undone and it is counterproductive to focus excessively on how people feel about the past (Ellis, 1991b).

Another lady holds: *"My experience of my dad was very bad, and from this, I never wanted to have anything to do with men. In fact, this explains why I never got married. I can't trust men, the only man I trusted in my life—my father—betrayed me, and therefore I have no confidence to be in a relationship with any man."*

The lady had a very negative experience with the father figure, which gave rise to negative ideas and attitudes towards men in general. These provoked feelings of anger and hatred towards men, and eventually, generated an attitude where men are to be avoided under all circumstances.

Another lady shares: *"We were made to believe that it was useless to send girls to school, and therefore we were subordinate to boys or men. I was taught to be respectful of men, since they were the heads of the family, as well as the ones who provided for the entire family. My role as a woman was to serve them and accept whatever they offered even when I was not convinced. I was made to sacrifice my needs for my brothers and my family."*

Three of the ladies interviewed have children that were not planned for, and, as one of them put it, by accident. The fathers of their children abandoned them. All those whose mothers are alive report getting a lot of encouragement from their mothers to keep the pregnancy. Their mothers took charge of these children in order to allow the ladies to pursue something different, seeing as they were very young.

Interviewer's personal experience: I could identify with the negative experience of the father figure in my life. I never related well with my father as I would have loved to. He was too authoritarian, and this left me with no choice but to carry out his orders and to avoid him under all circumstances. I feared my dad. I thought he never cared a whit about us but was only concerned about his image, seeing as he was a public figure. Working with the police force did not help, because he expected us to act like soldiers. I remember when he used to come home, we all had to line up outside when we heard his car coming, like soldiers, and greet him. Only when he dismissed us could we disperse. I felt terrorised by this feeling, and I did not like it all. In fact, I had a negative attitude towards men until I went through therapy while I was doing my undergraduate studies. Getting married at a later age in itself was an indication that I had to be very careful of the kind of man I wanted to spend my life with.

SELF-DENIAL, DENIAL OF PERSONAL NEEDS

"When I was born, I found other two female children, whom I took to be my sisters. My mother had taken these cousins of mine in with her because they had been abandoned by their parents. They were homeless and my mom decided to take care of them despite her meagre salary and the fact that she was single, and the fact that my aunt and uncle were in horrible economic and mental conditions."

"My mom was on a constant struggle due to the many mouths she had to feed. However, she did not give up on anyone. She was always there to save everyone, and that behaviour continues till today."

"Currently, I work as a baby sitter, residing in this family with 3 young children, where the mom mistreats me and expects me to work so much for a low pay. I decided to just bite the bullet and stay put, since I need the job, and I can not afford to be a failure in this job, and I can not risk to lose it, otherwise my people back home will think that I am incapable of handling a job." The lady is willing to subdue her emotional needs in order to continue working for her current employer and providing for her family back in her country. This is a lesson she learned from her mother. This fits the criteria of ego disturbance, where the belief that *"I must do well and win the approval for all my performances..."* prevails. This leads to one thinking and feeling inadequate and undeserving when they do not do as well as they believe they must. Here, one demands that they be special, perfect, outstanding, superhuman, and hence godlike (Jones, 1995). In both discomfort and ego anxiety, individuals have a belief that if they don't get or do what they want, the results will be awful or catastrophic (Sharf, 2012).

Working in the here and now and disputing irrational beliefs could be helpful to the ladies, seeing as they can not change the past, and can not change their mother's beliefs and attitudes. Each one of these ladies is only responsible of themselves and no one else.

Community and familial expectations condition people remarkably. For instance, one lady argues that *"when one has a problem, the family and community get together and help them out. I have learned from my family to do exactly this. Currently, I send significant amounts of money home, to help different family members in their situations. I sacrifice plenty of things in order to help my people at home. It is actually expected that I do so. If I don't, I will be considered selfish and transgressing our values, so I have to help them. In fact, if there is a pressing need at home, people get together to help out. It is expected that one asks for help when they need to, and everyone comes together to give a hand. There is a strong sense of solidarity especially in matters to do with illnesses, studies, calamities, among others."*

Another lady reports: *"When I was growing up, as a girl child, I was taught to let others take the first place. I was taught to respect boys, because boys have more worth than us girls. For this reason, I had to sacrifice myself totally in order to reach out to the others. I remember when I used to cook, I would serve everyone else, and only when and if food remained would I eat. I learned this from my mother. She was always the last to eat, and usually she ate leftovers. She made me internalize these concepts and so that explains why even now, when guests come to visit me, I am always the last to eat, and sometimes I don't eat at all. I think this is not a fair game but I accept it all the same. What I was taught by my mother is important and I will observe it as long as I live."*

The lady believes that in order for her to be accepted by others, she has to live up to their expectations, I must do well and win the approval of others for my performances or else I am no good at all. Even if she feels bad about doing what she learned from her mother, she feels tied to it and does not have the courage to change this behaviour. She is heavily conditioned by what she learned, and this makes it difficult for her to see other alternatives. This belief often leads to anxiety, depression, shame, and guilt. The lady reports suffering periodically of ailments she hardly understands.

TRAUMA AND TOUGH LIFE EXPERIENCES

Most of these ladies have gone through difficult experiences, and three of them experienced trauma once or more times in their life, but have not been able to process the trauma, so they are still living with its consequences. Their experiences have been stifling. In most cases, they sought to interpret these traumatic experiences in the eyes of faith, however, the inner processes have been compromised. They were made to believe that all these experiences were a form of atonement for something they or their family members might have done that displeased God.

"I was an only child. My mom died when I was 4. When my mom died, I was lying down with her on the bed. No one has ever told me if my mom was sick or if it was a sudden death, but what I can vaguely remember is calling her out to wake up, and she was not responding. I vaguely remember that as I called out, I felt very frustrated, and then my father came in and took me away. After a week, we buried my mom. I did not understand then what all this meant. The only thing I can remember is calling out for my mom all the time, but she never answered me." This lady experienced a series of traumas which would need a structured program to work through. She felt abandoned by her mom, and later she blamed herself for not having saved her mom. Part of her died when her mom died, and she has not been able to reclaim that lost part so far. She still feels responsible for all that happened, at the same resentful to her father for not intervening and preventing the death of her mom.

REBT emphasizes self-talk that influences both the conscious and the unconscious decisions people make. It helps individuals to identify, challenge, and replace their self defeating thoughts and beliefs with healthier thoughts that promote emotional wellbeing and goal achievement. It focuses on educating people about the relationships between thoughts and emotions, exploring common negative thoughts held by trauma survivors, identifying personal negative beliefs, developing alternative interpretations and judgements, and practicing new thinking (Rubush, 2013).

"I thought I made my mom die." The lady still experiences guilt for the death of her mother, and this is still stifling and it sometimes prevents her from living out her life in the fullest way possible.

Another lady reports: *"I was born in a remote village in Somalia where there was no food and we were living in constant fear of bandits. We were being attacked every now and then and the fear and terror were constant. My parents separated, my mom went to Nairobi while my dad went to Libya. I was left back in Somalia with my siblings. I did not go to school because I did not have the money to pay school fees. I had to learn early to take care of my own needs because my parents had left us on our own. I did menial jobs in order to survive, and I also worked as a domestic help where I made do with very little, to say nothing of all the mistreatments I got from my employer. People used to take advantage of me because I was desperate. I did not have other choices but to persevere hoping that some better days would come."*

This lady was living in constant fear and insecurity right from when she was born. She experienced one trauma after the other. Being abandoned by her parents added to the traumatic experiences. As with the lady cited earlier, REBT trauma therapy might be helpful in this situation as well. She continues:

"In 2009, I decided to leave Somalia and go to Europe via Libya. I had nothing to lose, I had lost so much in my life, so I looked for money and paid for the trip—which was not guaranteed. It was a hefty sum of money but I was sick and tired of living the kind of life I was leading in Somalia. I left, through the desert, with a group of 10 other people. We walked for 3 months through the desert. I came face to face with death on a constant basis. We were attacked, raped, robbed, threatened, and I thought I would die any time. Through the desert, we did not have food, and we used to drink our own urine, disgusting as it was at the beginning. I however got used to it, I did not have a choice. We went hungry for prolonged periods of time. We walked endlessly, I could not see the end of the desert. It was infinite. However, I always had hope that over the horizon, we would get to a place where we could have our basic survival needs guaranteed."

The lady confirms that she wanted change, she was not happy with the life she was leading back home, so she was willing to do anything possible to change the situation, even to risk death. This is the beginning of change. This is where the theory of constructivism comes in. Constructivism, as indicated earlier, holds that people have considerable power to construct self-helping thoughts, feelings, and actions, as well as to construct self-defeating behaviours (Ellis, 2011). Despite some biological and societal limitations, people generally have a choice in how they conduct their lives, and therefore with effort, they can become what they want to be. People can motivate and work towards change. Having highly developed language skills, they can think, think about their thinking, and think about thinking about thinking (Ellis, 2005). Thinking, feeling, and acting influence and interact with each other, hence, when people think, they also feel and act; when they feel, they also think and act, and when they act, they also feel and think.

This lady showed a lot of resilience, which could be useful in the ABC process. It may take time for the lady to deal with her trauma seeing as she had a series of traumatic experiences right from the time she was little. In this case, REBT may need to adapt to the need of time that this lady may have.

RESILIENCE

It is evident how each of these ladies was able to persevere through very tough and at times traumatizing experiences. Each one of them, in their own way, demonstrated how strong they were inwardly and the courage they had to face life despite all odds. Their capacity for growth through adversity is remarkable. In extreme circumstances, they still found inner strength to go on. REBT could build on this resilience in that the inner strength demonstrated by the ladies could be used to help them change the way they relate to themselves, others, and life in general.

SOCIAL PROBLEM SOLVING ASPECT

Problem solving is considered a collective task by all these ladies. When one has a problem, everyone comes together to help resolve the issue and move on. One's problem is the community's problem, and problems are dealt with in a collective way. In fact, the saying *"I am because we are"* is very deeply rooted in the East African culture, and these ladies confirmed this. Being in an individually oriented community after an experience of a well-knit social system is itself very daunting, and some of the ladies' report getting shocked by such individualism in Italy. Integration becomes difficult because some of these values are absent in this particular community, therefore going through individualized therapy is itself very difficult for these ladies, because it reverses the whole process—that the problem is individual not communal. REBT might have a problem addressing this issue seeing as it emphasizes personal responsibility over one's choices. It would take lengthy work for the ladies to accept the fact that they are solely responsible of their choices despite living in a well-knit society. Seeing as REBT does not emphasize staying in therapy for a long time, it might not be applicable in these cases, unless the ladies are willing to make an about turn in the way they view life.

DIFFICULTIES IN SETTLING AND LACK
OF EMOTIONAL SUPPORT.

The ladies express difficulties in settling down in Trieste, and live in anxiety over economic insecurity. One lady posits that *"my life here is a struggle. I don't feel at home here, and I feel discriminated against. This is due to my colour, difficulty in learning the local language, and the fact that I did not study here. I feel discriminated against because my academic certificates are not recognised here. As far as getting relevant documents is concerned, it is a real strenuous effort, and it has been very frustrating. One constantly needs the help of others in order to get anything done".*

Adjusting to a new life has been very difficult, and each reports that they would like to move on to other countries because they don't see their future in Italy. Lack of emotional support has contributed towards this sense of loss. They hardly get to talk about their past experiences with anyone, because they feel that no one is available for them. They fear seeking help because they might be considered mentally ill. This is one of the strongest earlier conditioning that these women face. They claim to have mental health issues, but these issues are not adequately addressed. They report experiencing discrimination. They feel the need to talk to someone about their problems but they don't get the right person who would understand them without judging them, someone who can speak their own language and empathize with them. They experience lack of emotional support.

"Settling here in Italy has been problematic right from the moment I set foot here. My main problem is that I feel discriminated against. Racism is still very rampant here, and I don't see my future here. I would like leave this country and move on, I don't actually like living here. I would like to go to UK or other countries." The lady feels that everyone is out there to get her, and she feels defenseless. *"I have all along felt misunderstood, by my parents, friends, acquaintances. I continue to feel the racism all around me, and I also feel betrayed by so many people."*

This lady and those others who experience this hardship might need to review their earlier conditioning. Feeling discriminated upon is attached to their past experiences and the beliefs they have concerning how they should be treated. It might help them to dispute their irrational beliefs. Developing the following types of thinking could help the ladies in their process and in their relationships with other people:

Unconditional self-acceptance: I am a fallible human being, I have both my good and bad points. There is no reason why I should be flawless, and despite my good and bad points, I am no more worthy and no less worthy than any other human being.

Unconditional other acceptance: Other people will treat me unfairly from time to time. There is no reason why they must treat me fairly, and the people who treat me unfairly are no more worthy and no less worthy than any other human being.

Unconditional life acceptance: Life doesn't always work out the way I would like it to. There is no reason why life must go the way I want it to, and life is not necessarily pleasant but it is never awful and it is nearly always bearable.

Interviewer's Personal Experience: I can relate to this experience, although I made a conscious decision to relocate to Italy from my country, albeit with great difficulty. I had to leave everything that was familiar to me, my home, my family members, friends, lifestyle, everything, and settle in an individually oriented society. I lived in a great home, and I had to abandon that. I came to a tiny apartment, with no help, I had to do everything all by myself. When I arrived in Trieste, I was in my 8 months pregnant with my son. It was very hot—I was not used to such heat, although I had visited Italy other summers. After my son was born, I felt very lonely. My daughter was 18 months old when my son was born, and my husband would be away the entire week for work purposes. It was very difficult for me to deal with two babies, and the loneliness I felt was beyond words. As a result of constant stress, I got very ill. I felt abandoned. Back in my country, when a baby is born, close and extended family members, friends, and neighbours all get together to encourage and support the new mom. She is never alone, she is not allowed to do any housework because her duty during the first three months is to recuperate and nurse her newborn. This is what I experienced when my daughter was born back in Kenya. Then, here I was in Italy, all alone, after a C-section, left all by myself to face everything. I wanted to go back home. It was very traumatic, the culture shock, and I felt that no one understood what I was going through. I would have liked to have someone to share all my frustrations with, but no matter where I turned, I felt hostility, whether it was intended or not. It took me two years to start appreciating my life in this community and creating new friends, despite being a very outgoing person. I enrolled in a Masters program and this helped a great deal.

DESIRE FOR PSYCHOLOGICAL, EMOTIONAL, AS WELL AS ECONOMIC SUPPORT IN SETTLING.

"I think it would help if people trying to settle here could get the right counselling that could help them adjust to situations. Life is very difficult here and it is difficult for someone to face it alone. The services currently given do not answer to the needs of those who seek them, because they are not made for this purpose." The lady feels that there is room for change, that she can improve things. Here, REBT could work. In REBT, the client acknowledges the existence of a problem and identifies any form of 'meta-disturbances'

about the problem (problems about the problem, for instance, feeling guilty about being depressed) (Mulhauser, 2013). The client goes on to identify the underlying irrational belief that caused the original problem and comes to understand why it is irrational, and why a rational belief would be a healthy alternative. The client therefore challenges this irrational belief system and adapts a range of cognitive, behavioural, emotive, and imagery techniques to strengthen their conviction in a rational alternative. Rational emotive imagery (REI) helps clients to practice changing unhealthy negative emotions into healthy ones at C, while imagining the negative event at A, as a way of changing their underlying philosophy at B, helping clients move from an intellectual insight about which of their beliefs are rational and which are irrational, identifying impediments to progress and overcoming them, as they work continuously to consolidate their gains and to prevent relapse (Mulhauser, 2013). Another lady says:

"I think it would really help those women who come here with the aim of getting a better life to receive help in coping with their traumas. I feel that I need to talk to someone, I have always had that need, but I never got the right chance and the right person. I want to put my experiences in writing so that others can know what some of us have gone through before getting here."

"I love my baby, but she is a constant reminder of the terrible experience with my dad and her father. She is a pretty girl, but her presence will always remind me of the men in my life who did not protect me, and who destroyed my life."

DESIRE TO BE HAPPY AND TO LIVE A
FULFILLING LIFE (HEDONISM).

"It has been very stressful trying to settle here in Italy. At one point, I wanted to go back home, but I knew that I had reached a point of no return, so I had to persevere like my mom taught me, and continue hoping for better times." Ellis emphasizes that people have an underlying goal to be happy. They strive for the best in life, want to live as stress free a life as it is humanly possible. This lady wanted to achieve this goal, but she felt conditioned by her past, her culture, her family, and her surroundings. REBT posits that people have it within their power to profoundly change their beliefs and philosophies, and therefore to radically change their state of psychological health. This lady did not experience this power; it was very hard for her to think independently. She felt that her life was not her own, and the way she lived was to be dictated by others. The cultural convictions make it very hard for East Africans to

internalize this truth. It requires colossal emotional and psychological commitment to achieve this goal. What could be useful to this lady might be the theory of constructivism, where emphasis is on the considerable power people have to construct self-helping thoughts, feelings, and actions, as well as to construct self-defeating behaviours (Ellis, 2011).

"Many times I am under stress and I overeat. I have a bad metabolism and sometimes I suffer stomach problems. My aim is to go back to school and take a college degree." The lady feels that she is capable of improving things, so this is a good beginning and a strong ground to work on.

"Here in Italy, I am living in dire need. I have a simple job which earns me very little money. I get rent and food stamps but that is not enough. I have to take care of my daughter single handed, and it is not easy. I would like to leave this place and go to another country. Maybe the fact that I have a baby might help to get me the necessary help I need to survive. I am fed up with this place. I have met very pleasant people, but there is no future in this country. I want to leave, to go away to another country. The problem is that I have a refugee status, therefore I can not leave this county and settle in another one. I will wait and see if I can apply for permanent residence after 5 years of my stay." Ellis holds that the first step of the journey towards healing is readiness to challenge one's irrational beliefs, which cause people's emotional and behavioural responses. REBT views human beings as responsibly hedonistic in that they strive to remain alive and to achieve some degree of happiness (Mulhauser, 2013). However, Ellis advocates responsible hedonism, which seeks to focus on long-range rather than short-range hedonism (Sharf, 2012). Individuals with a responsible attitude towards hedonism think through the consequences of their behaviour on others as well as on themselves.

According to REBT, all people want to be happy, whether alone or in company. People seek to have fulfilling relationships, and get along well with others. People desire the best in life, they want to be educated, well informed, and at the top of things. People want a good job, a good remuneration, and the ability to enjoy their leisure time without being conditioned by other factors. When people want to survive and be happy, they have several desires to perform important tasks well, to relate successfully to others, and to do what it takes to help them reach their goals (Ellis, 2011). This is the ideal situation, but concrete life shows that people hardly get all they want, and instead, are thwarted by the *"slings and arrows of outrageous fortune"* (Ross, 2006). When people's goal to be happy is blocked, they may respond in ways that are healthy and constructively happy, or in unhealthy and unhelpful ways. These reactions are determined by people's beliefs. These beliefs cause people's emotional and behavioural responses. People's irrational beliefs and behaviours often take the form of extreme or dogmatic 'musts', 'shoulds', or 'oughts', contrasting with the rational and flexible desires, wishes, preferences, and wants (Mulhauser, 2013). REBT holds that people have it within their power to profoundly change their beliefs and philosophies, and therefore to radically change their state of psychological health. The ladies interviewed, if empowered, can make a difference in their own lives.

AREAS THAT MAY NOT BE ADEQUATELY ADDRESSED BY REBT

Some cultural practices in the community of these ladies may not facilitate the use of REBT. For instances, one lady reports: *"Handicapped and sick people are considered bad omen, and their handicap is associated with something wrong that the parents may have done. The blame is on the parents or someone who might be jealous of the family and wants to destroy them. Some rituals are performed to kick out the evil spirits. It is the hope of the people that this lesson serves to warn others against doing evil."* In this situation, the strength of these cultural beliefs makes it a collective responsibility for whatever may go wrong. No one individual is to blame for what happens, therefore there is a chance that no one will see the need of working through their own conditioning, beliefs, and thinking about their way of thinking. Room is not given to people to address their personal issues, because the sense of collective responsibility prevails. This makes it difficult for personal inner work, as the *"blame"* is placed on something outside of the person.

CHAPTER CONCLUSION

REBT emphasizes the importance of preferences in life when processing thoughts versus the inflexibility of absolute thinking with respect to the outcome of events (Greenfield, 2011). In counselling East African women, REBT is a good starting point but other counselling approaches might be needed in order to address all the needs of the women. Cultural characteristics such as the group identity, silence, non verbal language, among others, need to be understood within the context of the culture. REBT gives little focus on delving into a client's past. It provides short term, solution-focused treatment that helps clients cope with their current problems while they develop healthier ways of thinking and coping (Miller, 2014). For this reason, REBT may not exclusively be effective with the East African ladies cited above.

REBT's goal is to reduce or eliminate irrational behaviour. In order to achieve this, the client needs to learn how their thinking, emotions, and behaviour are interrelated. Seeing as REBT is frequently relatively short-term, it may not be helpful with seriously disturbed clients, for example, those who have lived through traumas and continue doing so. REBT's approach needs to be focused in that it doesn't bring into question the client's cultural values and background.

REBT emphasizes reinforcements. However, reinforcements in the East African culture are not appreciated as reinforcements, but as everyone's duty, so these may not work in this case.

REBT, for these ladies, would promote cognitive restructuring, through the ABC charts, paradoxical homework, reverse role play and referencing (Greenfeld, 2011).

CHAPTER FOUR

PREFERENCE OF REBT OVER OTHER PSYCHOLOGICAL THEORIES

INTRODUCTION

Rational Emotive Behaviour Therapy was chosen over other therapies in this research. The reasons for this choice are developed as the chapter unfolds and as other theories are considered alongside REBT. In this chapter, most of the main psychological theories are briefly described, and then compared with REBT. The theories are grouped and clustered as per their approaches namely Psychodynamic, Cognitive, Behavioural, Existential, Family, Group, and Multicultural.

There is no one single theory that can satisfy all clients' needs, therefore it is essential to integrate different theories based on the needs of the clients as shall be seen in this research. Each theory has much to offer, but it may not, independently of others, satisfy all the needs of clients. Theories have been developed within certain contexts, and this itself is proof that certain needs of a particular environment called for the development of tailor made approaches depending on the cultural background and exigencies at hand. For this reason, it would not be helpful to use a theory blindly. The choice of the relevant theory depends on the therapist, hence, the need for training in a wider perspective to accommodate arising needs as well as needs of a population different than the environment within which the theory was created.

REBT is seen as an approach that can be implemented with various clients/contexts. Ellis himself said that *"personally, I favour counsellors taking socio-cultural and socio-political stand"* (Ellis, 2000). This means that he was open to widening his clients and adapting the theory to fit clients' needs.

REBT also empowers people against conforming too much to social values and family expectations. This fits the needs of the East African ladies as they experience social and family pressures. REBT advocates accepting the consequences of one's choices, thus empowering people to take responsibility over their actions, which is one of the main felt needs of the East African women interviewed in this research.

41. PSYCHODYNAMIC THEORIES

These theories emphasize the inner conflict and seek to reconcile our biological selves with our social selves. They hold that the unconscious influences behaviour without one's awareness (Strisik, 2014). Psychodynamic approaches work to make the unconscious conscious so people can have greater insight into their needs and behaviours and therefore more control on how they allow these conflicts to affect them (Strisik, 2014).

PSYCHOANALYSIS

Sigmund Freud held that inborn drives, particularly sexual, are very important in determining later personality development. His structure of personality is based on the ego, id, and superego. Traditional psychoanalytic methods require several years of treatment. Will to pleasure is the underlying motivation of all human behaviour according to Freud. We constantly act out our developmental history and our unconscious biological drives. This means that one is so influenced by their childhood and their inner mechanisms that they do not have the free will to make choices and decide. According to Freud, we are products of other forces and not ourselves. His theories ignore mediational processes (McLeod, 2007), there is no room for thinking, reflection, and memory. This limits the human being and fails to encourage free choice and the responsibility that comes as a result of one's choices and the consequences of one's actions. Free will therefore has no place in Freud's theory.

Freud's theory was created for a specific audience, and may not be able to address current issues such as multicultural aspects, feminist theories, and audience other than Westerners.

Albert Ellis differed with Freud and held that the past is only as important as the client wants it to be. It is the person who gives importance to their past. REBT does not necessarily require long years of therapy as does psychoanalysis.

Psychoanalysis is extremely time consuming and expensive. When psychoanalytic concepts are used in brief therapy, therapists are limited in their goals and in the type of patients they can work with, whereas REBT does not operate with such restrictions. Looking at the needs expressed by the East

African women, time is of essence, and they would find it hard to stay in therapy for prolonged periods of time. This favours REBT over psychoanalysis in addressing the needs at hand.

The concept of family within East Africa is largely felt, every child is everyone's child, and this cultural characteristic may not favour the childhood experiences Freud emphasizes. The fact that REBT does not dwell on the past for its own sake is favourable to the audience at hand.

JUNGIAN ANALYSIS AND THERAPY

Jung places great emphasis on the role of unconscious processes in human behaviour. Jungians are particularly interested in dreams, fantasies, and other material that reflects unconscious processes (Sharf, 2012). Symbols of universal patterns that are reflected in the unconscious processes of people from all cultures are important. Therapy therefore focuses on the analysis of unconscious processes so that clients can better integrate them into conscious awareness.

Jung's psychotherapy bridges the gap between spirituality and science. Jung's work concentrated on digging deep into one's own soul and cultivating a relationship with the divine. He talked about spirituality, not religion. Spirituality is about wholeness and unity of body and mind and not their separation. Personality, for Jung, is the psyche, and it includes all thought, feeling, and behaviour, whether conscious or unconscious (Roya, 2010). This is what helps us to adapt to social life and our environment. The psyche needs to be explored in order to find a state of wholeness. Within a person's problems lies the hidden wisdom which a person can use to find solutions to these problems and transform one's shortcomings into a spiritual compost for a more integrated, conscious, and holistic life. Murray (2010) notes that

> *the end result of a Jungian psychoanalysis is not principally to better functioning or improved coping skills, nor is it a greater emotional sense of wellbeing, happiness, or self-worth. The primary result is awareness of personal life patterns of coherence and direction that are rooted deeply in the psyche as a whole – in the Self. One gains a wide perspective on how one belongs to one's personal, cultural, and historical context. Personal and cultural context complexes and archetypal images rise to the surface of consciousness and merge with the ego consciousness to form an image of self that is much greater than it had before therapy (pg. xvii).*

Jungian theory considers the importance of different cultures and social contexts. This could favour the East African reality. However, Jung's emphasis on dreams, fantasies and other unconscious material differs with REBT's approach of dwelling in the here and now. East African women expressed the need to reinforce their personal identity in order to settle with more ease. REBT empowers the person to change their irrational beliefs which eventually helps them to live free creative lives. Jungian psychoanalysis works towards awareness of personal life patterns of coherence and direction that are rooted deeply in the psyche as a whole, and not necessarily better functioning or improved coping skills or greater emotional sense of wellbeing, happiness, or self-worth. REBT instead teaches people to be responsible of themselves and their choices, that they are the authors of their own happiness, and the goal of therapy is to bring change in their belief systems which consequently leads to behaviour change. The East African ladies interviewed expressed the need to be happy, to be independent, to make healthy choices. They eventually learn new coping skills as they attain greater emotional sense of wellbeing, happiness, and self-worth.

The aspect of spirituality could be applicable in counselling East African ladies. Jung emphasizes on one's spirituality, connectedness, and individuation. The spiritual aspect of East Africans is strong and so borrowing this aspect from Jung could strengthen REBT.

ADLERIAN THERAPY

Alfred Adler believed that the personality of individuals is formed in their early years as a result of relationships within the family (Sharf, 2012). He emphasized the importance of individual's contributions to their community and to society. This therapy is practical, and it seeks to help individuals to change dysfunctional beliefs and encourage them to take new steps to change their lives. It also emphasizes teaching and educating people about dealing with interpersonal problems (Sharf, 2012). Adler also saw people as largely responsible for who they are, and disputed the idea that people have little or no choice in shaping their personality. Adler considered present behaviour as being shaped by people's view of the future, as opposed to people being dependent on their past experiences. Adler reckoned that psychologically healthy people are fully aware of their choices and the reason behind them, (McGraw Hill, undated), and that it is not the unconscious propelling people's choices.

Adler differed with Freud in that he believed that the human being cannot be divided into parts (id, ego, superego), but is a unity, indivisible units (Manaster & Corsini, 2009). Individual psychology deals with subjective reality – our impressions, views, perceptions, apperceptions, and conclusions, not with physical reality – the concept of phenomenology (Manaster & Corsini, 2009). What is important, according to Adler, is not what happens to us, but how we react to what happens. This then gives remarkable power to an individual to decide their destiny.

However, although events in the environment influence the development of personality, such events are not the causes of what people become (Curtis, 2010). Every individual is endowed with the ability to become what they choose to become.

According to Adler, each person is endowed with the power to create their own style of life. Their creative power gives them control over their lives, is responsible for their final goal, determines the method of striving to that goal, and contributes to the development of social interest (McGraw, undated). This leads to freedom, which is dynamic – involving movement towards a goal. Despite being products of heredity and environment, people are creative beings who not only react to their environment but act on it and cause it to react to them.

The focus of Adlerians is to re-educate individuals and shape the society, focusing on internal determinants of behaviour such as values, beliefs, attitudes, goals, interests, and the individual perception of reality (Curtis, 2010).

The counselling process centres on providing information, teaching, guiding, and offering encouragement to discouraged clients.

According to Curtis (2010), people fail to change because:

→ They do not recognize errors in their thinking or the purposes of their behaviours.
→ They do not know what to do differently.
→ They are fearful of leaving old patterns for new and unpredicted outcomes.

Adlerian Therapy has several similarities with REBT's approach to therapy. The fact that each person is responsible of their choices empowers people to stop blaming others for their conditions. However, none of the things it promotes is done in depth (Sharf, 2012). Too much emphasis is given to individuals' perceptions of early recollections, and, by focusing on the importance of social interest, the theory tends to ignore important aspects of individual development. Too much emphasis is given to changing beliefs and not enough on changing behaviours. East African ladies are rooted in a society which follows the axiom *"I am because we are"*, and while this is considered a cultural strength, Adlerian approach is likely to emphasise extensively on this aspect as opposed to the identified current needs of these ladies – to address their own individual needs, since they have all along sought to satisfy the needs of others at the expense of their own. REBT in this case empowers the ladies to attain this goal.

4 2. EXISTENTIAL THEORIES

This approach considers the holistic approach to a person – mind, body, and soul. It recognizes the self-healing capacities of clients (Strisik, 2014). It enables clients to find constructive ways of coming to terms with the challenges of everyday living. Focus is on the client's concrete individual experience of anxiety and distress leading to an exploration of their personal beliefs and value system, in order to clarify and understand this in relation to the specific physical, psychological, and social-cultural context (Strisik, 2014). The past, present, and future experiences are given equal emphasis. The four existential problems to be dealt with are death, freedom versus responsibility, isolation, and meaninglessness.

This is a philosophical approach to people and problems relating to being human or existing, it deals with life themes rather than techniques (Sharf, 2012). Goals of existential therapy include becoming aware of oneself and developing the ability to look beyond immediate problems and daily events, and developing honest and intimate relationships with others.

Existential therapy emphasizes a keen respect for the person (Park, undated). Human beings change constantly, and are ever in evolution. Existential theory presupposes that humans are free to make the choices that they consider worthwhile for them, are capable of taking responsibility over their choices, and experience self-determination. In this theory, loneliness is seen as a natural condition of life. People create meaning in their lives by posing important questions such as who they are, where they come from, where they are heading, and what they want to become, among other fundamental questions. However, the present is emphasized. Existential approaches to counselling go beyond dealing with the surface problems to assist clients to confront the basic issues of their existence; anxiety, despair, death, loneliness, alienation, and meaninglessness (Jones, 1995). How honestly and authentically individuals deal with these themes affects their existence and psychological well-being (Sharf, 2012).

Existential therapy is about taking personal responsibility for the choices that one faces on a daily basis. One's destiny is shaped by themselves and not the outside world. Existential therapists view life in dialectical extremes and then gather knowledge and meaning from an integration of these two extremes (Flanagan, 2009). The aim is to embrace all existence and be fully alive. The goal of this therapy is to attain greater awareness or existential integration.

Existentialists hold that people have an underlying biological or transpersonal real or true self that they can discover and actualize. REBT teaches that one's true self is unique, and that with experimentation and hard work, it can be significantly changed (Albert Ellis, 1998). REBT also looks at the individual as well as the society and environment in which one lives, not either/or.

The existential approach to therapy offers highly intellectual ideas about human existence, and lacks guidelines for therapists. It is more philosophical in nature, and may be difficult to understand by people who have a simple educational background. Most of the ladies interviewed have a low level educational achievement, and may find it difficult to grasp the concepts detailed in existential therapy. It also emphasizes the negative aspects of life (death, meaninglessness, and anxiety) which may be counter-productive in dealing with East African women who already have had to face so much negativity, adversity, and trauma in their life. REBT instead helps them to live the here and now and take charge of their lives, giving quality and positivity to their lives and improving their growth process. REBT's goals are to help individuals overcome their emotional blocks and disturbances, as well as to help them become more fully functioning, self-actualizing, and happier than they otherwise would be. East Africans are not attuned to abstract issues, and are much more concrete.

PERSON-CENTRED THERAPY

Carl Rogers emphasized understanding and caring for the client, as opposed to diagnosis, advice, or persuasion. Unconditionally accepting clients for who they are is important. Clients are empowered to take responsibility for making positive changes in their lives. Person centred therapy (PCT) defines human behaviour as being motivated by the good in people and the desire to reach one's highest potential (Pickren, 2010).

Carl Rogers believed that everyone has the resources for personal growth and healing within themselves, and they can work towards personal development – becoming their best self. This form of therapy gives more responsibility to the client and views humans in a positive manner. The principle of non-directivity underpins PCT (Wilkins, 2010). The client is seen as the goal of the therapeutic relationship.

One of the fundamental concepts in PCT is power and how it is exercised. This refers to working towards reducing the power that others may have had on a client which has impeded the client from being fully functional. This increases the client's power to make decisions and be responsible for those decisions. Clients begin to trust themselves and their own sense of judgement, leading to becoming more creative and compassionate towards themselves and others. At the heart of this therapy is the actualizing tendency (Wilkins, 2010), which implies the drive within every individual towards accepting important experiences into the self-structure – thus, into awareness (Tolan, 2012).

Assessment and diagnosis are viewed as on-going processes by the PCT therapist, not as formal procedures undertaken at the beginning of the therapeutic relationship (Corey, 2001). As the relationship progresses, client aspects become clearer to both the therapist and the client, and the client is assisted to find alternative ways of living in order to function fully.

Bozarth (1999) summarizes PCT in the following three points:

→ There is one motivating force in a client – the actualizing tendency
→ There is one directive to the therapist – to embody the attitudinal quality of genuineness and to experience empathic understanding from the client's internal frame of reference and to experience unconditional positive regard towards the client
→ When the client perceives the therapist's unconditional positive regard and empathic understanding, the actualizing tendency of the client is promoted.

The essence of PCT is the therapist's dedication to going with the client's direction, at the client's pace, and in the client's unique way of being (Bozarth, 1999), the full commitment to trust in the client's own way of going about dealing with their problems and their life. The therapist does not disagree or point out contradictions, nor does he/she delve into the unconscious. Focus is on the immediate conscious experience (Pescitelli, 1996). This gives direction to the therapeutic relationship and empowers the client to take charge of their life.

The main goal of PCT is for clients to fully understand themselves, accept themselves, and extend this achievement to others. This is through a self-directed manner, being less concerned about pleasing others and meeting the expectations of others (Sharf, 2012). Individuals then become more realistic in their perceptions, better at problem solving, and less defensive (Sharf, 2012). This leads to a fully functional person.

According to Seligman (2009), there are a few goals of PCT namely

- → To facilitate client's trust and ability to live the here and now, which promotes honesty without one feeling judged by the therapist
- → To promote client's self-awareness and self-esteem
- → To empower the client to change
- → To encourage congruence in the client's behaviour and feelings
- → To help people gain the ability to manage their lives and become self-actualized.

Corey (2009) and Seligman (2007) outline a few weaknesses in PCT namely

- → The approach may lead therapists to be just supportive without challenging clients
- → There is often a difficulty in therapists allowing clients to find their own way
- → If the therapist is non-directive and passive, it can be an ineffective way to facilitate therapy
- → It tends to be simplistic and unrealistically optimistic
- → It does not draw on developmental, psychodynamic, or behavioural therapy, thus it limits the overall understanding of the patient
- → Listening and caring for clients may not be enough
- → This therapy may not be effective in psychopathological situations
- → It is not appropriate for those who are not motivated to change
- → It fails to prepare clients to face the world through the unconditional positive regard
- → It lacks techniques to help clients solve their problems

PCT has several aspects in common with REBT, and most of these could be borrowed to reinforce REBT. The living here and now, self-awareness and self-esteem, being responsible of one's choices, and giving no importance to what others say or think about the person, are some of the common characteristics found both in PCT and REBT. However, East African ladies need to be guided, they may not be in a position to know how to deal with their current problems. PCT does not offer training or education, therefore clients may be lost. REBT instead trains the clients on how to deal with their belief systems and gives homework in order for the client to continue the process outside the therapy setting. PCT lets the client determine the direction the therapeutic relationship takes, and this may not be helpful for this particular audience since they may not even know how to proceed and progress. Therapeutic progress requires structure and direction for specific change (Sharf, 2012), which PCT does not offer but REBT does. Clients need direction and suggestions which are not provided by PCT.

GESTALT THERAPY

This therapy helps a client become more aware of themselves and others both physically and psychologically. Everyone is responsible of themselves and needs to be attuned to their language, non-verbal behaviours, emotional feelings, and conflicts within themselves and others (Sharf, 2012).

The term gestalt means form, shape, pattern, or configuration (Jones, 1996). This signifies that the human organism is a unified whole which can only exist in an environmental field. This alludes that any split of the human being is erroneous. The gestalt process is based on the relationship between the client and the therapist and the experience in the current moment – the here and now. One's past is important only in as much as it sheds light to the present; the patient learns self-regulation and methods to tackle the load of the past which gets into the way of adequate perception of the present moment. One does not deny the past, but acknowledges it and uses it to understand the present and grow in it.

The aim of the gestalt therapy is awareness. Awareness refers to knowing the surroundings, responsibility for decisions, knowledge of the self, acceptance of the self, and the capability to contact (Gestalt Theory, 2013). The awareness is of the *"what"* and *"how"* not the *"why"* clients do what they do. Self-acceptance, knowledge of the environment, responsibility for choices, and the ability to make contact with their field (a dynamic system of interrelationships) and the people in it are important awareness processes and goals, all of which are based in the here and now experience that is constantly changing (Corey, 2012). This theory is grounded in experience and observation. The basic premise of gestalt therapy is that human nature is organized into patterns or wholes, that it is experienced by the individual in these terms, and that it can only be understood as a function of the patterns of wholes of which it is made (Perls, 1973). This signifies that human beings organize what they perceive into meaningful wholes. Gestalt aims at searching for the overall pattern rather than false dichotomies. Gestalt therapists value being fully present during the therapeutic relationship since this unconditional presence is good ground for growth due to the genuine contact between the client and the therapist.

Gestalt therapy seeks to clarify thinking, explicating beliefs, and mutually deciding what fits for the client, de-emphasizing thinking that avoids experience (obsessing) and encourages thinking that supports experience (Yontef, 1989). Yontef further posits that people manifest their distress in how they behave, think, and feel. Gestalt therapy views the entire bio-psychosocial field, including organism/environment as important, actively using physiological, sociological, cognitive, and motivational variables.

Gestalt notes that a person exists by differentiating themselves from others, and by connecting self and other – the two functions of a boundary. A person therefore assimilates what is helpful and discards what is toxic. This process is known as mental metabolism, where a person bites an appropriate amount of food (ideas, relationships, among others), chews it (considers it), and discovers in it toxins and healthy nourishment, assimilating what is healthy and spitting out what is toxic. This requires people to be willing to trust their taste and judgement (Yontef, 1989).

Faced with challenges, individuals often seek to restore equilibrium or to work towards change and growth. In fact, gestalt focuses more on process (what is happening) than content (what is being discussed) – the emphasis being on what is being done, thought, and felt at the moment rather than what was, might be, could be, or should be (Yontef, 1989), hence, the emphasis on the here and now.

Human organism is a unified whole, thus the split between body and mind, subjective (emotional) and objective (real), spiritual and profane, infantile and mature, love and aggression, conscious and unconscious, is erroneous. According to gestalt therapy, people's actions provide clues to their thoughts, and their thoughts demonstrate what their actions will be. Instead of *having* organisms, people *are* organisms engaged in activities of the same order which are often strongly dichotomized into mental and physical activities (Jones, 1996). People are not self-sufficient, but can only exist in an environmental field. A person and their environment are what they are because of their relationship to each other and to the whole. The whole therefore is different from the sum total of different parts. Gestalt therapists attend to attending to the obvious, while paying attention to how the parts fit together, how the client makes contact with the environment, and integration (Corey, 2012).

Field theory is a method of exploring that describes the whole field of which the event is currently a part rather than analysing the event in terms of a class to which it belongs by its nature or a unilinear, historical, cause-effect sequence (Yontef, 1989). This field is a whole, where parts are in relationship one with the other, and responsive to each other. No part is uninfluenced by what is happening with the other. A person constitutes a field. The client is seen as a whole, with all the parts working towards a description of who the person is. Everything is inter-related, what has effect must touch that which is affected in time and space. Field theory is descriptive rather than speculative, interpretive, or classificatory. The emphasis is on observing, describing, and explicating the exact structure of whatever is being studied (Yontef, 1989).

Gestalt therapy holds that emotion, the organism's direct evaluative experience of the organism/environment field, is immediate rather than regulated by thoughts and verbal judgements – a continuous process since all instances in people's lives carry some feeling tone of pleasantness and unpleasantness (Jones, 1996). Jones further argues that excitement is modified into specific emotions according to the situation that has to be met and the emotions mobilize the sensory and motor system so that needs may be satisfied. Through emotions, people become aware of their concerns, and therefore what they are and what the world is.

Gestalt approach has several characteristics that are similar to REBT and therefore it could be integrated with REBT to form a more holistic approach to therapy. Gestalt approach, however, over-emphasizes emotions, which could lead an individual to become vulnerable and confused. It hardly integrates body and mind into feelings. The East African culture over-emphasizes the separation between the body and mind, therefore the gestalt approach may reinforce this reality and hence fail in helping the client see themselves holistically and as interconnected. REBT helps clients to understand how their thinking affects their feelings and acting, how their feelings influence their thinking and acting, and how their acting influences their feelings and thinking. This leads to a sense of wholeness.

Therapists in gestalt therapy are accommodating and highly empathic. This could lead to a client getting confused about their own needs and those of the therapist. REBT on the other hand is directive, and the therapist leaves no doubt about their role, which helps the therapist differentiate their own issues from those of the clients.

Clients may not be aware of how stifling and limiting their beliefs are, therefore they need to learn these issues in therapy. Empowerment to reach out to others helps the client to stay on track.

4 3. COGNITIVE BEHAVIOUR THEORIES

This form of therapy defines concrete goals and uses active techniques to teach these goals. Patterns of thinking and behaviour and how they are re-inforced and maintained within one's environment are emphasized (Strisik, 2014). Functional analysis of thinking and behaviour are performed. In this approach, attention to irrational thinking is central. The techniques used here are relation training, systematic desensitization, assertiveness training, and social skills training. Symptoms reduction is achieved when symptoms are accepted and fighting against them ceases.

Cognitive behavioural therapy (CBT) is about the way one thinks about themselves, other people, and the world, and how what one does affects their thoughts and feelings. CBT focuses on the here and now, as opposed to fo-cusing on the causes of one's problems or symptoms in the past. It seeks ways to improve one's state of mind in the now. Behavioural interventions aim to decrease maladaptive behaviours and increase adaptive ones by modifying their antecedents and consequences and by behavioural practices that result in new learning, while the cognitive interventions aim at modifying mal-adaptive cognitions, self-statements, or beliefs (Craske, 2012).

COGNITIVE THERAPY

Aaron Beck developed a form of psychotherapy in the early 1960's that he originally called cognitive therapy, which later came to be called cognitive behaviour therapy. Beck decided to test the psychoanalytic concept that de-pression is the result of hostility turned inwards toward the self. He investi-gated the dreams of depressed patients, and found that they contained fewer themes of hostility and far greater themes of defectiveness, deprivation, and loss (Beck, 2011). These themes paralleled clients' thinking while awake. Beck devised a structured, short term, present-oriented psychotherapy for depression, directed toward solving current problems and modifying dys-functional thinking and behaviour (Beck, 2011). Beck also reckoned that people have their own internal communication system which leads to the formation of sets of beliefs, which later lead to the formulation of rules or standards for themselves called schemas, or thought patterns that determine how experiences will be perceived and interpreted (Sharf, 2012). Beck therefore formulated the concept of negative cognitive shift, in which individuals ignore much positive information relevant to themselves and focus instead on negative information about themselves (Sharf, 2012).

CT holds that dysfunctional thinking is common to all psychological disturbances. People have inherent tendencies to certain negative thoughts that evoke unhappiness and disturbance, especially in response to certain trigger situations (Webber, 2012). When people learn to evaluate their thinking in a more realistic and adaptive way, they experience improvement in their emotional state and in their behaviour (Beck, 2011). For this reason, CT attempts to reduce excessive emotional reactions and self-defeating behaviour by modifying the faulty or erroneous thinking and maladaptive beliefs that underlie these reactions (Vivyan, 2009).

Psychological disorders can be connected to a combination of biological, environmental, and social factors, interacting in a variety of ways, so that there is rarely a single cause for disorder (Sharf, 2012). For instance, early childhood events may lead to later cognitive distortions. Scarcity of experience or training may lead to ineffective or maladaptive ways of thinking, such as unrealistic goals or making inaccurate assumptions (Beck, et. al. 2004). When under duress, when someone anticipates or perceives a situation as threatening, their thinking is likely to be distorted. It is therefore not the inaccurate thought that causes the psychological disorder, but a combination of biological, developmental, and environmental factors (Beck & Weishaar, 1989). Automatic thoughts are likely to be a significant part of the processing of the perceived distress regardless of the cause of the psychological disturbance (Sharf, 2012). Automatic thoughts occur easily, spontaneously, and without much effort or choice. Automatic thoughts are not deeply buried as schemas and reflect schema content (Jones, 1997). In psychological disorders, these thoughts are often distorted, extreme, or otherwise inaccurate (Sharf, 2012). Automatic thoughts are part of people's internal monologue. These can take the form of words, images, or both. Such thoughts occur very rapidly and usually at the fringe of awareness. Automatic thoughts precede emotions, including feelings and inhibitions (Jones, 1997). People acquire cognitive vulnerability through childhood traumas, negative treatment in childhood, social learning, and inadequate experiences for learning coping skills (Jones, 1997), among others.

Jones (1997) further underscores that people maintain their psychological disorders through failure to turn off hypervalent modes, inability to reality-test dysfunctional interpretations, resistances to change, and unhelpful influences in their daily lives.

CT works best with clients who can focus on their automatic thoughts and take some responsibility for self-help (Jones, 1997). Some of those who have benefited from this therapy include people with schizophrenia, substance abuse problems, post-traumatic-stress-disorder, dissociative disorders, among others. It is not recommended to persons experiencing impaired reality. For some disorders, a combination of CT and pharmacological therapy is recommended.

CT posits that events or situations in life do not cause problematic emotions such as guilt, depression, and hostility; rather, it is mainly the evaluation of the event and the beliefs people hold about these events that get them into trouble (Corey, 2001). The past has influence over the present only by way of a person's present interpretation of past experiences.

Aaron Beck's concepts of automatic thoughts and cognitive schemas may not be easy for clients to grasp, as they are constructs rather than observable behaviours (Sharf, 2012). As noted earlier, East African ladies in question have minimal educational background and therefore they might find it hard to grasp these concepts. This approach over-emphasizes the client's responsibilities for problems and not enough attention to social forces such as violence that cause problems (Sharf, 2012). REBT is the foundation of CBT's (Daniels, 2014). Ellis came up with the unconditional regard to self, others, and life. This empowers the East African ladies to accept themselves as they are, without judging themselves, but to deal with their distorted beliefs that lead to the unmanageability of their lives. REBT emphasizes on the unity among cognitive, emotive, and behavioural dimensions of human functioning (Corey, 1982). It challenges the *absolutist musts* aspect of human behaviour, perfectionism. Through this, people make themselves panicked, depressed, indecisive, and often inert.

BEHAVIOUR THERAPY

Behaviour therapy (BT) is a psychological technique based on the foundation that specific, observable, maladaptive, badly adjusted, or self-destructing behaviours can be modified by learning new, more appropriate behaviours to replace them (FordMartin, 2013). This signifies that behaviour that has been learned can be unlearned. BT, unlike psychodynamic theories, does not focus on uncovering or comprehending the unconscious motivations that are behind behaviour. BT concentrates on changing behaviour. This form of therapy advocates that human beings respond predictably to stimuli, and the people who control these stimuli consequently control the person. There is no free will but only responses to perceived pleasures and pains. The basic idea of BT is that if one wants to treat irrational behaviours, one needs to make sure that the irrational behaviour is punished, and the rational behaviour rewarded, leading to the disappearance of the irrational behaviour because it leads to pain (Walter, 2013). BT posits that all behaviour is acquired through conditioning, and that people's responses to environmental stimuli shape their behaviours. According to behaviourism, behaviour can be studied in a systematic and observable manner with no consideration on internal mental states, because internal states such as cognitions, emotions, and moods are too subjective (Kendra, 2013).

BT has its roots in experimental psychology and the study of the learning process in humans and animals (Sharf, 2012). It is a collaborative, active-oriented therapy, empowering clients to take an active role in therapy and discouraging dependence on the therapist. Treatment does not last long. The assumption in behavioural therapy is that any behaviour that is positively reinforced will certainly repeat itself, and over time, it becomes a habit. This habit spills over other areas of a person's life, hence influencing the client to become different in more than one aspect of their life. Utilitarian calculus (Walter, 2013) is the centre of this therapy – pursuing things that produce pleasure and avoiding those that generate pain. According to Skinner, the mental make-up of a person could be understood (and behaviours predicted) through the history of what has been provided or deprived from that person's life with sufficient frequency to create a habitual attitude (Walter, 2013).

Pavlov conducted research into the functioning of the cerebral hemisphere of dogs, and discovered the conditioned reflex – classical or respondent conditioning. Watson viewed human behaviour as an objective experimental branch of natural science focused on the behaviour of human beings, distinguishing between unlearned and learned responses, detailing three main habit systems that are formed by conditioning, namely visceral or emotional, manual, and laryngeal or verbal (Jones, 1996). Skinner viewed behaviour as being shaped and maintained by its consequences. He acknowledged the importance of classical conditioning, but went beyond this to focus on the action of the environment after the response has been made (Jones, 1996).

BT emphasizes the overwhelming role of environmental contingencies in influencing the acquisition and perpetuation of behaviour (Jones, 1996). Learning is a process involving acquisition and retention of behaviours.

Skinner regarded the self as a repertoire of behaviours appropriate to a given set of reinforcement contingencies (Jones, 1996). People are not necessarily autonomous agents responsible for their own lives, but are shaped by evolutionary contingencies of survival and their behaviour is under the control of the environment they live in. Consciousness and awareness are a social product shaped by the environment.

Since much of the behaviour involved in mental disease is learned, the role of psychotherapy is therefore to change behaviour by manipulating the client's contingencies of reinforcement. Psychotherapy is also perceived as a form of control whose aim is to correct the undesired effects of excessive or inconsistent control exercised by other agencies (parents, guardians, teachers, among others) to restrict the individual's selfish, primarily reinforced behaviour. The therapist needs to be able to be a controlling agent or potent reinforcer (Jones, 1996). The therapist needs to avoid any punishment. This helps the client to bring out some of their behaviour which might be repressed, as well as extinguishing some of the effects of punishment. In situations where ethical or parental control have been inadequate, therapy may consist of supplying additional controlling contingencies. Teaching the client self-control techniques, especially when the client is subject to continued excessive or inconsistent control, is an important characteristic of therapy. Change of behaviour is important in the therapeutic relationship, where clients find solutions to their situations by themselves, and the clients' behaviour in respect to their problem is a relevant intervening variable.

Generally, behaviour therapy seeks to create new conditions for learning (Corey, 2001).

Behaviour is shaped and maintained by consequences, therefore changing behaviour requires changing consequences, the operant behaviour.

This approach hardly focuses on the person as a whole. It focuses prevalently on changing one's behaviour without any regard on where that behaviour originates from. It tends to ignore important existential and social constraints on behaviour. This change of behaviour may not be long lasting because it is symptomatic. REBT on the other hand makes use of many different strategies and techniques, helping the client to change their irrational beliefs so that future crises and problems may be avoided (Sharf, 2012). This approach is active, featuring homework and role playing as well as record keeping. Clients do not need to blame themselves. East African ladies have overly emphasized on doing rather than on being, and BT may reinforce this concept. They need to be able to see themselves from the perspective of who they are, and REBT helps this process. Whenever something goes wrong, it is a tendency of these ladies to blame themselves or others as this is what they have been taught in the past. A type of therapy that perpetuates this attitude may not be helpful to clients.

REALITY THERAPY

Reality therapy was developed by William Glasser. Glasser was dissatisfied with psychoanalytic psychiatry because he thought that too much emphasis is put on clients' feelings and past history, and insufficient emphasis on what clients were doing (Jones, 1996). Individuals sense the world outside of themselves, process these perceptions in their brain, and then choose how to respond to them. The brain then organises or reorganizes this behaviour, resulting in thoughts, actions, and feelings (Sharf, 2012). Glasser argued that psychoanalysis did not teach people to be responsible for their behaviour but to look at their past in order to blame others for it (Sharf, 2012). The deficits he saw in psychoanalysis led him to develop reality theory. The heart of reality therapy is what one chooses to do in a relationship and not what others choose to do (Glasser, 2000). Glasser also reckons that happiness and fulfilment depend on the quality of our relationships, that choice determines the kind of relationships we have and will have, and that controlling others is not the way to get what we want (pg. xii). Reality therapy suggests that all human issues derive from a lack of fulfilling relationships with others, and its main goal is to provide a connection for people, beginning with the therapist/client connection. When people fail in the effort to connect with other people, they suffer because the need to do so is as much built into our genes as the need to survive (Glasser, 2000).

In reality theory, perceptions of reality, rather than reality itself, determine behaviour: actions, thoughts, and feelings.

The therapist in reality therapy asks the client to gauge their behaviour and the effects it has had on their life thus far (Good Therapy.org, 2012). The therapist and the client do not dwell on the past; they only refer to the past in as much as it will help the present's choices. The past should illuminate the actual situation, otherwise it is of no use. The client however is the architect of their own transformation, and this transformation leads to self-confidence. The client needs to get and be real, and be honest and sincere if or when things do not work. Reality therapy is compassionate, empowering, and focuses on building a better life for the future. It utilizes thinking, decision making, and action steps to help people create fulfilling lives. The core principle of reality therapy is that everyone is always attempting to meet one of the five core needs (survival, love, freedom, fun, and power), sometimes unconsciously. If one's actions are ineffective, one will be unsuccessful in getting what they want (Jacqueline, 2011). Reality therapy teaches people how to direct their lives, make more informed and effective choices, and how to develop the strength to handle the stresses and problems of life. No matter what has happened in the past, one can always choose how to live their present life. In reality therapy, there is no focus on symptoms because the symptom is always chosen to deal with the present unsatisfying relationship (Corey, 2001). The symptom disappears when the relationship is improved. People are not victims of the past unless they choose to be so.

Glasser held that mental illness, regardless of causation, is one of the hundreds of ways people choose to behave when they are unable to satisfy basic genetic needs such as love and power, to the extent they want – hence disconnection (Glasser, 2000). Relationships are core in one's health or lack of it. Glasser reckons that people do not act irresponsibly because they are ill, they are ill because they act irresponsibly (Glasser, 1975). This then sets the basis of reality therapy – the importance of behaviour. External control psychology does not serve a person any good, and clients need to learn to defend themselves against it and use choice theory. Reality theory has been used with institutional populations and difficult clientele with remarkable success.

Jones (1996) sums up reality therapy in the following way:

→ Reality therapy is based on choice theory, whose assumption is that people's behaviour is always their best attempt to control the world to satisfy their needs, which comprise of the need to survive and the psychological needs for belonging, power, freedom, and fun

→ People develop personal picture albums consisting of pictures in their heads of how to satisfy their needs. Total behaviour is the sum of the four components of acting, thinking, feeling, and physiology. People, as control systems, behave to get the pictures they want

→ Children develop pictures in their heads through experiences of getting their needs satisfied. They learn total behaviours by creatively choosing different ways to control the world and by imitation

→ Reasons that people choose to maintain their misery are: to keep angering under control, to attract help, to excuse not taking more effective action, and to control others

→ Reasons that most people remain unaware that they choose misery are: mistaking short-term pure feelings for long-term feeling behaviours, most of their painful choices becoming automatic, and not wanting to lose self-esteem. People can also choose to stay controlled by others' misery

→ Reality therapists always require a clear choice theory reason for anything they do. The main goal of reality therapy is to help clients take effective control of their lives

→ The therapeutic relationship is characterised by involvement, compassion, caring, honesty, and not giving up on clients. Reality therapists teach choice theory through their initial structuring, using choice theory concepts, and direct teaching.

→ No excuses and no punishment are two principles when evaluating the client's progress in implementing plans

→ Applications of reality therapy and control theory include marriage counselling, group counselling, and working with school administrators and teachers to assist students (pg. 92).

RT has several similarities with REBT, one of which is that it holds that no matter what happened in the past, people can always choose how they will act here and now. Changing behaviour is the core goal of this therapy. However, this theory tends to be simplistic and superficial. Using the car analogy oversimplifies very complex human behaviour (Sharf, 2012). It may not be very easy to use in the real world. REBT concentrates less on behaviour because it is considered a consequence of thought change. For the East African ladies, the main issue is their thought patterns which need to be addressed. Behaviour change will come as a result of disputing irrational beliefs. These ladies also tend to be very defensive when it comes to being criticised regarding behaviour. It is a cultural characteristic. For this reason, RT would not be very effective with them.

4 4. FAMILY SYSTEMS THEORY

Family systems therapy is a type of family therapy that concentrates on the interactions of family members and views the entire family as a unit or system (Sharf, 2012). In family systems therapy, treatment is designed to understand and bring about change within the family structure. The family is a central system that significantly impacts a person's psychological development and sense of personal well-being. Families often take on the function of protecting other family members in response to what occurs in the broader social environment (Ivey, et. al. 2002).

Family systems theory views the family as a unit, a network of interlocking relationships, which have a remarkable influence in the thinking, feelings, and behaviour of each member of the family members. The psychology of the individual is not ignored in family theory; it is only put into a larger context (Kerr & Bowen, 1988). Bowen focused on patterns that develop in families in order to diffuse anxiety. A main generator of anxiety in families lies in the perception of either too much closeness or too great a distance in relationships (Brown, 1999). Brown further posits that the degree of anxiety in any family will be determined by the current levels of external stress and the sensitivities to particular themes that have been transmitted down the generations. If families do not have the capacity to think through their responses to relationship dilemmas, but rather react anxiously to perceived emotional demands, a state of chronic anxiety or reactivity may be set in place (Brown, 1999). Family systems theory is based on the assumptions that the human being is a product of evolution and that human behaviour is significantly regulated by the same natural processes that regulate the behaviour of all other living things (Kerr & Bowen, 1988). Emphasis in family systems theory is on process rather than content: focus is in what is happening in the present rather than what happened or the sequence of events that led up to an event (Sharf, 2012).

Of the many different family systems therapy approaches, this work will address four of these approaches namely intergenerational therapy, structural therapy, strategic therapy, and experiential therapy.

Family systems therapy focuses not just on the individual but on the entire functioning of the family. Bowen's inter-generational theory deals not only with relationships between two family members and how they involve a third but also on relationships that back one or more generations (Sharf, 2012). Minuchin's structural approach addresses the flexibility of boundaries within the family and how members can become too close or too distant, thus inhibiting proper family functioning. The strategic therapy of Haley concentrates on resolving symptoms within the family through direct or indirect means, besides incorporating concepts about family boundaries. The experiential approaches of Whitaker and Satir are partly based on intuitive reactions of the therapist to the family and making therapeutic interventions that lead to healthier family functioning (Sharf, 2012).

The East African ladies going through therapy do not have their family members with them. This makes it difficult for this theory to work. East Africans value family a great deal, but in the Italian context, it is not feasible. It could help in reflecting on how the family directly or indirectly influences the thought patterns of these ladies as well as their behaviour, and deal with the relationships within the families that may be significant in therapy.

However, this theory tends to ignore individual dysfunction and focuses on interactions between family members. It looks at the family's responsibility over the problems in the family. REBT instead helps the individual to understand how their irrational beliefs lead to thought formation and eventually to behaviour, therefore the person is solely responsible over what happens in their life. Proper integration of FT with REBT could yield good fruits in counselling the East African ladies.

4 5. GROUP COUNSELLING THEORY

When one is placed within the context of a group, they come to terms with who and what they are because the group serves as a mirror for them to view themselves. The group helps one to gain a wider perspective of the self, which leads to self-awareness. The group also helps one to see themselves from different perspectives (Berg, 1971). Cohn (1967) reckons that it is only in the light of the enlightened awareness that a person gains from the group that they are able to gain a more complete awareness of their substance, and it is this more enriched concept of self that enables a person to release their full positive potential to society. Group counselling provides individuals with the kinds of group experiences that help them learn to function effectively, to develop tolerance to stress and anxiety, and to find satisfaction in working and living with others (Corey, 2004). Members are able to benefit from the feedback and insights of other group members as well as of the facilitator. Learning by imitation also helps group members to grow, when they see others with problems similar to theirs cope well.

Group counselling would work best if the group is cohesive and has a common denominator. Even though these ladies come from East Africa, each of them has gone through different experiences and the traumas are different. However, they could benefit from group therapy because members would be able to share their experiences and how they are able to be deal with problems. It would however be necessary to do some individual work first before forming the group, and the work done using REBT could be a good beginning.

Group interventions based on REBT are brief and intensive (Corey, 2004). Corey further states that Albert Ellis posited that group members can quickly learn how they disturb themselves. The A-B-Cs of their problems can be clearly and simply shown, easily grasped, and quickly put to use in therapy. Because of the active, directive nature of REBT, members can alleviate their disturbances in the shortest feasible time. Also, by using the cognitive, emotive, and behavioural methods of REBT for even a brief period of time, members can internalize a constructive philosophy that shows them new ways of approaching situations. It seeks to eliminate the clients' irrational and self-defeating outlook on life and replace it with a more tolerant and rational one.

Group members are taught the ABC of REBT in that the irrational beliefs they learned in the past can be disputed, the active disputation of faulty beliefs through checking and modifying their values and attitudes towards themselves and others, coping self-statements through learning to change how they speak, psycho-educational methods where they practice and implement what they learn in the group, and cognitive homework (Corey, 2004).

Group members are taught unconditional self-acceptance as well as unconditional other-acceptance. Role playing also helps demystify emotions and thoughts. Reinforcement and penalties are also practiced in the group, as well as skills training.

REBT demonstrates some techniques that can be used in the group through:

- The activity oriented homework assignments that are vital components of REBT are more effectively carried out in the group context that in one-to-one therapy
- The group offers an effective milieu for several active/directive procedures, such as role playing, assertion training, behaviour rehearsal, modelling, and risk taking exercises

- The group serves as a laboratory in which behaviour can be directly observed in action
- Clients are often asked to complete homework report forms, which require going over the ABCs of upsetting situations and then learning how to correct faulty thinking and behaving. By hearing other members' reports and learning how they have dealt with the situations in question, participants can better deal with their own issues. Members can then practice together behaviours they would like to increase or decrease in the real world
- By watching other members, participants are able to see that treatment can be effective, that people can change, that they can take steps to help themselves, and that successful therapy is the product of hard and persistent work
- Disclosing intimate problems, some of which the person considers shameful, is therapeutic. Self-disclosure enables participants to realize that taking risks pays off
- Group procedures are especially useful for people who are rigidly bound by old patterns of dysfunctional behaviour; the group setting provides the challenge necessary to re-evaluate these patterns and adopt healthier ones (Corey, 2004, pp. 410-411)

REBT can be applied in multicultural groups. Since it challenges faulty beliefs and the cognitive restructuring process, involves confronting group members with their self-defeating thinking, members are likely to benefit greatly from group work. Most of the immigrant women are likely to have faulty beliefs which they have learned and assimilated with time. They need to be helped to see that these beliefs no longer serve any positive purpose, and they would do well to challenge them and replace them with new, conscious, positive, beliefs which will lead to unconditional self as well as other acceptance.

Group living is an essential part of human nature, and people learn to relate with the people they share their life with. This means that working in groups is an extension of day to day life, and that people's happiness depends largely on the quality of their functioning within their community, a very relevant concept in the East African cultural context.

4 6. CROSS CULTURAL THEORY

It is not possible to fully understand the psychology of a certain people without a complete understanding of the social, historic, political, ideological, and religious premises that have shaped the people of this group (Shiraev & Levy, 2004).

A holistic view of persons implies willingness to cross boundaries created by labels and categorization which includes beliefs, values, rituals, customs, and other types of behaviours (Van Beek, 1996). Van Beek goes on to affirm that counsellors need to be actively sensitive to the inter-related processes at work in the life of the client, the expectations of the counsellor in a particular encounter, the client's place on a gender role and identity awareness scale, the variations within cultural codes, the manifestation of class differences, the possibility of other different world views emerging in the interaction, the influence of inter-generational tensions as a result of cultural traditions, and the nature of culture as processes that provide meaning.

According to Repetto (2002), cross cultural counselling is defined as psycho-pedagogical intervention based on metatheory which

- Recognizes that all counselling approaches and theories are developed in a specific inter-active context
- Refers to inter-action in which two or more participants come from different cultures
- Includes any combination of the techniques involved in a culture
- Is characterised by professional assistance with the knowledge, skills, and attitudes that are culturally appropriate
- Recognizes the use of western and non western approaches in assistance
- The changes involve not only the introduction of cross cultural counselling programs but also the inclusion of this approach in the curriculum and in all the dimensions of the educational system such as teaching techniques, motivation, grouping, student assessment, and teacher training.

REBT may need to consider these factors in order to be effective with the audience at hand.

Van Beek (1996) says that cross cultural counselling aims at encouraging persons away from brokenness and toward wholeness in all areas of their life. Wholeness includes reconciliation and the restoration of communication in personal relations, acceptance of one's own talents and shortcomings, integration of one's value system-in-process, a harmonious experience of one's faith, as well as behaviour consistent with one's self-concept, values, faith, and the nature of one's relationships. Many of the clients in this research come from traumatised backgrounds, and there is a close connection between their culture and the way they live their traumatic experiences. Many of them may experience both physical as well as psychological trauma effects. An important aspect to consider in counselling is the fact that different cultures deal with trauma differently, and therefore therapists need to be conversant with the various ways clients have experienced and have dealt with trauma in their cultural context. Most East Africans may be used to alternative means of healing namely medicine men, traditional healers, culture specific rituals, conventional medical practices, and community based practices that offer forms of social and emotional support for the person suffering the trauma (Wilson & Tang, 2010). This renders the therapeutic relationship quite tricky in that the counsellor needs to be well aware of these factors. Clients may at first be suspicious of the counsellor because they do not know what to expect. It is the counsellor's responsibility to help the clients experience trust in the relationship and consequently start to talk about their experiences.

4 7. MULTICULTURAL COUNSELLING AND THERAPY

Multicultural counselling and therapy (MCT) does not discount the importance of any theoretical orientation, rather, MCT recognizes, adapts, and supports all approaches to therapy (Ivey, et. al. 2002). Individuals present themselves with specific problems within specific circumstances, and these need to be addressed as per need, tailor-making the treatment plan to fit specific individual needs. Working with only one approach may not adequately address all problems, and an umbrella approach is bound to leave remarkable grey areas. A holistic approach is better placed to effect the desired outcome of treatment. Issues such as race, ethnicity, gender, age, socio-economic status, religion, lifestyle, and sexual orientation are crucial when establishing a therapeutic relationship with clients (Corey, 2001).

With the current globalization trend witnessed in the current world, diversification is happening at a fast rate, and clients' needs are becoming increasingly diverse, requiring a culture-centred metatheory. Understanding the cultural and socio-political context of a client's behaviour is essential to accurate assessment, interpretation, and treatment (Sue, et. al. 1996). However, each person has many different cultures or identities with each identity becoming relevant at different times and places, therefore MCT emphasizes both the way people are different from and similar to other people (Pederson, 1994).

MCT recognizes the value of traditional methods of helping as long as they are employed in a culturally meaningful and culturally sensitive fashion (Ivey, et. al. 2002). MCT begins with the assessment of the client, family, and cultural experience. It seeks to find how the client constructs and makes meaning in the world, stressing an egalitarian, non-hierarchical therapist-client relationship. The main issue in MCT is to work with the client in a culturally sensitive way to find a technique, strategy, theory, or set of theories that meet the client's needs.

MCT needs to include differences based on religion, sexual orientation, socio-economic factors, age, gender, physical handicaps, and levels of acculturation and assimilation (Sue, et. al. 1992).

Repetto (2001/2002) details five assumptions that can be identified in multiculturalism, namely:

→ Multiculturalism accepts the existence of many points of view, none of which are considered good or bad, correct or incorrect.

→ Multiculturalism involves social constructionism, in that people construct their world through social processes (historical, cultural, and social experiences) which contain cultural symbols and metaphors.

→ It is contextualistic in that conduct can only be understood within the context in which it takes place. This challenges the psychological and counselling theories that arise out of a specific cultural context.

→ It offers different approaches to the world because each perspective captures a different, valid approach.

→ It defends a relational sense for language rather than just a representational one, because language has a high correlation with culture and the perception of reality. The relational approach allows truths and realities to be seen beyond western scientific traditions.

4 8. COUNSELLING IMMIGRANT WOMEN

In counselling East African immigrant women, it is important to recognize that they have one foot in their old culture and the other in their new one.

They may experience real conflicts, feelings neither fully East African nor Italian, and at times, they may be uncertain on how to integrate the two aspects of their life. Based on their culture, they may be wary about disclosing their own personal material, not necessarily because they do not want to, but because a certain cultural tradition may have encouraged them to be emotionally reserved, which is a strong characteristic in this group.

When talking about the East African cultural traits, it is important to consider the role shame and guilt play in people's lives, especially people who have had difficult past experiences, and more so, for people who migrate to another country and find themselves faced with challenges they had not anticipated. Experiencing psychological distress and feeling the need for professional help may also trigger stigma and shame. These aspects need to be taken into account in the counselling process.

Non verbal behaviour is also another aspect to be taken into consideration in the therapeutic relationship. For instance, these women may be cautious in attempting eye contact with the therapist, which is often considered a sign of respect. Looking directly into the eyes of the other person is considered rude and disrespectful, especially when it comes to authority and people in leadership positions, and this gesture may be interpreted differently in a culture where eye contact is encouraged constantly, and avoiding it may be interpreted as resistance or evasiveness.

Expecting these women to reveal themselves immediately is not practical. This is not a sign of defensiveness. Rather, it may be a sign that they may need time to feel comfortable, and may not relate well with a high level of directness (Corey, 2001). Sometimes these women may demonstrate long periods of silence. This is not rudeness, being stoic, or unemotional. Rather, relating with someone who appears more advanced and ahead than they are may trigger feelings of suspicion on what the person may think about them, and hence silence becomes the coping mechanism. They may not trust the therapist, which has nothing to do with the therapist per se, but may reflect past experiences that may have conditioned them to be cautious.

Discrimination may also be an experience that these women have gone through, either in their home country, or where they settle. It is essential to understand where these women are coming from, what motivates them to seek therapy, and why they want to stay in therapy. Continuous learning from them is prerogative, for without this, misinterpretations are likely to occur.

Most African talk in terms of *"we"* as opposed to *"I"*. Traditional counselling and psychotherapy theories emphasize the use of *"I"* statements in order to own one's feelings and reactions/responses to situations. The sense of self in this particular community is collective in nature, and their being may be authenticated mainly in terms of others (Ivey, et. al. 2002). This calls for addressing their relationships with significant others in order to help the individual, as well as the cultural, contextual, and environmental issues.

While emphasizing the importance of multicultural approach to therapy, it is important to recognize that universal human themes unite people in spite of whatever factors differentiate them. Irrespective of one's culture, everyone needs to receive and give love, to makes sense of their psychological pain, and to make significant connections with others. It is important however, to explore any difference that has the capacity to create a gap in understanding namely age, gender, lifestyle, socio-economic status, religion, and sexual orientation (Corey, 2001).

MCT focuses on the individual in a family and cultural context (Ivey, et. al. 2002). This seeks to show clients how their difficulties may be tied to societal and social justice issues concerning race or ethnicity, gender, or socio-economic status.

MCT is a practical approach to therapy, as it forces therapists to deal with realities of difference. The very complexity and high demands of MCT are simultaneously its strength and weakness, providing challenges and opportunities (Ivey, et. al. 2002).

Multicultural counselling needs to consider the client's context (family and society), cultural beliefs and practices, communication, and the entire *"way of doing things"* in order to address real needs.

Richard Nelson-Jones (2002), in his article *Diverse Goals for Multicultural Counselling and Therapy*, details the twelve goals for multicultural counselling and therapy namely:

- → Reconciliation
- → Support
- → Coping with post-traumatic stress
- → Assisting acculturation and assimilation
- → Avoiding further marginalization
- → Addressing racial and cultural discrimination
- → Assisting clients to manage close cross-cultural relationships
- → Assisting clients to manage inter-generational conflict
- → Assisting long stay transients and expatriates

- → Assisting with gender roles and equality issues
- → Attaining higher levels of development
- → The formation of the good society.

MCT therefore aims at improving the client's life, inspiring them to change and become better people, and improve their relationships. REBT, used along with MCT, can yield remarkable results.

4 9. INTEGRATION OF REBT WITH OTHER THERAPIES FOR EFFECTIVE COUNSELLING

Rational emotive behaviour therapy (REBT) is a comprehensive approach to psychological treatment that deals not only with the emotional and behavioural aspects of human disturbance, but places a great deal of stress on its thinking component (Abrahams, undated). Human beings are highly complex, and there is no one single way that can effectively deal with the disturbances that characterize humanity. Psychological disturbances arise from misconceptions and mistaken cognitions about their perceptions, from emotional under-reactions or over-reactions to whatever stimuli they face, and from habitually dysfunctional behaviour patterns, which enable them to keep choosing and repeating unhealthy responses despite their failure to work.

REBT is based on the assumption that how we label our emotional reactions is largely caused by our conscious and unconscious evaluations, interpretations, and philosophies (Abrahams, undated). This means that we feel angry because we strongly convince ourselves that we are being treated unjustly and that the other person has something against us. We feel hostile because we believe that people who act against us should not act the way they do therefore their behaviour in our regard is unjustified. REBT focuses on uncovering irrational beliefs which may lead to unhealthy negative emotions and replacing them with more productive rational alternatives (Mulhauser, 2013). It aims at reducing emotional pain and helping clients make healthy choices. REBT is based on the idea that it is not external circumstances that make a person happy or unhappy, but internal thoughts about events, others, or self. Thinking, feeling, and behaviour are seen as linked and influencing one another (Ellis, 2011). REBT therefore focuses on changing one's thinking.

REBT is holistic in its approach, in that it teaches many types of thinking, feeling, and behavioural techniques to identify, investigate, and change dysfunctional behaviours. It encourages insight, realistic perspective, reasoning, and logic, but holds that these rational elements alone, without strong emotion, motivation, and action, are not enough for lasting change (Ellis, 2006).

REBT is the founding cognitive, multimodal, and integrative therapy approach, although it differs from other cognitive behaviour therapies in that it has a strong philosophical emphasis. It emphasizes the importance of unconditional acceptance.

Much of what is called emotion is nothing more or less than a certain kind – a biased, prejudiced, or strongly evaluative kind – of thought (Ellis, 2011). Ellis' emphasis in therapy is more on how people sustain their irrationality than on how they initially acquired it: the past cannot be undone and it is counterproductive to focus excessively on how people feel about the past (Ellis, 1991b).

The main goal of REBT is to empower clients to internalize healthy and undefeating philosophies and meanings and quickly react sensibly and fulfillingly to unfortunate life events, hence minimising emotional disturbances, decreasing self-defeating self-behaviours, and becoming more self-actualized so that they can lead a happier existence (Ellis, 2005). Rationality in this context is seen as the use of reason in pursuit of chosen short-range and long-range hedonism (Jones, 1996). Not only should a client remove symptoms of disturbing behaviour in their life, but they also need to develop what Ellis (1980) calls disturbability. One develops new philosophies and internalizes them, choosing to think in flexible and preferential rather than rigid and musturbatory ways. People with effective philosophies keep working on disciplined, goal-oriented reactions to everyday obnoxious activating events (A's) so that such reactions become somewhat automatic; they also think scientifically and fight and act against narrow-mindedness and arbitrary intellectual-emotional-behavioural restriction (Ellis, 1991b, pg. 166).

Sub-goals of REBT include helping the individual think more clearly and rationally, feel more appropriately, and act more efficiently and effectively in achieving goals of living happily (Sharf, 2012).

CHAPTER CONCLUSION

In addressing the needs of the East African ladies, it suffices to say that different aspects of counselling influence the outcome of therapy. Besides the psychotherapeutic approaches used, it is essential to note that there are other factors that determine the success or lack of it of a therapeutic relationship. One of these factors is the relationship that exists between the client and the therapist. The condition of the client also plays a major role in determining whether the approach is effective or not. The therapist's skills matter significantly.

Irrespective of what therapy approach one chooses, there are some fundamental principles that characterize the counselling relationship that go beyond any specific culture. There are some universal human themes that unite people regardless of their cultural background, and transcend culture, namely that everyone has a need to receive and give love, to makes sense of their psychological pain, and to make significant connections with others (Corey, 2001). In order to have an integrated approach to clients' situations, it is essential to ask some few questions namely: "Which theories provide a basis for understanding the cognitive dimension? Which theories facilitate understanding the feeling dimension? Which theories address the behavioural dimension? (Corey, 2001). Knowing the unique needs of clients, a therapist's own values and personality, and the theories themselves is a good basis for developing an integrated approach towards therapy. This requires knowledge, ark, skill, and experience. Knowing when and how to use a particular therapeutic intervention is essential.

Integrative psychotherapy brings together the affective, cognitive, behavioural, and physiological systems within a person, with an awareness of the social and transpersonal aspects of the systems surrounding the person (Erskine, undated). It takes into account all the theories discussed above namely psychodynamic, client-centred, behaviourist, cognitive, family therapy, Gestalt therapy, REBT, object relations theory, psychoanalytic self-psychology, and MCT. Each of these theories by themselves provide a partial explanation of behaviour and each is enhanced when selectively integrated with other aspects of the therapist's approach. The aim of integrative psychotherapy is to facilitate wholeness in such a way as to enhance the quality of a person's being and functioning in the intrapsychic, interpersonal, and socio-political space.

There is a clear value to the role of theory in psychotherapy integration, whether the theory deals with the way integration works (theoretical integration), the framework that governs the choice of interventions (assimilative integration), or the organizing principle for understanding the common factors that are present in all psychotherapy (Stricker, 2013).

Having addressed these different theories, it is clear that different theories work with different people, and that there is no one single theory that works with and for all and in the same way. It is therefore the therapist's responsibility to work towards continual training and own process in order to be able to assess client's real needs, and work with the client towards achievement of goals and objectives.

CHAPTER FIVE

REFLECTIONS, CONCLUSIONS, AND SUGGESTIONS FOR FURTHER RESEARCH

INTRODUCTION

The main purpose of this study is to allow the immigrant ladies' realities unfold, and hence add knowledge to the counselling profession especially in Italy. Seeing as there are hardly any formal counselling theories based on the African population and needs, Rational Emotive Behaviour Therapy, being a western theory, was chosen in order to establish if and how it could be used as a theory in counselling East African immigrant women. Narratives from these ladies were used to identify their felt needs vis-à-vis REBT. Without the narratives, it could have been impossible to arrive at any tentative conclusions. The findings from the research revealed some of the needs that these women face, and as well, added new findings to immigrants' mental health literature.

These findings, the impact of narratives, implications on counselling in Italy, recommendations for future research, and limitations of the study are addressed in this chapter.

5 1. IMPACT ON NARRATIVES

In this research, the needs of the immigrant women were recorded as they expressed themselves in the interviews. As seen in the common themes, it is seen that through giving them a voice, they manifested their desires and the researcher sought to evaluate these desires in view of REBT and its effectiveness or lack of it in assisting them in their adjustment process.

The narratives suggest that most of these immigrants experience survivor guilt. Having left suffering family members back home, they expressed deep concerns for them. Some of them also lost significant others in different circumstances, and they expressed the difficulty of living with this reality. They are aware that their family members are living in dire need. This guilt is experienced deeply, and once they found someone who could speak their language and who did not represent the authority that their stay depended upon, they opened themselves up and poured their hearts out.

According to some authorities, narratives are seen to improve immigrants' mental health (Groleau and Kirmayer, 2004). As they narrated their stories, they noted that they felt better (see explication of data). They were able to listen to themselves talking, and this was a challenge for them. Narratives can sometimes be seen as helping to piece together one's alienated selves (Ochs and Capps, 1996). Most of the immigrants held that their life was fragmented. There were issues that they did not even realize were present. For instance, one immigrant woman noted: *"I did not realize how angry I was towards my father for abusing me until now that I speak with you"*. In order to survive, the lady had decided to shelf this anger towards the father because she needed this energy for other areas of her life.

Narratives also appear to have an impact on clinicians, making them learn so much while working on their own issues. As the ladies shared their life experiences, they reported experiencing some sort of relief. This may lead to the conclusion that there is a therapeutic value in narratives, as they express emotions and offer the ability to come to terms with one's repressed material, both in participants and interviewer. As this researcher interviewed the immigrant women, she came to terms with her own anger towards situations that cause so much suffering to helpless people. The narratives of the women triggered a strong desire to work towards empowering helpless people who fall prey to bad governance, greed, and chauvinistic mentality. In these ladies, the researcher could see a representation of continual suffering and helplessness, and this strengthened her resolve to do whatever is in her capacity to work towards social change.

5 2. IMPLICATIONS FOR MULTICULTURAL SOCIAL WORK PRACTICE

In the helping profession, Doan (2011) argues that it is prerogative to begin from where the immigrant is in order to support them as they move on. A total assessment of their current state is important, namely physically, emotionally, mentally, and socially. Clinicians need to understand the use of defence mechanisms including repression, suppression, or disassociation in response to traumatic experiences (Doan, 2011). As seen in the narratives, most of these ladies had experienced trauma, be it in small or large doses, a one-time experience or a series of traumas. Each of these ladies shared how they tried to survive and how they had to shelf so much in order to have the energy to face much more urgent situations. This does not mean that the issues had been resolved, but they had to adapt ways of survival in the midst of extremely difficult situations.

Clinicians need to be multiculturally trained. They need to have training and cultural competency as well as other skills. Awareness of their own prejudices and biases, transference and counter-transference issues, among others, is essential in order to be able to separate their own issues from those of clients, and to work well with immigrants. Working on their own issues and growth is important. Social work requires a spirit of service, social justice, dignity and worth of the person, importance of human relationships, integrity, and competence (Doan, 2011). Therapists need to be living examples of these values in order for them to have an impact on their clients. Therapists need to examine their own perceptions, attitudes, and values that may influence the ability to effectively engage and work with multicultural populations (Chung, 2010).

No two immigrants' experiences are the same, even if they may be similar, the way their experiences influence their identity, relationships with others, mental health, and ways of understanding self all vary (Geib, 2012). This calls for a therapist's openness and willingness to learn, as well as continuous readiness to challenge their status quo. Therapists who are constantly ready to learn have been seen to work better with varied groups and their work tends to be more profound. This is an experience that this researcher has had with the social services in Trieste, Italy. Interacting with psychotherapists, psychoanalysts, psychiatrists, social workers, educators, and other clinicians has been an eye opener because it has confirmed the need for mental health workers to keep themselves abreast and informed in areas regarding culture, mental illnesses, and interactions that immigrants hold important.

It's prerogative to really hear what the immigrant is saying as opposed to relying on theories and schools of thought. Translated words may have different meanings for both therapist and immigrant; therefore, there is dire need for cultural training. This researcher, in her work in Trieste, has been in situations where there was a need for cultural negotiators whose role was to translate and interpret what immigrants were trying to say. In many cases, there were misunderstandings because what the client may have intended experienced change in the process of translation and interpretation, and this led to misdiagnosis at worst and utter misunderstanding at best. At times, there were no corresponding words in both languages, and only words close in meaning could be used, and this was a big drawback.

Having said all these, from the interviews and the comparison of REBT with other theories, it is evident that REBT as a theory can be used with East African ladies in their integration process in Trieste, Italy. The above comparison shows that REBT can safely be used with these ladies in that it advocates changing thought patterns, does not dwell on the past for the sake of it, empowers people to be responsible of their choices hence also the consequences, works towards overcoming emotional blocks and disturbances leading to full functioning, self-actualization, and happiness, and involves training which is highly needed for the ladies. REBT also recognizes the differentiation between the therapist and the client, and this becomes essential seeing as there is a strong emphasis on the collective identity of people which often leads to confusion and hence conflict that can not be traced to people's thought patterns.

5 3. RECOMMENDATIONS FOR PROFESSIONAL COUNSELLING IN ITALY

As noted in an earlier chapter, counselling is a relatively new discipline in Italy, but it is growing steadily as needs arise and as clinicians recognise its importance in mental health. As can be seen in this research, in most cases, office restricted counselling may not work with immigrant women. This challenges the setting in a therapeutic one-on-one relationship between therapist and client. Immigrants come with so many issues that ensuring their comfort in the counselling setting is paramount if the relationship is to be established and become therapeutic. It could help to make home visits, offer community based counselling sites (Baker, 2007), as well as mobilize other circles that could offer particular services to the immigrant. This was seen as a felt need which goes beyond classic counselling settings. From the narratives, it was noted that the most important needs for an immigrant are basic survival necessities as detailed by Abraham Maslow, hence food, shelter, clothing, safety, belonging, and esteem needs come first. The immigrants expressed anxiety over these basic needs. The need to learn basic skills namely language, western culture, and other basic skills was considered a necessity. This makes it difficult to respect the counselling setting and insist on immigrants following suit. Person-centred counselling theories as well as psychosocial support could help at the beginning in order to create a rapport with the immigrants and to gain understanding of their cultural practices, as well as to demonstrate respect for their coping mechanisms. Psycho-educational approaches are necessary in order to help them adjust to life in Italy (Baker, 2007). Thankfully, Italy makes use of various types of educators and psycho-education is given its importance. Educators serve several clients' needs and offer support in day to day life in empowering clients and furnishing them with skills that they need to live their life fully. In fact, most educators wear different huts depending on the needs at hand.

Therapists need to be flexible and creative, while seeking to walk with the client in their difficult process.

Seeing as Italy emphasizes more on psychotherapy and psychoanalysis, it would be helpful to introduce counselling in the various training programs. Counselling institutions could also be set up. Those that are present are not enough and they do not satisfy the high demand for counsellors. Mental health workers could also be trained while they work in order for them to gain skills that would equip them to deal with the varied immigrants' needs. Counselling and therapy need to be empowering for women, hence supporting their development of skills that will allow them to effect change across ecological contexts (Yakushko & Chronister, 2005). Psycho-education provides relief and support by explaining and normalizing the nature of symptoms and experiences (Van der Veer, 1998).

This research could be a basis on what to build future training.

5 4. RECOMMENDATIONS FOR FURTHER RESEARCH

The immigration influx into Europe in general and Italy in particular calls for deeper research on the mental health needs of immigrants. Seeing as there is a huge number of people immigrating to Italy, and Italy is being used as an entry point to other countries by immigrants, it is worth researching on how their mental health affects the country and the community in general, and the immigrant in particular. This research is a starting point, as there has not been, to the best of this researcher's knowledge, any previous work done on addressing the mental health needs of East African immigrants in Trieste through counselling. There is a great need for other approaches and how other theories could be used in addressing the immigrants' needs.

This research suggests the need to train therapists on multiculturalism. This researcher, being an immigrant herself, having been trained in western counselling theories in Western countries, living in a western context with particular cultural needs, and working in mental health area, appreciates the need for training in multicultural counselling. This study, therefore, is not conclusive. It is an opening to a wider area of research, as felt needs keep changing, and as the plight of immigrants becomes more and more complex.

Further research with more participants, a greater range of participants in terms of demographics (race, status, age, among others), and inclusion of men in the research might be helpful in future research. As noted earlier, only six East African immigrant ladies were interviewed, and this is a very small number which can not be representative of the entire population. Including men in future research could open a whole new perspective in counselling immigrants.

A strong need to examine post-immigration stressors in the lives of immigrants was seen from the narratives. Spiritual intervention could also be used as an effective therapy tool with immigrants. As seen earlier in the narratives, all the six immigrants, and most of East Africans in general, are very religious right from childhood. Religion is something that gets inculcated into one's system and it becomes part and parcel of one's life. However, not everyone who is religious is spiritual, and vice versa, hence the reason to treat each person's experiences in a unique way seeing as each immigrant experiences religion and spirituality in a very unique way.

The aspect of survivor guilt could also be good grounds for future research.

Traditional healing therapies practiced back in their homes could also be a field that could enrich future research in counselling, and it could possibly be compared to western counselling therapies.

The purpose of the current research is to generate additional hypothesis (Creswell, 1998). It would help to reflect on whether men would respond in the same way as women. This would lead to changing the counselling approach and the research questions.

From the interview with an Italian Professional Psychotherapist, it was clear that REBT as a theory is not commonly used in Italy, so it could be opportune to assess whether it would help to use other theories alongside REBT or independently. It would help future research to assess the ability and willingness of immigrants to go through therapy, sometimes a lengthy one, their personal beliefs about it, and whether for them therapy is helpful or not.

It could also be helpful to explore whether the participants have any faith in the helping process.

The possibilities of future research are immense, and the researcher believes that this work is only a starting point, the sky is the limit.

5 5. INTERVENTIONS THAT COULD BE USED IN COUNSELLING

According to Yakushko and Chronister (2005), some interventions could facilitate the counselling process of immigrants as they work on their settling process. Counsellors may need training on these interventions. These include:

1. **Bronfendbrenner's (1979) ecological framework** to increase their understanding as counsellors of the impact of multiple contexts on immigrant women's cultural beliefs and experiences (Baker, 2007). The need to empathize with the women through creating a rapport and a safe atmosphere where their cultural experiences are valued should be at the basis. Balance between short-term mental health needs including housing and employment, and long term ones such as dealing with stress and anxiety (Yakushko and Chronister, 2005; Wang and Freeland, 2004) needs to be emphasized. This framework offers education on how counselling works in Italy as well as awareness of discrimination and prejudice that many immigrants experience. Providing information that deals with discrimination based on nationality, religion, gender, race, language abilities, among others, is essential for counsellors.

2. **The Empowerment Program:** this is a program addressing approaches to meet immigrants' needs namely counselling, visits, psycho-educational workshops, and support from counsellors and other immigrant women. Women need empowerment, giving importance to what they consider vital. Workshops could be held to provide culturally sensitive psycho-education in group settings focused on topics such as mental health, acculturation and adjustments, physical health, family and gender roles, parenting, health, loss and grief, legal issues, and stress-self-care (Doan, 2011).

Taking a holistic approach in counselling, as seen from the interviews, may work better than looking at just one area of needs. Another aspect that was deduced from the interviews is that it could be helpful to create groups where immigrants experience a sense of belonging. Kenzie (2001) offers guidelines for establishing an effective clinical practice for refugees namely well-trained, bilingual staff that's prepared to treat major mental illnesses, a location that is easily accessible by immigrants, and an approach that integrates physical and mental health. Formation of cultural negotiators is necessary too. From this researcher's experience, most of the cultural negotiators in Italy are people chosen at random who happen to speak the immigrant's language, and most of them may not have any background preparation at all. Cultural negotiators' work is not only to translate, but to interpret certain words and terminologies/concepts that direct translation would do injustice to. This researcher has witnessed situations where cultural negotiators were in actual fact scarce in their ability to transmit the very and real message, feelings, and experiences of the immigrant. This made it difficult to address the immigrant's needs, and consequently led to gross misunderstandings by the mental health workers. Misinterpretation of facts, experiences, and feelings can damage the whole process and therefore it is prerogative for mental health workers to pay careful attention to nuances expressed by the immigrant. Counsellors need to give value to the immigrants' coping mechanisms and to believe with them in their desires to get better. As seen from the narratives, therapists may need to appreciate the spiritual and religious life of the immigrants even though they may not be believers themselves.

Continuous research on cultural and mental health issues related to displacement is an area that could be ventured in. Ongoing formation is priceless in this process, and therapists need to be committed to their own training. Training in spiritual and theological precepts is necessary, irrespective of whether the mental health worker is a believer or not. Counsellor training programs need to encourage bilingual/bicultural students needed in a fast changing society. Counsellors need training to learn how to identify mental health immigrant issues and be able to provide appropriate referrals.

5 6. LIMITATIONS OF STUDY

This research involved just a handful of participants. This limited number did not allow the researcher to reach major conclusions that could be representative of the general population of East African immigrants. The participants in this study were seen only once for the interviews except for one. More sessions could have helped to deepen the knowledge gathered.

The ladies had to meet a stranger who, despite coming from the same country, was not known to them, so inhibitions were to be expected. The interviewer did not speak all of the languages that the participants spoke, though all of them could speak either English, or Swahili, or Kikuyu, or Italian. In the East African languages, emotions or sentiments have no specific name. They are associated with other senses like hearing and seeing, as well as living itself. This made it difficult for the immigrant women to name what they were experiencing emotionally and to express their emotions using the right terminologies. The fact that the interviewer is aware of this reality helped the situation and made it easier to place emotions in perspective.

The researcher's background, being an immigrant herself, albeit by choice, influenced the research. This was an advantage as well as a disadvantage. It was an advantage in that she could grasp the hidden meaning of terminologies and non verbal language, and also she had witnessed, although not lived, some of the traumas the immigrant women talked about. It was a disadvantage because at times, the researcher could *"predict"* what the immigrant wanted to say and could often find herself completing their sentences. Being aware of some of the traumas made the interviewer relive some painful experiences, and at one point, the interview had to be suspended in order for the researcher to deal with the triggered issues with her supervisor. Identification with the immigrants, especially when they shared very deep traumatic experiences, provoked emotional distress to the researcher when listening to their sad stories.

In many cases, immigrants have no voice, though the media reports everyday of new influx and the alarming situation facing the country. Through the interviews, immigrants were given a voice; they had the chance to verbalize their issues to a person who did not judge them harshly, and someone who could empathise with them. This, however, is a drop from the bucket of the many issues that immigrants face, and it is not sufficient because wounds were opened but no further follow up was done.

GENERAL CONCLUSION

This chapter closes with the reflections that are the results of the research. As noted earlier, the aim of this study is to lay a foundation for future study, and to contribute to the already existing literature. The narratives show that immigrants' needs are immensely complex, and no one single theory can claim sole ability to deal with all of them. It would help to come up with theories based on the East African context, which would include traditional healing interventions. This could be a topic for future research.

This study is justified in that the needs of immigrants are left to fate, and most therapists and mental health workers are not trained to handle such complex issues. Issues are often interpreted based on the local filters, which, as has been seen and proved, leave grey areas. Training is necessary for a holistic approach to counselling when dealing with such particular, specific, and complex populations.

As indicated right from the beginning, this study aims at exploring the validity of REBT as a counselling tool with immigrant women settling in Trieste. This research has been very enriching mainly to the researcher and hopefully to future research. As noted earlier, this is only the beginning of a wide area of research and it opened up many possibilities that could be explored in the future. Little has been done on this topic, mainly due to two reasons: first, immigration is a relatively new phenomenon in Italy and it is becoming an issue only now that things are getting out of hand. Second, counselling is a relatively new discipline in Italy and its full importance is yet to be appreciated.

The qualitative phenomenological approach used in this study included interviews, personal journal weekly entries, behavioural observations, free interaction between the researcher and the participants, and reflections by the researcher of all what was happening. Weekly supervision was also an integral part of the whole process, without which the researcher could have experienced difficulties. The researcher's growth is notable in this whole process, and her appreciation of diversity and resilience is remarkable.

During the process, several emotions were triggered, and the researcher sought to apply REBT in dealing with these emotions and disputing her thoughts. She therefore had a first hand experience of the technique before recommending it to others.

This study has left the researcher with a strong desire to pursue more focused research in the future, and this is one of the projects in the limelight. The researcher also desires to offer counselling to immigrants in their settlement process after this study. Some participants keep in touch with the researcher expressing the need to address their issues, and this is a sign that there is a strong need for this service.

The whole process was a continuous challenge and inspiration to the researcher, and it is her hope and prayer that it may serve to empower other people in the field of counselling, and that social change may come as a result.

BIBLIOGRAPHY

ABRAHAMS, M. (undated). *The Essence of Rational Emotive Behaviour Therapy: A Comprehensive Approach to Treatment.* Retrieved from http://www.rebt.ws/albert_ellis_the_essence_of_rebt.htm

ADLER, A. (1958). *What Life Should Mean to You.* New York: Capricorn

AFRICAN FATHERS INITIATIVE. (undated). *African Baby Naming Ceremonies.* Retrieved from events.sweetmotherinternational.org

AFRICAN NEWS (2014). *Give Jobs First to Italians, then to Immigrants,* says Italy's Former Minister. Retrieved from www.africanews.eu

AIPC A. L. (2010). *Person-Centred Therapy.* Retrieved from http://www.aipc.net.au/articles/?p=190

ALLEN, J. G. (2005). *Coping with Trauma: Hope Through Understanding.* American Psychiatric Publication.

AMERICAN ACADEMY of CHILD & ADOLESCENT PSYCHIATRY (2010). *Your Child—Childhood Trauma and Its Effects.* Retrieved from http://www.aacap.org/cs/root/publication_store/your_child_childhood_trauma_and_its_effects

AMERICAN COUNSELLING ASSOCIATION CODE OF ETHICS (2005).

American Psychological Association (1993). *Guidelines for Providers of Psychological Services to Ethnic, Linguistic, and Culturally Diverse Populations.* Washington, Author.

ANSA (2014). Italy's *Immigration Triples.* Retrieved from www.ansa.it

APA (1982). *Ethical Principles in the Conduct of Research with Human Participants.* Washington DC: Author

ARREDONDO, P. et. al. (1996). *Operationalization of the Multicultural Counselling Competencies.* Alexandria: AMCD

ARTHUR, N. (2004). *Counselling International Students: Clients from Around the World.* New York: Kluwer Academic/Plenum Publishers.

AZAR, T. P. (2007). *Cross Cultural Counselling: A Pastoral Perspective.* Usaf Academy.

BAKER, R. E. (2007). *A Phenomenological Study of the Resettlement Experiences and Mental Health Needs of Somali Bantu Refugee Women.* MI: UMI Dissertation Publishing.

BAUER, E., & THOMPSON, P. (2004). She's Always the Person with a Very Global Vision: The Gender Dynamics of Migration, Narrative Interpretation and the Case of Jamaican Transnational Families. *Gender and History, 16* (2), 334-375. Blackwell Publishing.

BAUMAN, S., & WALDO, M. (1998), Existential Theory and Mental Health Counselling: If it Were a Snake, It Would Have Bitten! *Journal of Mental Health Counselling, 20* (1), 13-27.

BBC NEWS. (2006). *Italian Women Shun "Mamma" Role: Birth Rates in the European Union are Falling Fast.* Retrieved from www.bbc.co.uk/1/hi/world/europe/4739154.stm

BECK, A. T. & WEISHAAR, M. (1989). Cognitive Therapy. In A. Freeman, K. M. Simon, L. E. Beutler, & H. Arkowitz (Eds.). *Comprehensive Handbook of Cognitive Therapy* (pp. 21 – 26). New York: Plenum.

BECK, A. T. (1976). *Cognitive Therapy and the Emotional Disorders.* New York: International University's Press.

BECK, A. T. (1978). *Anxiety Checklist.* Philadelphia: Centre for Cognitive Therapy.

BECK, A. T. (1988). *Love is Never Enough: How Couples Can Overcome Misunderstanding, Resolve Conflicts, and Solve Relationship Problems Through Cognitive Therapy.* New York: Harper &Row.

BECK, A. T., FREEMAN, A., DAVIS, D., & ASSOCIATES. (2004). *Cognitive Therapy of Personality Disorders* (2nd ed.). New York: Guilford.

BECK, A. T., WARD, C. H., MENDELSON, M., MOCK, J. E., &ERBAUGH, J. K. (1961). An Inventory for Measuring Depression. *Archives of General Psychology*, 4, 561-71.

BECK, A. T., YOUNG, J. E., & EL SHAMMA, K. (1979). *Competency Checklist for Cognitive Therapists*. Philadelphia: Centre for Cognitive Therapy.

BECK, S. J. (2011). *Cognitive Behaviour Therapy: Basics and Beyond* (2nd ed.) New York: Guilford Press.

BECKER, H. S. (1986). *Writing for Social Scientists*. 2nd ed. Chicago: University of Chicago Press.

BENEDUCE, R., & TALIANI, S. (2006). Embodied Powers, Deconstructed Bodies: Spirit, Possession, And The Search for Wealth of Nigerian Immigrant Women. *Anthropos 101* (1): 9-20.

BENSLAMA, F. (200). Epreuves De L'Etranger: Clinique De L'Exile. *Cahiers Intersignes 14-15*: 9-29.

BENSON, M. (2007). *There's More to Life: British Lifestyle Migration to Rural France. PhD Thesis*: Comparative and Applied Social Sciences. University of Hill.

BENSON, M., & O'REILLY, K. (2009). Migration and the Search for a Better Way of Life: A Critical Exploration of Lifestyle Migration. *The Sociological Review*, 57: 4. Oxford: Blackwell Publishing Inc.

BERGMANN, M. M. (2008). *Advances in Mixed Methods Research: Theories and Applications*. London: Sage Publications.

BEYSTEHNER, K. M. (2001). *Psychoanalysis: Freud's Revolutionary Approach to Human Personality*. Retrieved from http://www.personalityresearch.org/papers/beystehner.html

BINSWANGER, F. 1958). The Case of Ellen West, in Existence: *A New Dimension in Psychiatry and Psychology*. Ed. Rollo May, Ernest Angela, and Henri F.E. 237-364. New York: Basic Books.

BISHAW, M. (1991). Promoting Traditional Medicine in Ethiopia: A Brief Historical View of Government Policy. *Social Science and Medicine*, 33 (2), 193-200.

BLAUSTEIN, M. E., & KINNIBURGH, K. M. (2010). *Treating Traumatic Stress in Children and Adolescents: How to Foster Resilience Through Attachment, Self-Regulation, and Competency*. New York: Guilford Press.

BOEHLEIN, J. K. (2006). Religion and Spirituality in Psychiatric Care: Looking Back, Looking Ahead. *Transcultural Psychiatry*, 43, 634-651.

BOEREE, G. (2006). *Personality Theories: Victor Frankl*. Shippensburg University. Retrieved from http://webspace.ship.edu/cgboer/frankl.html

BONANNO, G. A. (2005). Clarifying and Extending the Construct of Adult Resilience. *American Psychologist, 60* (3), 265-267.

BOOTH, W. C. et. al. (2008). *The Craft of Research, 3rd ed*. Chicago: University of Chicago Press.

BOYNTON, P. (2005). *The Research Companion: A Practical Guide for the Social and Health Sciences*. Hove, Sussex: Psychology Press.

BOZARTH, J. (1999). Person-Centred Therapy: A Revolutionary Paradigm. *Person-Centred.com*. Retrieved from http://www.personcentered.com/pcch1.html

BRAHM, E. (2004). Trauma Healing. *Beyond Intractability*. Eds Burgess G. & Burgess H. Conflict Information Consortium, University of Colorado. http://www.beyondintractability.org/bi-essay/trauma-healing

BREAKWELL, G. M., HAMMOND, S., & SCHAW, C. F. (eds.) (1998). *Research Methods in Psychology*. London: Sage Publishers.

BRIERE, J., & WILSON, J. P. (2004). Uncovering: Trauma Focused Treatment Techniques with Asylum Seekers. In J. P. Wilson & B. Drozdek (eds), *Broken Spirits*. (243-276). New York: Brunner-Routledge.

BROWN, J. (1999). *Bowen Family Systems Theory and Practice*. Retrieved from http://www.familysystemstraining.com/papers/bowen-illustration-and-critique.html

BRUNER, J. (1990). *Acts of Meaning.* Cambridge, MA: Harvard University Press.

BRYCESON, D., & VUORELA, U. (2002). *The Transnational Family: New European Frontiers and Global Networks.* New York: Berg.

CALESTRO, K. (1972). Psychotherapy, Faith Healing, And Suggestions. *International Journal of Psychology, 10* (2), 83-113.

CALLAGHAN, K. (1988). Movement Psychotherapy with Adult Survivors of Political Torture and Organized Violence. *The Arts in Psychotherapy, 20,* 411-421.

CARDAMONE, A. F. (1990). Urbanization in Italy. *Journal of Regional Policy, 10,* 135-145.

CARVALHO, J. (2014). *Impact of Extreme Right Parties on Immigration Policy. Comparing Britain, France, and Italy.* London: Routledge Taylor and Francis Group.

CHAMBERS, J. C., & SMITH, A. J. (2006). *A Hermeneutic Approach to Culture and Psychotherapy.* London: Routledge.

CHANGING MINDS. (2012). *Jung's Archetypes.* Retrieved from http://changingminds.org/explanations/identity/jung_archetypes.htm

CHARLESON, S. B. (2010). *Reflective Practice in Counselling and Psychotherapy.* Middlesex: Sage Publications.

CHATTY, D. (2013). Forced Migration. *The Encyclopaedia of Global Human Migration.* London: Blackwell Publishers.

CHIEN-JUH. G. (2012). Women Status in the Context of International Migration. *Sociology Compass, 6/6.* 458-471. Western Michigan University.

CHRISTOPHER, J. C. (2001). Culture and Psychotherapy: Toward a Hermeneutic Approach. *Psychotherapy: Theory, Research, and Training, 38,* 115-128.

CHUNG, J. (2010). *Refugees and Immigrant Survivors of Trauma: A Curriculum for Social Workers.* MI: UMI Dissertation Publishing.

CINDEE, G. (2008). *Holistic Self-Care for Post-Traumatic Stress and Dissociative Identity*. Open Source.

CLARK, D. A., BECK, A. T., & ALFORD, B. A. (1999). *Scientific Foundations of Cognitive Theory and Therapy of Depression*. New York: Wiley.

CLARK, M. (1993). *Integration and Orient: Implications of Carl G. Jung's Concept of Persona, Shadow, and Theory of Psychological Types*. Retrieved from http://epages.wordpress.com/2012/08/18/integration-and-the-orient-implications-of-carl-gustav-jungs-concepts-of-persona-shadow-and-theory-of-psychological-types/

COHEN, M. (2000). Ten Steps to Healing Trauma. *A Psychological Counselling Corporation*. http://www.martinvcohen.com/trauma1.html

COLANGELO, J. (2009). The Recovered memory controversy: A Representative Case Study. *Journal of Child Abuse, 18* (1), 103-121.

COMANT, S. A. (1999). Using the Sweat Lodge Ceremony as Group Counselling for Navaja Youth: *The Journal for Specialists in Group Work, 24* (1), 155-173.

CONNOR, P. C. (2010). *A Theory of Immigrant Religious Adaptation: Disruption, Assimilation, and Facilitation*. MI: UMI Dissertation Publishing.

CONSIGLIO NAZIONALE DELL'ECONOMIA E DEL LAVORO (2005). *Rapporto di Monitoraggio Sulle Professioni non Regolamentate*. Roma.

COON, D, & MITTERER J.O. (2012). *Introduction to Psychology: Gateways to Mind and Behaviour*. Belmont: Wadsworth Cengage Learning.

COREY, G. (2001). *Case Approach to Counselling and Psychotherapy* (4th Ed.). California: Brooks/Cole Publishing Company.

COREY, G. (2012). *Theory and Practice of Counselling and Psychotherapy* (9th ed.). Belmont: Brooks/Cole Publishers.

CRASKE, M. G. (2012). *Cognitive Behavioural Therapy: Theories of Psychotherapy*. Washington: APA.

CRESWELL, J. W. (1998). *Qualitative Inquiry and Research Design: Choosing Among Five Traditions*. Thousands Oak, CA: Sage.

CRESWELL, J. W. (2002). *Research Design: Qualitative, Quantitative, and Mixed Methods Approaches* (2nd ed.) Thousand Oaks, CA: Sage Publications.

CRESWELL, J. W. (2005). *Qualitative Inquiry Design: Choosing Among Five Approaches.* Los Angeles: Sage

CURREN, L. (2010). *Trauma Competency: A Clinician's Guide.* Wisconsin: Pesi LLC.

CURTIS, R. (2010). *Counselling Theories: Adlerian Therapy.* Retrieved from http://counsellingtheories.blogspot.it/2011/01/adlerian-therapy.html

CUSHNER K., & BRISLIN, R. W. *Improving Intercultural Interactions: Modules for Cross Cultural Training Programs, Vol. 2.* London: Sage Publications.

DAAS-BRAILSFORD, P. (2007). *A Practical Approach to Trauma: Empowering Interventions.* Thousand Oaks. CA: Sage.

DANA, R. H. (1993). *Multicultural Assessment Perspectives for Professional Psychology.* Needham Heights, MA: Allyn and Bacon.

DANA, R. H. (2000). *Handbook of Cross-Cultural and Multicultural Personality Assessment.* London: Lawrence Erlbaum Associates Publishers.

DANIELS, D. (2014). *Rational Emotive Behaviour Therapy in the Context of Modern Psychological Research.* The Albert Ellis Institute. Retrieved from http://albertellis.org/rebt-in-the-context-of-modern-psychological-research/

DAVID, D. (2014). *Rational Emotive Behaviour Therapy in the Context of Modern Psychological Research.* The Albert Ellis Institute. Retrieved from http://albertellis.org/rebt-in-the-context-of-modern-psychological-research/

DAVIS, N. (2012). Theories of Counselling: Why are They Important? *Health Psychology Consultancy.* http://healthpsychologyconsultancy.wordpress.com/2012/10/01/theories-of-counselling-why-are-they-important/

DE LUCA, D., GALLIVAN, M. J. & KOCK, N. (2008). Furthering Information Systems Action Research: A Post-Positivist Synthesis of Four Dialectives. *Journal of the Association for Information System, 9*, (2), 48-72.

DOAN, D. (2011). *Row, Row, Row your Boat: A Personal Narrative of Immigration*. MI: UMI Dissertation Publishing.

DOAN, D. (2011). *Row, Row, Row Your Boat: A Personal Narrative of Immigration*. Long Beach: California State University.

DOUGLAS Eds. (2009). *Dream Psychology: Psychoanalysis for Beginners by Sigmund Freud*. Douglas Edition.

ECHEMA, A. (1995). *Corporate Personality in Traditional Igbo Society and the Sacrament of Reconciliation*. Indiana: Indiana University.

EGAN E. (1998). *The Skilled Helper*. London: International Thomson Publishing Europe.

EISENBRUCH, M. (1991). From Post-Traumatic Stress Disorder to Cultural Bereavement: *Diagnosis of Southeast Asian Refugees*. Social Sciences and Medicine, 33, 673-680.

EISENHAVER, E. R., MOSHERT, E. C., LAMSON, K. S., WOLF, H. A., & SCHWARTZ, D. G. (2012). Health Education for Somali Bantu Refugees Via Home Visits. *Health Information and Libraries Journal*, 29, pp. 152-161.

EISENMAN, D. P. et. al. (2007). PTSD in Latino Patients: Illness Beliefs, Treatment Preferences, and Implications for Care. *Journal of Internal General Medicine, 23* (9). 1386-1393.

EJIZU, C. I. (undated). *African Traditional Religions and the Promotion of Community-Living in Africa*. Retrieved from www.africaworld.net/afrel/community/htm

EKUE', A. A. A. (2009). Migrant Christians: Believing Wanderers Between Cultures and Nations. *World Council of Churches, The Ecumenical Review, 61*, No. 4.

ELLIS, A. (1962). *Reason and Emotion in Psychotherapy* (rvsd). Secaucus, NJ: Carol Publishing Group, 1994.

ELLIS, A. (1987). The Impossibility of Achieving Consistently Good Mental Health. *American Psychologist, 42,* 364-75.

ELLIS, A. (1988). *How to Stubbornly Refuse to Make Yourself Miserable About Anything, Yes, Anything.* Sydney: Pan Macmillan.

ELLIS, A. (1993b). Reflections on Rational-Emotive Therapy. *Journal of Consulting and Clinical Psychology, 61,* 199-201.

ELLIS, A. (2004). Why Rational Emotive Behavioural Therapy is the Most Comprehensive and Effective Form of Behaviour Therapy. *Journal of Rational Emotive & Cognitive Behaviour Therapy, 22(2),* 85-92.

ELLIS, A. (2011). *Rational Psychotherapy and Individual Psychology.* www.all-about-psychology.com Kindle edition

ELLIS, A., & ELLIS, J. D. (2005). *Rational Emotive Behaviour Therapy: A Therapist's Guide.* (2nd ed.). New York: Prometheus Books.

ELLIS, A., & JOFFE, D. (2011). *Rational Emotive Behaviour Therapy: Theories of Psychotherapy.* Washington: APA.

ELLIS, B. H. et. al. (2008). Mental Health of Somali Adolescent Refugees: The Role of Trauma, Stress, and Perceived Discrimination. *Journal of Consulting and Clinical Psychology, 76* (2), 184-195.

ELLIS, T. J., & LEVY, Y. (2009). Towards a Guide for Novice Researchers on Research Methodology: Review and Proposed Methods. *Journal of Issues in Informing Science and Information Technology, 6.*

ELLIS, T. J., and YARIS, L. (2009). Towards a Guide for Novice Researchers on Research Methods. *Issues in Informing Science and Information Technology, Vol. 6.*

ENG. A. L. (1998). Faith and Psychology: Integration or Separation. *Journal of Religion and Health, 37,* 45-47.

ERKSINE, R. (undated). *What is Integrative Psychotherapy?* Retrieved from http://www.integrativetherapy.com/en/integrative-psychotherapy.php

ERRINGTON, E. J. (2007). *Emigrant Worlds and Transatlantic Communities.* Montreal: McGill-Queens University Press.

FAN, C. (1999). A Comparison of Attitudes Towards Mental Illness and Knowledge of Mental Health Services Between Asian Immigrants and Anglo-Australians. *Community Mental Health Journal, 35* (1), 47-57.

FARLEX (2014). *Counselling and Psychotherapy in Italy: A Profession in Constant Change.* Retrieved from http://www.thefreelibrary.com/Counseling%20and%20psychotherapy%20in%20Italy:%20a%20profession%20in%20constant...-a0132162680

FAWCETT, J. (1999). *The Relationship of Theory and Research.* Philadelphia: F. A. Davis.

FELDMAN, M. (1993). The Dynamics of Reassurance. *International Journal of Psycho-analysis, 74,* 275 – 284.

FLANAGA, S., & FLANAGA R. (2012). *Counselling and Psychotherapy Theories in Context and Practice.* New Jersey: John Wiley & Sons.

FONG, R. (2004). *Culturally Competent Practice with Immigrant and Refugee Children and Families.* New York: The Guilford Press.

FONG, R. (2004). Overview of Immigrant and Refugee Children and Families. In R. Fong (ed), *Culturally Competent Practice with Immigrant and Refugee Children and Families,* (pp.1-18). New York: The Guilford Press.

FORDMARTIN, Paula, (2013). *Behavioural Therapy.* Retrieved from http://www.healthline.com/galecontent/behavioral-therapy#1

FRANKL, V. (1975). *The Unconscious God: Psychotherapy and Theology.* New York: Simon and Schuster.

FRANKL, V. (1978). *The Unheard Cry for Meaning.* New York: Touchstone Publishers.

FRANKL, V. (1992). *Man's Search for Meaning: An Introduction to Logotherapy.* Boston: Beacon Press.

FREUD, S. (1933). New Introductory Lectures on Psycho-analysis. *Lecture 33: Femininity.* Standard Edition, v. 22. Pp. 136 – 157

FREUD, S. (1949). *An Outline of Psychoanalysis.* New York: W. W. Norton

FUNNELL, S. C., & ROGERS, P. (2011). *Purposeful Program Theory: Effective Use of Theories of Change and Logic Models*. San Francisco: John Wiley & Sons.

GASHAW-GANT. G. G. (2004). *Culture and Mental Illness: A Review of a Model for Providing Mental Health Services to East African Refugees/Immigrants*. Proquest Dissertations. UMI.

GATHOGO, J. M. (undated). African Hospitality: Is It Compatible with the Ideal of Christ's Hospitality? Part 1. *Churchman*.

GEIB, M. (2012). *Coming to Terms with Abusive Childhood Sexual Experiences: A Listening Guide Study of Women's Stories*. MI: UMI Dissertation Publishing.

GERMIGNANI, M., & GILIBERTO, M. (2005). Counselling and Psychotherapy in Italy: A Profession in Constant Change. *Journal of Mental Health Counselling*.

GERSTEIN, L. H. et. al. (2009). *International Handbook of Cross Cultural Counselling: Cultural Assumptions and Practices Worldwide*. California: Sage Publications.

GESTALT THEORY. (2013). Gestalt Psychotherapy. *Oneness and Integrated Wholeness*. Retrieved from http://gestalttheory.com/psychotherapy/

GIDDENS, A. (1991). *Modernity and Self-Identity: Self and Society in the Late Modern Age*. Cambridge: Polity Press.

GILBERT J. (2001). Cross Cultural Issues in Counselling Skills Training: Lessons from Lesotho. *The Health Exchange*, April, 18-19).

GIORDANO, C. (2014). *Migrants in Transition. Caring and the Logics of Difference in Contemporary Italy*. Berkeley: University of California Press.

GLASSER, W. (1975). *Reality Therapy: A New Approach to Psychiatry*. New York: Harper and Row Publishers.

GLASSER, W. (1985). *Control Theory: A New explanation of How We Control Our Lives*. New York: Harper and Row Publishers.

GLASSER, W. (1990). *The Basic Concepts of Reality Therapy*. Canoga Park, CA: Institute for Reality Therapy.

GLASSER, W. (2000). *Counselling with Choice: The New Reality Therapy*. New York: Harper Collins.

GLASSER, W. (2010). *Choice Theory: A New Psychology of Personal Freedom*. New York: Harper Collins.

GLYNIS, B. et. al. (1994). *Research Methods in Psychology*. London: Sage Publications

GOBLE, F. G. (2004). *The Third Force: The Psychology of Abraham Maslow*. www.maslow.com

GODE, Y. (2010). Data Analysis Explained. *Buzzle*. http://www.buzzle.com/articles/data-analysis-methods.html

GOLDEN, C. (undated). *The 12 Common Archetypes*. Retrieved from http://www.soulcraft.co/essays/the_12_common_archetypes.html

GONG-GUY, E., CRAVENS, R., & PATTERSON, T. (1991). Clinical Issues in Mental Health Service Delivery to Refugees. *American Psychologist, 46* (6), 642-648.

GOOD THERAPY.ORG (2012). *Reality Therapy*. Retrieved from http://www.goodtherapy.org/reality-therapy.html

GOZDZIAK, E. M. (2004). Training Refugee Mental Health Providers: Ethnography as a Bridge to Multicultural Practice. *Human Organization, 63*, (2), 203-211.

GRAZIANO, A. M., & RAULIN, M. L. (2007). *Research Methods: A Process of Inquiry*. (6th ed.). Boston: Pearson Allyn and Bacon.

GREENFELD, J. M. (2011). *Using Rational Emotive Behaviour Therapy to Initiate and Maintain Regular Exercise in College Aged Men: A Qualitative Investigation*. Ann Arbor: UMI.

GROENEWALD. T. (2004). A Phenomenological Research Design Illustrated. *International Journal of Qualitative Methods, 3* (1).

GROLEAU, D., & KIRMAYER, L. (2004). Sociosomatic Theory in Vietnamese Immigrants Narratives of Distress. *Anthropology and Medicine, 11* (2), 117-133.

GUIGNON, C. (1984). Moods in Heidegger's being and Time, in C. Calhoun and R. C. Solomon (eds). *What is an Emotion?* New York: Oxford University Press, pp. 230-243.

HACKNEY, H. L., & CORNIER, S. (2008). *The Professional Counsellor.*

HALLING, S. & NILL. J. D. (1995). A Brief History of Existential-Phenomenological Psychiatry and Psychotherapy. *Journal of Phenomenological Psychology, 26,* 1-45.

HAMILTON, K. (2003). Italy's Southern Exposure. *Migration Information Source.* Retrieved from Migration Information Policy www.migrationinformation.org/Profiles/display.cfm?ID=121

HARLEY, J. (1976). *Problem-Solving Therapy.* San Francisco: Jossey-Bass.

HARRIS, M. (1998). *Trauma Recovery and Empowerment: A Clinician's Guide for Working with Women in Groups.* Free Press.

HAYS, P. (2008). *Addressing Cultural Complexities in Practice. Assessment, Diagnosis, and Therapy.* 2nd ed. American Psychological Association.

HEATH, A., NEIMEYER G. J., & PEDERSEN, P. The Future of Cross Cultural Counselling: A Delphi Poll. *Journal of Counselling and Development.* September 1988, Vol. 67.

HEINEN, J. R. (1995). A Primer on Psychological Theory. *Journal of Psychology.* 119, 413 – 421.

HERMAN, J. (1997). *Trauma and Recovery: The Aftermath of Violence from Domestic Abuse to Political Terror.* New York: Basic Books.

HERR, E. L. (1991). Challenges to Mental Health Counsellors in a Dynamic Society: Macrostrategies in the Profession. *Journal of Mental Health Counselling,* 13, 6-20.

HILES, D. (2001). *Heuristic Inquiry and Transpersonal Research.* Retrieved from www.psy.dmu.ac.uk/drhiles/HIpaper.htm

HIRAY, J. (2008). *The Research Process: Independent and Dependent Variables*. Retrieved from http://businessmanagement.wordpress.com/2008/03/16/the-research-process-independent-and-dependent-variables/

HOFFMAN, L. (2004). *Existential Therapy*. Retrieved from http://existential-therapy.com/Index.htm

HOLM/HADULLA, R. M. (2004). *The Art of Counselling and Psychotherapy*. London: Karnack Books.

HOOK, D. (2010). *Foucault Psychology and The Analytics of Power*. London: Palgrave Macmillan.

HORNUNG, M. (2002). *The War Children: The Son's Perspective on Nazism*. Paper to European Social Science History Conference. The Hague.

HUMAN RIGHTS TODAY (Aug. 2014). *Over 2,500 Migrants Reach Italy in 24 Hours*, More Expected to Follow. China Economic Net.

HYCNER, R. H. (1999). Some Guidelines for the Phenomenological Analysis of Interview Data, in A. Bryman & R. Burgess (eds). *Qualitative Research, 3*, pp. 143-164. London: Sage.

HYPSO Risk Advisor (2008). Cross-Cultural Counselling: How to be More Effective. *American Counselling Association Journal Vol. 2.*

IANS (13th July, 2014). *12 Dead. Illegal Immigrants Found Off Libyan Coast.* Human Rights Today.

IDOWU, E. B. (1973). *African Traditional Religion: A Definition*. London: SCM Press.

ISTAT (8th May, 2014). Non EU Citizens Holding a Resident Permit on 1st January 2014. *Welfare Society Territory*. Retrieved from www.istat.it

ISTAT. (2007). *La Popolazione Straniera Regolarmente Presente in Italia*. Nota Informativa, 11 Aprile.

ISTITUTO GESTALT TRIESTE (undated). *Gestalt Counselling Training*. Retrieved from www.istitutogestalt.net/counselling.aspx

IVEY, A. E. (1996). *Research Methods in Psychology.*

IVEY, A. E. et. al. (2002). *Theories of Counselling Psychotherapy: A multicultural Perspective*. (5th ed.) Boston: Pearson Education Company

JACKSON, C. L., & TAYLOR, G. R. (2008). *Demystifying Research: A Prime for Novice Researchers*. Sense Publishers.

JAHODA, G. (2002). Reflections of a Pre-Nominal Cross Cultural Psychologist. *On line Readings in Psychology and Culture, Unit 2*. Retrieved from http://scholarworks.gvsu.edu/orpc/vol2/iss1/2

JONES, R. N. (1995). *The Theory and Practice of Counselling*. London: Redwood Books.

JOSEPH, S., WILLIAMS, R., & YULE, W. (1997). *Understanding Post-Traumatic Stress: A Psychosocial Perspective on PTSD and Treatment*. London: John Wiley & Sons.

KENDRA, C. (2013). *Introduction to Classical Conditioning*. About. com Psychology. Retrieved from http://psychology.about.com/od/behavioralpsychology/a/classcond.htm

KENYATTA, J. (1965). *Facing Mount Kenya*. New York: Random House.

KERR, M. E., & BOWEN, M. (1988). *Family Evaluation: An Approach Based on Bowen Theory*. London: W. W. Norton & Company

KHAMPHAKDY-BROWN, S. et. al. (2006). The Empowerment Program: An Application of an Outreach Program for Refugee and Immigrant Women. *Journal of Mental Health Counselling, 28* (1), 38-47.

KHAN, S.R., BENDA, T., & STAGNARO, M.N. (2012). Stereotyping from The Perspective of Perceivers and Targets. *Online Readings in Psychology and Culture, Unit 5*. www.scholarworks.gusu.edu/orpc/vol11/iss1/1

KINZIE, J. D. (2001). Psychotherapy for Massively Traumatized Refugees: The Therapist Variable. *American Journal of Psychotherapy, 55* (4), 475-490.

KIRMAYER, L. J. et. al. (1994). Inuit Concepts of Mental Health and Illness. *Culture and Mental Health Research Unit Report No. 4*. Montreal.

KITAYAMA, S., & MARKUS, H. R. (2000). The Pursuit of Happiness and The Realization of Sympathy: Cultural Patterns of Self, Social Relations, and Well-Being, in *Culture and Subjective Well-Being*. Cambridge, MA: The MIT Press, pp. 113-161.

KOPALA, M. (1996). *Topic, Methods, and Qualitative Training*. New York: Fordham University.

KOSSAK, M. S. (2008). *Specialization in Transpersonal Psychology and Expressive Arts Therapies*. MI: UMI

LAFOUNTAIN, R., & BARTOS, R. (2002). *Research and Statistics Made Meaningful in Counselling and Student Affairs*.

LAGO, C. (2006). *Race, Culture, And Counselling: The Ongoing Challenge* (2nd ed.). England: McGraw-Hill Education.

LEE, C. C. (1991). Cultural Dynamics: Their Importance in Multicultural Counselling. In G. Corey, et. al. (eds). *Issues and Ethics in The Helping Professions*, (pp 239-265). Pacific Grove, CA: Brooks/Cole.

LEE, E. O. (2007). Religion and Spirituality as Predictors of Well-Being Among Chinese American and Korean American Older Adults. *Journal of Religion, Spirituality, and Aging, 19* (3), 77-100.

LEEDY, P. D., & ORMROD, J. E. (2005). *Practical Research: Planning and Design* (8th ed.). Upper Saddle River, NJ. Prentice Hall.

LEONARD, A. G. (1968). *The Lower Niger and its Tribes*. London: Frank Cass.

LERNER, R. (2002). *Concepts and Theories of Human Development*. (3rd ed.). New Jersey: Lawrence Erlbaum Associates.

LEVINE, P. (1997). *Waking the Tiger: Healing Trauma: The Innate Capacity to Transform Overwhelming Experiences*. North Atlantic Books.

LIN, E. H. et. al. (1985). An Exploration of Somatisation Among Asian Refugees and Immigrants in Primary Care. *American Journal of Public Health, 75*, 1080-1084.

LINLEY, P. A., & JOSEPHS, S. (2005). The Human Capacity for Growth Through Adversity. *American Psychologist, 60* (3), 262-264.

LOEWY, M. I., TOLLIVER, W. D. T., & KELETA, A. (2002). Group Counselling with Traumatised East African Refugee Women in the US: Using the Kaffa Ceremony Intervention. *Journal for Specialists in Group Work, 27* (2), 173-191.

M. J. (2011). *Reality Therapy: The Basics.* Retrieved from http://reality.therapyhub.com/

MAKE OF YOURSELF A LIGHT (undated). *Jungian Theory: A Synopsis.* Retrieved from http://roccovision.com/markmcmanus/?page_id=746

MANASTER, G. J. & CORSINI, R. J. (2009). *Individual Psychology: Theory and Practice.* Austin: University of Texas.

MASLOW, A. (1943). Hierarchy of Needs: A Theory of Human Motivation. *Amazon Digital Services.* www.all-about-psychology.com

MASLOW, A. (2011). Dynamics of Personality Organization. *Amazon Digital Services.* Retrieved from www.all-about-psychology.com

MAZZUCATO, V., & SCHANS, D. (2011). Transnational Families and The Wellbeing of Children: Conceptual and Methodological Challenges. *Journal of Marriage and Family, 73,* 704-712. Maastricht University.

MBITI, J. S. (1969). *African Religions and Philosophy.* London: Heinemann.

McGOLDRICK, M., GIORDANO, J., & GARCIA-PRETO, N. (2005). *Overview: Ethnicity and Family Therapy,* pp. 1-40. New York: Guilford Press.

McGraw Hill. (Undated). *Adler: Individual Psychology.* Retrieved from http://highered.mcgraw-hill.com/sites/dl/free/0073382701/600511/feist7_sample_ch03.pdf

McLeod, S. A. (2007). *Psychoanalysis | Freudian Theory.* Retrieved from http://www.simplypsychology.org/psychoanalysis.html

McLEOD, S. A. (2007). Psychodynamic Approach in Psychology. *Simply Psychology.* Retrieved from http://www.simplypsychology.org/psychodynamic.html

McLEOD, S. A. (2008). *Id Ego Super-ego.* Retrieved from http://www.simplypsychology.org/psyche.html

McLEOD, S. A. (2008). *Psychosexual Stages*. Retrieved from http://www.simplypsychology.org/psychosexual.html

McLEOD, S. A. (2009). *Defense Mechanisms*. Retrieved from http://www.simplypsychology.org/defense-mechanisms.html

McLEOD, S. A. (2009). *Freud - Dream Interpretation*. Retrieved from http://www.simplypsychology.org/freud-dreams.html

McLEOD, S. A. (2009). *The Unconscious Mind – Sigmund Freud*. Retrieved from http://www.simplypsychology.org/unconscious-mind.html

McNALLY, R. J. (2005). *Remembering Trauma*. Harvard University Press.

MEARNS, D. & THORNE, B. (2007). *Person-Centred Counselling in Action*. London: Sage Publications.

MENDEHALL, T. J. (2006). Trauma-Response Teams: Inherent Challenges and Practical Strategies in Interdisciplinary Fieldwork Family. *Systems and Health, 24* (3), 357-362.

MICHENBAUM, D. (1997). *Treating PTSD: A Handbook and Practice Manual for Therapy*. John Wiley and Sons. UK.

MILLER, A. (2014). The Role of the Counsellor in REBT. *Houston Chronicles*. Retrieved from http://work.chron.com/role-counselor-rebt-13029.html

MILLER, K., & RASCO, L. (Eds), (2004). *The Mental Health of Refugees: Ecological Approaches to Healing and Adaptation*. Mahwah, NJ. Lawrence Erlbaum Publishers, Inc.

MINUCHIN, S. (1974). *Families and Family Therapy*. Cambridge: Harvard University Press.

MOILA, M. P. (2002). *Challenging Issues in African Christianity*. Indiana: DB Powell Bible Centre.

MOJAB, C. G. (2006). Cross Cultural Counselling. *Life-circle Counselling and Consulting LLC.*

MOUSTAKAS, C. (1990). *Heuristic Research: Design, Methodology, and Applications*. New York: Sage Publications.

MOUSTAKAS, C. (2001). *Heuristic Research*. Retrieved from
www.unioninstitute.edu/Faculty/FacultyGrad/Moustakas.html

MULHAUSER, G. (2013). An Introduction to Rational Emotive Behavior
Therapy. *Counseling Resource Mental Health Library*. Retrieved from
http://counsellingresource.com/lib/therapy/types/rational-emotive/

MURDOCK, N. (2012). *Theories of Counselling and Psychotherapy: A Case
Approach*. Prentice Hall.

MURRAY, S. (2010). *Jungian Psychoanalysis: Working in the Spirit of C. G.
Jung*. Chicago: Carus Publishing Company.

MUSSER-GRAMSKI, J., & CARILLO, D. F. (1997). The Use of Bilingual,
Bicultural Paraprofessionals in Mental Health Services: Issues for Hiring,
Training, and Supervision. *Community Mental Health Journal, 33* (1). 51-
60.

NATIONAL CHILD TRAUMATIC STRESS NETWORK. (2005). *Mental
Health Interventions for Refugee Children in Resettlement White Paper II*.
Retrieved from www.nctsnet.org

NELSON, J. (2002). Diverse Goals for Multicultural Counselling and
Therapy. *Counselling Psychology Quarterly, vol. 15*, No. 1 June, 2002. pg. 133
– 143. Routledge: Taylor and Francis Group.

NGUIING, (2011). *Existential Therapy*. Retrieved from
http://nguiing.wordpress.com/2011/09/25/existential-therapy/

NICHOLSON, B. L. (1997). The Influence of Pre-Immigration and Post-
Emigration Stressors on Mental Health. A Study of South Asian Refugees.
Social Work Research, 21 (1), 19-31.

NOANXIETY.COM (undated). *Logotherapy: Victor Frankl*. Retrieved
from http://www.noanxiety.com/psychotherapies/logotherapy-victor-
frankl.html

NOOR, K. (2008). Case Study: A Strategic Research Methodology. *American Journal of Applied Sciences, 5* (11), 1602-1604.

NUDELMAN, A. (1993). The Importance of Traditional Healing for Ethio-
pian Immigrants in Israel. *Collegium Antropologicum, 17*, 233-239.

O'MAHONY, J. M., & DONNELLY, T. T. (2007). The Influence of Culture on Immigrant Women's Mental Health Care Experiences from the Perspective of Health Care Providers. *Issues in Mental Health Nursing, 28*, 453-471.

O'REILLY, K. (2007a). Intra-European Migration and the Mobility-Enclosure Dialectic. *Sociology, 41* (2), 277-293.

OLIKENYI, G. I. (2001). *African Hospitality*. London: Steyler Verlag.

ONYANGO, K. M., & ONYANGO, P. (1984). *The Sociology of the African Family*. New York: Longmans.

OYINKAN, M. (2009). *A Cross Cultural Study of Silence in Nigeria—An Ethnolinguistic Approach*. Retrieved from http://www.unilorin.edu.ng/publications/medubi/Oyin%20A%20cross-cultural%20of%20silence.pdf

PAPERO, D. V. (1983). Family Systems Theory and Therapy. In B. B. Wolman & G. Stricker (Eds.), *Handbook of Family and Marital Therapy* (pp. 137-158). New York: Plenum.

PARK, S. J. (undated). *Existential Theory*. University of North Texas. Retrieved from http://people.unt.edu/~sjp0013/existential

PARKER. A. H. (2011). *Psychology for Psychotherapy Counselling Types*. London: Alex H. Parker.

PATTERSON, C. H. (1996). Multicultural Counselling: From Diversity to Universality. *Journal of Counselling and Development, 74*, 227-231.

PATTON, M. Q. (2004). Heuristic Inquiry. *The Sage Encyclopaedia of Social Science Research Methods*.

PEDERSON, P. B. (1990). The Constructs of Complexity and Balance in Multicultural Counselling Theory and Practice. *Journal of Counselling and Development, 681*, 550-584.

PEDERSON, P. D. (1991). Multiculturalism as a Generic Framework. *Journal of Counselling & Development, 1991,* 70, 1: 6-12.

PERLS, F. S. (1969). *Gestalt Therapy Verbatim*. New York: Bantam Books.

PERLS, F. S. (1973). *The Gestalt Approach and Eyewitness to Therapy*. New York: Bantam Books.

PERLS, F. S., HEFFERLINE, R. F., & GOODMAN, P. (1951). *Gestalt Therapy*. London: Souvenir Press.

PESCITELLI, D. (1996). *Rogerian Therapy*. Retrieved from http://pandc.ca/?cat=carl_rogers&page=rogerian_therapy

PETRE, M., & RUGG, G. (2010). *The Unwritten Rules of PhD Research*. London: Open University Press.

PICKREN, Marc. (2010). Person Centred Therapy. *Helping Psychology*. Retrieved from http://www.helpingpsychology.com/person-centered-therapy

PINDERHUGHES, E. (1995). Empowering Diverse Populations: Family Practice in the 21st Century. *Family in Society: Journal of Contemporary Human Service, 76*, (3), 131-140.

POLDRUGO, F., & PATUSSI, V. (1996). Alcoholism and Alcohol Related Problems in Italy: An Overview on Recent Developments in Social Responses and Treatment Systems. *Journal of Addictive Diseases, 15*, 59-65.

POTOCHY-TRIPODI, M. (2002). *Best Practices for Social Work with Refugees and Immigrants*. New York: Columbia University Press.

POVOLEDO, E. (2003). In Italy, Summertime is for Divorce. *The International Herald Tribune*. Retrieved from www.nytimes.com/2003/08/08/news/09iht-divorce_ed1_.html

POWELL, J. (1989). *Fully Human, Fully Alive*.

PRESSE, A. F. (2014). 4,000 Immigrants Reach Italy by Boat in 48 Hours as Minister Calls for EU Help. *The Guardian*. Retrieved from www.theguardian.com/world/2014/apr/09/4000immigrants-Italy-boat-48-hours-eu-help

PRETORIUS, E. (1993). *The Traditional Healer in South African Health Care*. HSRC, SF: Pretoria.

RAPHAEL, B. (1986). *When Disaster Strikes: How Individuals and Communities Cope with Catastrophe*. New York: Basic Books.

REFERENCE.com (2012). *Alfred Adler*. Retrieved from http://www.reference.com/browse/Alfred+Adler

REMLEY Jr. P. T., BACCHINI, E., & KRIEG, P. (2010). Counselling in Italy. *Journal of Counselling and Development, 88.* American Counselling Association.

REPETTO, E. (2001-2002). *Cross Cultural Counselling: Problems and Prospects.* Universidad Nazionale de Educacion a Distancia (UNED): Madrid.

REYNERI, E. (2007). *Immigration in Italy: Trends and Perspectives.* IOM, Argo.

RICHMOND, A. H. (1994). *Global Apartheid: Refugees, Racism, and the New Order.* Oxford: Oxford University Press.

RIDGEWAY, I. R. (2007). *Reality Therapy: William Glasser.* Retrieved from http://myauz.com/ianr/articles/lect5realitytherapyglasser.pdf

ROBERTSON, R. (1992). *Beginner's Guide to Jungian Psychology.* York Beach: Nicolas-Hays.

ROBINSON, L., SMITH, M., & SEGAL, J. (2013). *Healing Emotional and Psychological Trauma: Symptoms, Treatment and Recovery.* Helpguide.org. Retrieved from http://www.helpguide.org/mental/emotional_psychological_trauma.htm

ROGERS, C. R. (1977). *Carl Rogers on Personal Power.* New York: Delacorte.

ROSENBLOOM, D., WILLIAMS, M. B., & WATKINS, B. E. (1999). *Life After Trauma: A Workbook for Healing.* New York: The Guilford Press.

ROSS, W. (2006). What is REBT? *REBT Network.* Retrieved from http://www.rebtnetwork.org/whatis.html

ROTHSCHILD, B. (2000). *The Body Remembers: The Psychophysiology of Trauma and Trauma Treatment.* Norton Publishers.

ROTHSCHILD, B. (2010). *8 Keys to Safe Trauma Recovery: Take Charge Strategies for Reclaiming Your Life.* Los Angeles: W. W. Norton & Company.

ROYA R. R. (2010). *Psyche and Self's Theories in Psychology.* Victoria, BC. Trafford Publishing.

ROYSIRCAR, G., & GARD, G. (in press). Research in multicultural counselling: Impact of therapist variables on process and outcome. In C. C. Lee (Ed.), *Multicultural Issues in Counselling: New Approaches to Diversity* (3rd edition). Alexandria, VA: American Counselling Association.

RUBUSH, C. (2013). *Cognitive Behaviour Therapy—Help for the Combat Vet with PTSD*. Retrieved from http://winoverptsd.com/wp/cognitive-behavior-therapy-cbt-help-for-the-combat-vet-with-ptsd/

SABATES-WHEELER, R. S., & KOETTL, J. (2010). Social Protection for Migrants: The Challenges of Delivery in the Context of Changing Migration Flows. *International Social Security Review, 63*, 3-4/2010.

SARTRE, J. P. (1956). *Being and Nothingness*. London: SCM Press.

SATIR, V. M. (1972). *Peoplemaking*. Palo Alto: Science and Behaviour Books.

SCHWEIGERT, W. A. (1998). *Research Methods in Psychology*. Pacific Grove: Brooks/Cole Pub.

SCHWEITZER, R. et. al. (2006). Trauma, Post-Migration Living Difficulties, and Social Support as Predictors of Psychological Adjustment in Resettled Sudanese Refugees. *Australian and New Zealand Journal of Psychiatry, 40* (2), 179-187.

SEAH, A. (2007). Multicultural Counselling and Therapy: A Model of Integrating. *Ashweek blog*. Retrieved from http://ashweek.blogspot.it/2007/06/multicultural-counselling-and-therapy.html

SELIGMAN, L. & REICHENBERG, L. W. (2009). *Theories of Counselling and Psychotherapy*. Pearson Prentice Hall

SHARF, R. (2012). *Theories of Psychotherapy and Counselling*. Belmont: Brooks/Cole Cengage Learning.

SHAUGHNESSY, J. J., & ZECHMEISTER, E. B. (1997). *Research Methods in Psychology*. New York: McGraw Pub.

SHIRAEV, E. & LEVY, D. (2004). *Cross Cultural Psychology: Critical Thinking and Contemporary Applications* (2nd ed.). Boston: Pearson Education INC.

SKINNER, B. F. (1974). *About Behaviourism*. New York: Vintage Books.

SKINNER, B. F. *Critique of Psychoanalytic Concepts and Theories*. www.all-about-psychology.com

SOCIETA' ITALIANA DI PSICOLOGIA (2009). Retrieved from www.sips.it

SOLOMON, M., & SIEGEL, D. (eds.) (2003). *Healing Trauma: Attachment, Mind, Body, & Brain*. London: W.W. Norton and Company.

SOMEKH, B. (2006). *Action Research: A Methodology for Change and Development*. Maidenhead, Eng: Open University Press.

SORSOLI, L. & TOLMAN, D. (2008). Hearing Voices: Listening for Multiplicity and Movement in Interview Data. *The Handbook of Emergent Methods in Psychological Research*. New York: Guilford Press.

SOUSSOU, M. A., CRAIG, C. D., OGREN, H., & SCHNAK, M. (2008). A Qualitative Study of Resilience Factors of Bosnian Refugee Women Resettled in the Southern United States. *Journal of Ethnic and Cultural Diversity in Social Work, 17* (4), 365-385.

SPONIAS, C. (2011). *Carl Jung's Dream Theories*. Retrieved from http://www.mindalignment.com/tag/psychotherapy/

STRAUSS, A., & CORBIN, J. (1990). *Basics of Qualitative Research: Grounded Theory Procedures and Techniques*. Newbury Park, CA: Sage.

STRICKER, G. (2013). Psychotherapy Integration. *Gale Encyclopedia of Mental Disorders*. Retrieved from http://www.encyclopedia.com/doc/1G2-3405700320.html

STRISIK, P., & STRISIK, S. W. (2014). Types of Psychotherapy Approaches. *Strisik.com*. Retrieved from http://www.strisik.com/therapy/approaches.htm

SUE, D. W., & SUE D. (2012). *Counselling the Culturally Diverse: Theory and Practice*. (6th Ed.). New Jersey: John Wiley and Sons.

SUE, D. W., ARREDONDO, P., & McDAVIS, R. J. (1992). Multicultural Competencies/Standards: A Pressing Need. *Journal of Counselling and Development, 70,* (4), 477-486.

SUE, D. W., IVEY, A. E., & Pedersen, P. B. (1992). *A Theory of Multicultural Counselling and Therapy.* Pacific Grove: Brooks/Cole.

SUMMERFIELD, D. (1999). A Critique of Seven Assumptions Behind Psychological Trauma Programmes in War-Affected Areas. *Social Science and Medicine, 48,* 1449-1462.

TASHAKKORI, A. & TEDDLIE, C. (eds.). (2003). *Handbook of Mixed Methods in Social and Behavioral Research.* Thousand Oaks, CA. Sage Publishers.

TAYLOR, G. (ed.). (2005). *Integrating Quantitative and Qualitative Methods in Research.* Maryland: UPA

TAYLOR, M. S. (2011). Analytical Psychotherapy: Ancient Archetypes, Modern Day Applications. *Therapy for the Soul.* Retrieved from http://www.therapyforyoursoul.com/carl-jung-psychology.html

THAVIS, J. (2004). Political Priorities: In Catholic Italy, Abortion is not an Issue. *Catholic News Service.* Retrieved from www.catholicnews.com

THOMAS, R. M., & BRUBAKER, D. L. (2008). *Theses and Dissertations: A Guide for the First Time Researcher.* (2nd ed.). Thousand Oaks: Corwin Press.

THOMPSON, J. B. (1998). *Research Methods in Psychology.* Belmont: Brooks/Cole Publishing.

THOMPSON, J. B. (1999). *Study Guide to Accompany Elmes, Kantowitz, and Roediger's Research Methods in Psychology.* (6th ed.). London: Brooks/ Cole Pub.

THORPE, S. A. (1991). *African Traditional Religions.* S. A.: University of S.A.

TITELMAN, P. (ed.). (2008). *Triangles: Bowen Family Systems Theory Perspectives.* New York: The Haworth Press.

TODD, Z. et. Al. (2004). *Mixing Methods in Psychology*. Sussex: Psychology Press.

TOLAN, J. (2012). *Skills in Person-Centred Counselling and Psychotherapy*. London: Sage Publications.

TRANS4MIND, (2012). *The Self: Jung's Definition*. Retrieved from http://www.trans4mind.com/jamesharveystout/self.htm

TRIBE, R. (2002a). Mental Health and Refugees. *Advances in Psychiatric Treatment, 8* (4), 240-247.

TRIBE, R. (2002b). Football for Facilitating Therapeutic Interventions Among a Group of Refugees. In: I, Cockerill (ed). *Solutions in Sports Psychology*. London: Thompson.

TRIBE, R. (2005). The Mental Health Needs of Refugees and Asylum Seekers. *The Mental Health Review, 10* (4), 8-16.

TRIMBLE & THURMAN. (2002). *Ethno-cultural Considerations and Strategies for Providing Counselling Services to Native American Indians*. P. Pederson J.

TURABIAN, K. L. (2007). *A Manual for Writers of Research Papers, Theses, and Dissertations*, 7th ed. Chicago: University of Chicago Press.

TUTU, D. (1989). *God is Not Christian*. London: Harper EBooks.

U.N. GENERAL ASSEMBLY, (1951). *Convention Relating to The Status of Refugees*. United Nations, Treaty Series, 189, 137.

VALENTI, T. R. (2010). *Dissociation and Trauma*. Retrieved from http://seattletherapist.wordpress.com/2010/06/28/dissociation-and-trauma/

VAN BEEK, A. (1996). *Cross Cultural Counselling*. Michigan: Augsburg Fortress

VESTI, P., & KASTRUP, M. (1995). Refugees Status, Torture, and Adjustment. In J. R. Freedy, & S. Hobfoil (Eds). *Traumatic Stress from Theory to Practice*, (pp. 213-235). New York: Prenum Press.

VIVYAN, C. (2007). *Introduction to Cognitive Behaviour Therapy*. Retrieved from http://www.cwgsy.net/private/get/CBT%20Intro.ppt#256

VOLKMAN, V. R. (2005). *Beyond Trauma: Conversations on Traumatic Incident Reduction*. Loving Healing Press.

VOLKMAN, V. R. (2005). *Traumatic Incident Reduction: Research and Results*. Loving Healing Press.

WALLIMAN, N. (2005). *Your Research Project: A step by step guide for the first time researchers* (2nd ed.). London: Sage Publications.

WALTER, J. (2013). *Skinner's Behavioural Theory*. Retrieved from http://www.ehow.com/about_5498343_skinner_s-behavioural-theory.html

WALTER, J. L., & MALPASS, R. (1994). *Psychology and Culture*.

WANG, L., & FREELAND, D. (2004). Coping with Immigration: New Challenges for the Mental Health Profession. In: J. L. Chin (Ed). *The Psychology of Prejudice and Discrimination*. Westport, Conn: Praeger Perspectives.

WEBBER, C. (2012). *Cognitive Therapy and Cognitive Behaviour Therapy*. Retrieved from http://www.netdoctor.co.uk/diseases/depression/cognitivetherapy_000439.htm

WEINE, S. M. et. Al. (2004). Family Consequences of Refugee Trauma. *Family Process, 43* (2), 147-160.

WEISSMAN, A. (1979). *The Dysfunctional Attitude Scale*. Philadelphia: Centre for Cognitive Therapy.

WENDY, S. A. (1998). *Research Methods in Psychology*. CA. Brooks/Cole Publishing Company.

WERTZ, F. J. (2005). Phenomenological Research Methods for Counselling Psychology. *APA Journal of Counselling Psychology 52* (2), 167-177.

WHITAKER, C. (1976). The Hindrance of Theory in Clinical Work. In P. J. Guerin, Jr. (ed.), *Family Therapy: Theory and Practice* (pp. 154 – 164). New York: Gardner.

WILKINS, P. (2010). *Person-Centred Therapy*. New York: Rutledge.

WILLIAMS, S. J. & CALNAN, M. (1996). The *"limits"* of Medicalization?: Modern Medicine and Lay Populace in *"Late"* Modernity. *Social Science & Medicine, 42*, 1609-1620.

WILSON, C. (2001). *New Pathways in Psychology: Maslow and the Post-Freudian Revolution.* Zorba Press.

WILSON, J. P., & TANG, S. C. (2010). *Cross Cultural Assessment of Psychological Trauma and PTSD.* New York: Springer Science + Business Media, LLC.

WINNETT, D.O. (1965). *Professional Counselling On Human Behaviour—Its Principles and Practices.*

WISKER, G. (ed). (2008). *The Post Graduate Research Handbook* (2nd ed.). Hampshire: Macmillan Publishers.

WRENN, C. G. (1985). Afterword: The Culturally Encapsulated Counsellor Revisited. In P. Pederson (Ed). *Handbook of Cross-Cultural Counselling and Counselling,* (pp. 323-329). Westport: Greenwood.

WUBBOLDING, R. E. (1998). Qualities of The Reality Therapist. *Journal of Reality Therapy, 18,* 47-49

WUBBOLDING, R. E. (2000). *Reality Therapy for The 21st Century.* Philadelphia: Brunner Rutledge.

YAKUSHKO, O. CHRONISTER, K. M. (2005). Immigrant Women and Counselling: The Invisible Others. *Journal of Counselling and Development, 83,* 292-298.

YALOM, I. D. (1980). *Existential Psychotherapy.* New York: Basic Books.

YEOH, S. A. B., & EN YI, C. (2013). Family Migration. *The Encyclopaedia of Global Human Migration.* London: Blackwell Publishers.

YONTEF, G. (1989). *Gestalt: An Introduction.* Retrieved from http://www.gestalt.org/yontef.htm

YOSHIHAMA, M. & HORRUCKS, J. (2002). Post-Traumatic Stress Symptoms and Victimization Among Japanese American Women. *Journal of Consulting and Clinical Psychology, 70,* 205-215.

ZHOU, M. (1997). Growing Up American: The Challenge Confronting Immigrant Children of Immigrants. *Annual Review of Sociology, 23* (1), 63-95.

ZIMMERMANN, K. A. (2012). *What is culture? Definition of Culture*. Retrieved from http://www.livescience.com/21478-what-is-culture-definition-of-culture.html

ZINKER, J. C. (1977). *Creative Process in Gestalt Therapy*. New York: Brunner/Mazel Zorba Press.

APPENDIX

INTERVIEW REPORTS

NARRATIVE OVVN1

My name is VVN, and I was born on October 23rd 1980. I was brought up by my mother, who was a Muslim, I never met my dad as they both separated soon after I was born. Since my father was a Christian and also a half cast of Indian and Kenyan origin, my clan could not allow my mother to marry a man from another ethnic group. According to my mom, my dad was a mean person and so my mom left him as soon as I was born. My mom openly talked about him to me. She never permitted him to even come closer to me, and even when he wanted to get involved in caring for me my mom distanced him completely. He used to attempt to come to visit me at school, he would wait at the school entrance, just to have a glimpse of me, but he would not talk to me or give me anything, because if my mom came to know that he came to visit me at school, he would face serious consequences.

When I was born, I found other two female children, whom I took to be my sisters. However, they used to refer my mom to as aunty, and so I also decided to call my mom aunty. Later, when I was around 7 or 8, my mom decided to reveal the truth that those were not my sisters, but were my cousins from my maternal aunt and uncle. I was not shocked because there was nothing new, whether they were sisters or cousins didn't make any difference in my life at all. My mother had taken these cousins of mine in with her because they had been abandoned by their parents. They were homeless and my mom decided to take care of them despite her meagre salary and the fact that she was single.

When I was 4 years old, another of my cousin was born by the same aunt whose daughters I had come to consider as my sisters. I was very excited about this birth, and I used to treat my baby cousin as a moving doll, with a lot of affection. My mother had decided to take in these cousins and take care of them because my aunt and uncle were in horrible economic and mental conditions.

My mom used to work with the government, but her salary was skimpy. She however used to do other odd jobs as a hairdresser, and this is how she managed to provide for us. We were poor, but we never lacked the basics. When I was 8, my mom got married to my step father and this man took us as his own children. He was also not well off economically, so my mom decided to take a loan from the government for him to start a business, which he did and prospered. As a result, our needs were taken care of adequately.

My mother moved to a small plot of land in the middle of nowhere, and she took her own mom with her. Later, she took my aunt and uncle with her. My aunt was suffering from depression, and when she got laid off from a good job – she had been working as an air hostess with Kenya Airlines – she deteriorated into a severe depression which was manifested through incoherence and mental confusion. She was even taken to a mental hospital but they were unable to help her. My uncle was also problematic. He was lazy and never wanted to do anything. He was spoilt and never learned to take any responsibility. My mom took him aboard and continued taking care of him. My mom was on a constant struggle due to the many mouths she had to feed. However, she did not give up on anyone. She was always there to save everyone, and that behaviour continues till today. She was always very busy, and had no time for entertaining anyone. In fact, discipline at home was very strict. If we misbehaved, we were thoroughly beaten – she would use any means to hit us and teach us that some things were better watched from afar than done. We grew up knowing clearly the difference between right and wrong. We acted right because we really feared the beating. For instance, I think I received the most beating from my mom as opposed to my cousins. Whenever anything went wrong, I would be beaten even before I was asked to explain, whether I was directly involved or not. I was a very reserved child, and the fact that I did not defend myself was taken to mean that I was guilty, so many times I suffered punishments that were unjust. I however accepted this as part of life and did not feel bothered much by it. My behaviour was highly conditioned by the look on my mother's face. If she frowned at us, we knew we were in trouble. Just a gaze was enough to make us understand that what we were doing at that moment was wrong. I did not have any choice,

I would either adhere to what my mom expected from me or face the thorough beating, which was terrible so I adhered.

In my family, illness was taken as normal, and recourse was made to a traditional medicine man who cured most illnesses. In fact, since I was born up till the age of 7, I used to have terrible fevers which would constantly recur despite the medical intervention in the local hospital. At one point, my mom was fed up with the situation, and she decided to resort to a traditional medicine man. This medicine man put his thumb at the centre of my diaphragm, and pressed so hard I can remember the pain as if it happened yesterday. This pain was excruciating, but after he let go of the grip, I immediately felt better. He gave my mom medicine for me to take orally, as well as apply on the skin. From that moment, my fever left me and never returned. The medicine man healed me once and for all.

I got a baby 11 years ago, just at the same age as when my mother gave birth to me (23) – and the father of my son was also unreliable. I decided to leave him as he was too involved in other things and neglected us. I told him that he would not have anything to do with my son, and much as he pleaded with me to stay, I decided to leave him any way.

I learned from my mom to sacrifice myself for others, as she constantly gave up her own needs and showed that hers did not matter. In fact, I am the one who provides for my mom, my son, my uncle, my grandmother, my aunt, and my cousins. I send money to them constantly and if I fail to do so, they have serious problems. My aunt is psychotic, and my uncle is always sick. He is totally dependent on my mom for everything. I want my mom to move out of that place and just take my grandmother along with her. Her brother and sister have made her start having mental confusion. She claims to see imaginary things in the house, she says people beat her and want to strangle her, and often, at night, she wakes up feeling strangled and choked. She has been sick recently and this situation has been very stressful for me. She has been experiencing these things for the past 5 years and I am now fed up. I want to remove my mom from where she is so that she can move away from those things that attack her. Finally, I have been able to convince her to move, and I am working on this. I would like to get a small apartment for her so that she can leave that sick environment and settle down elsewhere.

I came to Italy not by choice, but due to poverty. I needed to help my family, especially my mom and my son, so I left my son there with my mom, and came over alone. My desire was to settle first and then call my son over, but he did not want to leave his grandmother. It worked out to my advantage because I would not have been able to take care of him. When I arrived here, I was so homesick. Thankfully, one of my cousins – the eldest of the ones I lived with, was already here in Italy therefore she assisted me. It was very difficult to get legal documents to stay here, and I was being thrown from one place to the other. It was very stressful. At one point, I wanted to go back home, but I knew that I had reached a point of no return, so I had to persevere like my mom did.

I managed to get the right documents after a couple of years. This meant that I could work. In the meantime, I was constantly under duress. Even after I got a job, I was still living under stress because I had to sustain my family back home. I was struggling to get somewhere to stay, at the same time I was under pressure from home. I felt a lot of discrimination, and just the fact that I am black made it difficult for me to get a job easily. Having no college degree also contributed to lack of proper jobs. I regretted why I did not pursue higher education.

Currently, I work as a baby sitter, residing in this family with 3 young children, where the mom mistreats me and expects me to work so much for a low pay. I decided to just bite the bullet and stay put, since I need the job. I however hope to get another job and move on. I would like to bring my son over here, as well as my mother, even if it is just for a while. After that, I will settle her in a totally different place.

Many times I am under stress and I overeat. I have a bad metabolism and sometimes I suffer stomach problems. My aim is to go back to school and take a college degree.

NARRATIVE OJN2

I was born in October 1964 in the highlands of Kenya. I was the second born in a family of four siblings. I have an elder sister who is two years senior to me, and my two twin brothers, who are 18 months younger than me. My dad was an engineer, while my mom was a housewife. When I was 4, my mom left us, and we were taken to my paternal grandmother who took care of us while my dad worked in Nairobi. My dad had a good job, but he had a problem with alcohol. He used to spend all his money on alcohol, so we lived in extreme poverty. I remember I had only one pair of underwear, and I was afraid to wash them because I could not think of staying without underwear. My grandma could give me hers, but they were too large for me. My grandma tried to provide food for us, but it was never enough. In fact,

I never used to attend school regularly because we could not afford fees. In any case, I was intelligent, despite all odds. We feared our father because he used to come home drunk.

My dad and grandma denied my mom permission to see us, so we never saw her. Any time she attempted to visit us, my dad made sure that she was sent away and never saw us. They made us believe that our mom was bad and so we did not feel the need to see her since she had abandoned us.

My mom wanted to see us, so one day, she came over with a policeman, and attempted to take us away with her. When I saw her, I ran away into the bush and hid, and despite looking for me all over, they did not find me, so they left without us. They however promised they would return. I was scared of going away with my mom. Then one day, when I was 8, my mom showed up with a policeman unannounced, and they took us away. My dad discovered later that we had been taken away. On the way to Nairobi, we all cried so bitterly, because we did not want to go away from our grandma. We did not know our mom well, since she had abandoned us when we were so small. However, we did not have a choice. We arrived in Nairobi, and got into a tiny one room slum apartment, and we were horrified. Mom had put up a bunk bed which we all used, and she had a small side bed where she slept. We were squeezed. We started learning how to relate with our mom – something we did not have a clue about. Gradually, we started getting used to the environment and liking it. We had enough food, clothes, and we could go to school. We appreciated our mom, and actually never thought of our grandma and dad. They once tried to visit us, but my mom denied them the possibility of seeing us. In the process, grandma passed away when I was about 15, and we attended her funeral. I was very sad about this death. I had however gone to see her in the hospital, so we had made peace.

It was only when I was in high school that I could see my dad. He came to visit me when he had stopped drinking. He had even taken in another lady; with whom he was living happily. After some time, he relapsed, and his life deteriorated. He started going out with different women, until he got very sick of AIDS and passed away in 1985. While he was sick, I could visit him in the hospital.

My experience of my dad was very bad, and from this, I never wanted to have anything to do with men. In fact, this explains why I never got married. I can't trust men, the only man I trusted in my life – my father – betrayed me, and therefore I have no confidence to be in a relationship with any man.

When I finished high school, I got a job in a casino, where I used to work at night. My mom was not happy, but I needed my independence. In that environment, I learned how to drink due to peer pressure. It was a terrible experience, and when I could not take it any longer, I asked my mom to get me out of there. She got me a job as a clerk in an office, and I was saved from destruction. My mom also got another job, and she moved out into a larger house.

In my community, when a baby is born, there is a lot of celebration, since the child is considered a blessing. Elders come together to bless the child and welcome him or her into the family and community. They bring gifts, assist the new mom with counsel and material help, and offer to keep her company while she is learning to take care of her child. The baby is given a name immediately, because the name has a remarkable significance in the community. The name corresponds to some specific experiences, relatives, or phenomenological conditions. A baby should be born where there is a father and a mother. Single mothers are frowned upon, and considered outcasts. It doesn't matter whether a person is legally married or not, but the presence of both parents is crucial in child birth. Whoever has a child outside *"wedlock"* is considered an outcast.

Handicapped children are considered bad omen, and their handicap is associated with something wrong that the parents may have done. The blame is on the parents or someone who might be jealous of the family and wants to destroy them. Some rituals are performed to kick out the evil spirits. It is the hope of the people that this lesson serves to warn others against doing evil.

Discipline in my family was very clear. If you did anything wrong, you were punished by beating. I got beaten severally, even if I was not at fault. My baby twin brothers used to instigate me, and when I reacted, I was punished for it because I was considered older than them so I should never quarrel with them or fight. When something went wrong, there was no chance of explaining oneself. I got punished and that was all. Sometimes my mom did not have all the information she needed, but she went ahead and beat me. Discipline was in form of smacking, beating with a stick, belt, or slipper, or punishment to the effect of going without dinner.

Birthdays are celebrated in my community, people have lots of fun, and they dance, sing, eat, and tell stories. Death is seen as a passage. A funeral is a celebration of life, despite the sadness that comes with it. Life is not ended, but changed.

Religion is a very crucial aspect of our life. Everything is explained with the optic of religion. Religion is considered a way of life, and it offers one the basic principles of life. Those who do not profess their religion are considered strange. It moulds one to become a better person, and to have meaning in life. God is mentioned in every conversation. Suffering is also explained through the eyes of faith. Whatever one goes through is meant to purify them and make them better people. This explains why even when one is dying, they are serene.

When one has a problem, the family and community get together and help them out. I have learned from my family to do exactly this. Currently, I send significant amounts of money home, to help different family members in their situations. I sacrifice plenty of things in order to help my people at home. It is actually expected that I do so. If I don't, I will be considered selfish and against my values, so I have to help them. In fact, if there is a pressing need at home, people get together to help out. It is expected that one asks for help when they need to, and everyone comes together to give a hand. There is a strong sense of solidarity especially in matters to do with illnesses, studies, calamities, among others.

As far as marriage is concerned, people are free to choose their partners and their decision is often respected. However, there are some situations when the family intervenes especially if someone opts for an alcoholic or drug addict, or assassin, or any criminal.

I think my life here is a struggle. I don't feel at home here, and I feel discriminated upon. This is due to my colour, difficulty in learning the local language, and the fact that I did not study here. I feel discriminated upon because my certificates are not recognised here. As far as getting relevant documents is concerned, it is a real strenuous effort, and it can be very frustrating. One constantly needs the help of others in order to get to places.

I think it would help if people trying to settle here get the right counselling that could help them adjust to situations. People need to come to terms with their past as well as the struggles they are going through currently.

My desire is to make enough money and eventually go back home. No matter where I am, East or West, home is best, because I have my family and community there, I have a strong sense of belonging, since I am because we are.

NARRATIVE ONNK3

I was born on 27th October 1975 in a remote area in Kenya. At the time, my father was a businessman, and I was the 4th in a family of 5 siblings. My father used to work very hard in order to provide for us, while my mother stayed at home caring for us and the farm. We used to help my mother a lot in the farm, with the animals, and in the house. I was a very hard worker. My mother was a very religious woman, and we used to sit together every evening to pray. My mother taught us that there is nothing impossible before God, and we lived in this perspective. We were taught to respect our parents and our elders, and we never used to answer back when an elder talked to us. In fact, we never used to raise our eyes when our parents or elders talked to us. Our head was always bowed as a sign of respect. We never ever questioned what our parents told us to do, and even if we did not agree with what they told us, we had to accept it without questions. We however used to talk to each other about how we felt, though our parents never came to know. I was not very close to my mother, I never used to confide in her, and, although it was not verbalized, we felt that we had to deal with our problems on our own without resorting to our parents, except when the situation was critical. My mother was too busy taking care of many other issues to listen to our menial problems. I grew up knowing and believing that I had to solve my problems on my own, I could not just talk about them to other people. In fact, we were told that you don't wash your family dirty laundry in public, so we never used to discuss problematic situations.

I went through school without many incidents, but I never went to high school because I was a girl child. My brothers however had this possibility. My sister and I reached only up to 8th grade. We were made to believe that it was useless to send girls to school, and therefore we were subordinate to boys or men. I was taught to be respectful of men, since they were the heads of the family, as well as the ones who provided. My role as a woman was to serve them and accept whatever they offered even when I was not convinced. I was made to sacrifice my needs for my brothers and my family.

I left early to go and look for a job, and I was employed as a house help. I used to send all the money I earned to my mother who needed school fees to send my brothers to school. I did not have a choice about the jobs I performed. I was however a very hard worker. Later, I left this kind of job and started working in a hair salon. I learned to make hair and that opened me up to more job opportunities. Later, I was employed in a boutique, where I met different people from different cultures and for the first time, I discovered that people are not all the same – that there are other worlds that I am not aware of. I was impressed to see tourists and I wondered where and how they lived. It was an eye opener. In fact, I got involved with one of the tourists, but later I refused to continue with the relationship since I feared that he might take me away from my family.

In my community, when a child is born, there is a lot of merry making. If the child is male, there is more merry making than if it is female. This confirms that boys are superior to girls and therefore girls should be subordinate to boys. The baby is welcomed with lot ululations, and the whole neighbourhood joins in. If it is a girl, the ululation is repeated 5 times. If it is a girl, 4 times. People bring in gifts in form of clothes, farm produce, dry goods, and other foodstuffs. When a boy is born, a goat or a sheep is slaughtered and everyone joins together to feast. There are drinks of all types and it is a real celebration. The mother is treated like a queen, and she is not allowed to work. Everyday, for at least three months, someone comes home to help her, and relatives and neighbours take turns. During this period, a woman can not have intercourse with the husband, since she is considered unclean. It is only after the flow is finished that there can be sexual intercourse.

In my community, initiation ceremonies are held for both girls and boys. However, right now, girls do not go through the process. During my time, we all used to be circumcised. This was a special celebration where we were separated from other younger girls and taught to be *"women"*. This involved female older generations instructing us on how to be good and mature women. I was circumcised when I was 12, and it was normal for this process to take place. It was a painful experience but I was not allowed to even cry and whine. In fact, I was taught not to allow myself to feel pain, and when I did, I could not express it. I however felt terrible about it, but I could not verbalize it lest I be considered a weakling.

Illness in the family is considered some form of punishment from God. If someone falls sick, they need to do an exam of consciousness to understand where they have gone wrong. They need to purify themselves and go through a cleansing rite in order to get their health back. God communicates with us through illness. If God has a reason to keep one alive, no matter how serious one's illness is, they will recover, so I learned to accept illness the way it comes and wait on the Lord. Illness is therefore taken as a personal issue – one feels responsible for being ill. Some illnesses are treated in hospitals, while others are treated traditionally. It depends on the kind of illness and its duration. When one has a simple cold, they can not waste time in bed, they need to be strong and face the daily activities without retreating. If someone has malaria, some evil spirits might be involved, so some cleansing is required.

In my family and in my community, people have what we call "*harambee*" spirit. This means that if anyone has any kind of need, everyone comes together to help. For instance, if someone needs to go abroad to study, the family and friends organize a fundraiser and invite people from all walks of life to contribute towards this cause. There usually is a guest of honour, who is supposed to bring substantial amounts of money as well as invite as many friends as possible to contribute towards the harambee. One's needs are the community's needs. If you do not help someone in need, you will be treated the same – no one will help you at the hour of need. There is a strong spirit of generosity, we don't share only that which is a surplus, but out of our necessity. This is what I was taught by my mom and my community. When guests come to visit, we remove the best items, we cook the best food, and we wear the best clothes. This means that the guest is much more important that I am and therefore I should deny myself to give to the guest. We consider the guest as a river, they bring blessings with them and move on, so it is up to us to welcome them since by so doing we can partake of these blessings.

As for marriage, it is an important aspect of my family and culture. For instance, the choice of a spouse is highly influenced by the elders. If I choose someone that my parents do not approve of, it is likely that I will have problems for life. I should be able to find someone who is accepted by my family and community, in order for blessings to come my way. If parents do not approve of a partner, one is likely to be haunted by this all throughout their life. Eventually, they will return to their homes and seek forgiveness from the parents when things do not work out well. It is therefore important to appease family and community in choosing a spouse.

When I was growing up, as a girl child, I was taught to let the others take the first place. I was taught to respect boys, because boys have more worth than us girls. For this reason, I had to sacrifice myself totally in order to reach out to the others. I remember when I used to cook, I would serve everyone else, and only when and if food remained did I eat. I learned this from my mother. She was always the last to eat, and usually she ate leftovers. She made me internalize these concepts and so that is the reason why even now, when guests come to visit me, I am always the last to eat, and sometimes I don't even eat. I think this is not a fair game but I accept it all the same. What I was taught by my mother is important and I will observe it as long as I live. Even as things stand now, I always seek advice from my mother. She actually helps me interpret my dreams, deal with difficult situations, and advices me on each and every issue. Her advice is very important and I can never think of overlooking it, even when I don't agree with her. I take recourse to her constantly. My mother is very important in my life and I don't know what I would do without her.

In my family, silence is common. When we get angry, we prefer to keep silent. I don't talk to the person I am angry at for some time until the anger eases. Sometimes I also refuse to talk to other people, I prefer to keep things to myself and deal with them. It is not easy for me to let go of grudges. I cling to them because I think people are unfair to me. I feel as if people are out there to hurt me. Sometimes I prefer to close myself into my own world and ignore the rest of reality. I often do this through withdrawing and keeping silent. Even when people ask me what is happening, I don't tell them because I know that they will just continue judging me. I better deal with my problems by myself. When the going gets very tough, I call my mom and she helps me deal with the situation.

I came to Italy in search of a better life. I was working with an Italian gentleman who later died while I was in Italy with him. The local authorities wanted me to return to Kenya but I insisted and provided a story which made the commission accept my application. Thankfully, I was helped by the organization which deals with asylum seekers. I feel that this association did its job, I should not be thankful to them because they were just carrying out their responsibilities. It is their job to do so, while I happened to be here and needing their help. They should assist since they are here for that reason.

My aim is to be able to make good money and move on to another country, hopefully. I don't like it here and once I hate something I hate it with a passion.

NARRATIVE OAC4

I was born in a far off village in Ethiopia. I was an only child. My mom died when I was 4. When my mom died, I was lying down with her on the bed. No one has ever told me if my mom was sick or if it was a sudden death, but what I can vaguely remember is calling her out to wake up, and she was not responding. I vaguely remember that as I called out, I felt very frustrated, and then my father came in and took me away. After a week, we buried my mom.

I did not understand by then what all this meant. The only thing I can remember is calling out for my mom all the time, but she never answered me.

After some years, my father took in another woman. I was excited to have someone who would take care of me, although my father was doing the best he could. This lady started mistreating me. She made me carry out house chores, and she never let me go to school. This went on for a long time, and my father did not intervene. I wanted my father to help me out of this situation. There were days I would go without food because my step mother could not let me eat despite having cooked it myself. It was very difficult and I missed my mom so much. I thought I made my mom die. At one point, I could not take it any more, I decided to escape from home and go look for a better life. I was 9. I went to look for odd jobs, and a lady took me into her home where she told me that I had to do all house chores, till the land, and make sure that I took care of her young child. I started working, doing my best in order not to be sent away, as I did not know where to go. The lady never used to pay me, and many times she would not allow me to eat. I had to be content with the baby's leftovers, and sometimes I would really starve. I don't remember how long I stayed in this lady's home, but at one point, I could not handle it anymore. I decided to leave and change employer. While I was loitering around looking for somewhere to go, some nuns saw me and rescued me. They took me to the local orphanage, where I met many other children. They made me go to school, I had never gone to school. It was very difficult for me. I could sometimes hide and do my own things. I however made new friends, and I learned to cope in a disciplined environment.

Then when I was 12, some people came to the orphanage and wanted to adopt me. I was excited because I thought I would have a better life abroad. I was introduced to this couple from Italy, and I liked them immediately. They told me that I was their daughter whom they had been longing for. I was excited, but at the same time, full of apprehension because I didn't know how genuine these parents were. However, I thought there was nothing worse than what I had gone through. I was subjected to several health tests, then it was time to leave and go to a new country, a new world. I had to abandon my land, my people, everything that was familiar to me.

All this time, since I left home at the age of 9, my father never bothered about me. He never called to know where I was, he never checked to see if I was alright. He did not even know where I was. However, after arriving in the orphanage, I called him and told him where I was, and the possibility of being adopted. Only then did he show up, being sorry about what I had gone through and telling me that he loved me. I received him back because he was the only point of reference I had.

Then in August 2008, my new adoptive parents came to visit me in Ethiopia. I was scared to see this couple, and I did not know what to expect. I was however happy to see them, and for the first time in my life, I had hope for a better life. I could not wait to leave the orphanage and start a new life all together. I looked malnourished, I looked like a 9-year-old, while in truth I was 12. In fact, the orphanage staff told my adoptive parents that I was 9. This is because they knew that these parents would not have accepted me had they known that I was 12. I think they wanted to get rid of me from the orphanage. I was not the best of children and I used to commit many petty crimes. In fact, I would sneak out of school because I felt too imprisoned in that environment. I had been used to a free life and finding myself tethered to the orphanage did not auger well with me. I did not have anyone to talk to about my problems, and I was made to do things which I did not like, like work in the farm, clean up the compound, and do other chores. Life was very severe. Since I had not gone to school, I started schooling then, and it was very difficult for me to keep up. I did not have any base, and it was like torture to me. Several times, I attempted to run away from the orphanage, but I ended up being taken back by some people who knew me.

Time came for me to leave. My father came to say goodbye. He was very cold and did not talk much with my foster parents. He was silent all the time. We left for Italy, and I was overwhelmed by everything I saw in Italy because I had never travelled outside my village before. Everything looked so clean, so orderly, so organized. For the first time I could have tap water without limit, I could sleep on a clean bed, I could eat good proper food. On one side, I was delighted to have come to Italy. On the other hand, I missed my people, my country, and the life I was used to. I did not know the language, the food, the culture, the social life, etc. I could stay for lengthy periods of time without talking because I did not know how to express myself. Soon after, I was sent to junior high school, where I had to interact with other students who were much younger than myself. Everyone tried to be friendly, but I feared everyone and was suspicious of what they wanted from me. I could constantly defend myself and many times I was suspicious for no apparent reason, just the fact that I did not understand the language and the local culture. I could fight back every time I suspected any minimal provocation, discrimination, or observation. I could go physical several times. My parents used to be called to school to help the teachers understand me. I felt classified and pigeon holed.

Gradually I learned the language, and in a couple of months, I could understand pretty much. I started appreciating the others because I could understand what they were saying. I started making friends, but I was constantly suspicious of everyone who tried to come close, including my own foster parents. I could cry at night, I wanted to go back home where I knew the language and the people and the entire environment. But I knew that I had reached a point of no return, so deep down within me, I knew that there was nothing I could do. Life was difficult for both my foster parents and myself, they did not know how to help me. Whenever I got angry and was a bit downcast, I took it out on them, they paid for wrongs they hadn't committed, and I hardened my heart not to feel what they might have been feeling. At one point, since my parents did not know how to handle me, they went to the local health district to seek help, and I was given educators who helped me. At first I did not appreciate them, but I gradually came to like them and I would see them on a daily basis. I knew that I could count on them, tell them my story. I felt a bit more secure with them, and this helped a lot. However, I did not know how to express myself, and despite the availability of these educators, I continued having issues with my parents. We would have constant fights, and many times I would call these educators for help. Thankfully, they used to respond immediately and I felt protected.

Life went on and I finished my junior high school education.

During this time, the natural father that I never had could constantly get in touch with me. He wanted me to send him money. I felt guilty, helpless, but I told my foster parents that if they wanted to keep me, they had to send a certain amount of money regularly to my father. They did not have a choice, and they did. Even after all this, my father did not leave me alone in peace, he continued pestering me with a million demands. Then he ended up in jail, and he told me that he had been falsely accused of failing to pay some taxes to the government. He was condemned to three years' imprisonment, and I did not know what to think. He could make the cops call me asking me for money, and some of this money could go to the cops. He then fell ill and continued asking me for money to buy medication. My foster parents continued sending money, but the problems never ended. He continued pestering me and I felt guilty if I did not help him. I also felt guilty of having abandoned him. However, I knew that he had abandoned me first.

There were times I would vacillate between feelings of sympathy on my dad and feelings of revenge. I could not understand why he had abandoned me when I was little and now he was all over me like a rash. My parents and educators made me aware of this, but I did not have the courage to think differently.

I then went back to my country after 3 years, and my foster parents had given me a good amount of money to take there. My father made sure that he got a good share of the money. He actually did not show much interest in me, he was only interested in the money. He was still in prison.

As I continued growing, my doubts increased about myself and my father. I never had the courage to face my problems, and I avoided a situation where I would be exposed. I would talk a lot about what happened, but deep down, I felt scared, and avoided facing my feelings. This went on until now. I still feel insecure to face my traumas, which are many.

Settling here in Italy has been problematic right from the moment I set foot here. My main problem is that I feel discriminated against. Racism is still very rampant here, and I don't see my future here. I would like to move on and leave this country, I don't actually like living here. I would like to go to UK or other countries. I want to be able to make a life for myself, to have a good job, and be able to help my dad. I know he is suffering a lot, although he left the prison. It is taking him a long time to feel better, and he is entirely dependent on me for everything. He keeps calling me telling me that he is on his deathbed, but thankfully it does not happen. I think my father is selfish, he doesn't think about me. But then I don't know what to do, because in any case, he is my father, and the only biological point of reference I have. I would like to visit Ethiopia again and settle my father, but I know that it will be useless because he doesn't want to settle, he wants quick, free money, and he knows how to make me do everything possible to get him money. I am imprisoned in this web and I find it hard to come out of it. I don't even know if I will ever be free.

I have all along felt misunderstood, by my parents, friends, acquaintances. I continue to feel the racism all around me, and I also feel betrayed by so many people.

I hope to settle elsewhere and make a good living, in a different environment.

NARRATIVE OAK5

I was born in a remote village in Somalia where there was no food and we were living in constant fear of bandits. We were being attacked every now and then and the fear was constant. My parents separated, my mom went to Nairobi while my dad went to Libya. I was left back in Somalia with my siblings. I did not go to school because I did not have the money to pay school fees. I had to learn early to take care of my own needs because my parents had left us in charge of ourselves. I did menial jobs in order to survive, and I also worked as a domestic help where I made do with very little, to say nothing of all the mistreatments I got from my employer. People used to take advantage of me because I was desperate. I did not have other choices but to persevere hoping that some better days would come.

In 2009, I decided to leave Somalia and go to Europe via Libya. I had nothing to lose, so I looked for money and paid for the trip – which was not guaranteed. It was a hefty sum of money but I was sick and tired of living the kind of life I was living in Somalia. I left, through the desert, with a group of 10 of us. We walked for 3 months through the desert. I came face to face with death on a constant basis. We were attacked, raped, robbed, threatened, and I thought I would die any time. Through the desert, we did not have food, and we used to drink our own urine, disgusting as it was at the beginning. I however got used to it, I did not have a choice. We went hungry for prolonged periods of time. We walked endlessly, I could not see the end of the desert. It was infinite. However, I always had hope that over the horizon, we would get to a place where we could have our basic needs guaranteed.

After 3 difficult, unforgettable months, only 4 out of the 10 of us survived and arrived in Libya. I was glad to see my dad. He however was not glad to see me, as he forced me to do things his way. He got a man for me to marry, and since I did not want to, he threatened me and beat me up. He even cut my leg with a machete, and the scar is a cruel reminder of that action. This however did not make me change my mind, but my father did not want to hear any of my excuses. He made me sleep with the man so that I could get pregnant, and that meant that I would be bound to him forever. It was a forced relationship, tend I was not interested in him whatsoever. I wanted to leave Libya and go to Europe, where I hoped life would be decent. However, I did not have the means to do so, so I had to wait, get menial jobs, and live under terrible conditions.

Eventually, I made up some money and I could pay the boat owners for a risky trip to Europe.

When finally, I was assured of leaving Libya to go to Europe, I was pregnant, but that did not deter me from leaving, I knew it would be a risky trip on a huge dingy. It was in May. I left, together with my child's father, oblivious of what we were to face in the deep waters.

It took us 4 long days to cross over to Italy. We were not allowed any luggage, as room was reserved for people and not luggage. Everyone could only have a carry on bag. In there I put a bottle of water and a few cookies. I could not carry anything else. We were 1060 of us in that boat, and we were packed like sardines. Along the sea, 60 people lost their lives. It was very traumatizing to see someone you were talking to just die, and then get thrown into the sea. It was very scaring. Most of these people died of suffocation, the conditions were horrendous. The rest of us survived all the odds and we arrived in Sicily, Italy, where we were separated and placed in different houses. Some of us were sent to other parts of Europe, while a group remained here. I was sent to Trieste after some months at Lampedusa. I was on constant fear of being repatriated because I did not know if they would understand and believe my story.

I ended up in Trieste, where I was taken by Italian Consortium of Solidarity (ICS) as their guest. They gave me somewhere to stay and a home. In the meantime, my pregnancy was growing. I could wake up at night with nightmares about dying in the sea. This still continues.

After 4 months, my daughter was born. This was another trauma, because I knew I would be alone in bringing up this baby. However, I decided to keep my baby because I believe in life.

My baby's dad went to Norway, and I don't even want to know about him. I would not want to see him again. I want to forget him completely.

Here in Italy, I am living in dire need. I have a simple job which earns me very little money. I get rent and food stamps but that is not enough. I have to take care of my daughter single handedly, and it is not easy. I would like to leave this place and go to another country. Maybe the fact that I have a baby might help to get me the necessary help I need to survive. I am fed up with this place. I have met very pleasant people, but there is no future in this country. I want to leave, to go away to another country. The problem is that I have refugee status, therefore I can not leave this county and settle in another one. I will wait and see if I can apply for permanent residence after 5 years of my stay.

I think it would really help those women who come here with the aim of getting a better life to receive help in coping with their traumas. I feel that I need to talk to someone, I have always had that need, but I never got the right chance and the right person. I want to put my experiences in writing so that others can know what some of us have gone through before getting here.

I love my baby, but she is a constant reminder of the experience with my dad and her father. She is a pretty girl, but her presence will always remind me of the men in my life who did not protect me.

NARRATIVE OMK6

I was born in a remote area of Western Uganda where we were always afraid of rebels. I never met my father, and my mother used to tell me that he abandoned her when she got pregnant with me. My mother tells me that I have my father's features. I would have loved to meet my father but my mother considers him irresponsible because he should have come looking for us if he was interested in us. I used to suffer much when other children talked about their fathers and what these fathers did to them. I did not have any brothers or sisters, and my uncles and aunts lived far from our village. I used to see them only on special occasions so there was no real relationship with them.

My mother used to struggle to bring me up and to take care of all the household needs, so I was taught to be disciplined and to spend as little as possible. There was always something that was lacking at home, and my mom could show signs of great suffering due to this fact. She made me go through school with great difficulty. I was a bright child and I was determined not to let my mother down. I worked hard because I wanted to give my mother a better lifestyle. My mother sacrificed so much for me, and sent me to high school. Every now and then I used to be sent home for school fees, and at times I would spend weeks at home because my mother could not raise the money necessary for the fees. I did not like to stay at home when my classmates were at school, and sometimes I would get really sad. The security situation did not help matters, and I felt safer in school than at home. My mother used to do her very best, but she always had problems.

After a great struggle, I completed high school and decided to go to look for a job in order to relieve my mother of the burden. It was very difficult for me to leave my mom alone, and I was constantly thinking of her. I resolved to take her with me after I had settled in the big city of Kampala. I got a job as a babysitter, and gradually put up a small kiosk where I could sell almost everything. Thankfully, I was able to get a small apartment and as soon as I had some space, I got my mother to stay with me and we were finally reunited after 5 years of living apart. I felt born again.

My mother could help me in the kiosk, but we were not making money at all. However, we had very good neighbours who used to support us especially when we were down on resources. Many people used to pass by our kiosk to buy this or that, and one man could pass by more often than others. Eventually, he invited me out and he told me he wanted to marry me. I was so shocked by his words that I left him alone in the restaurant and returned home. It was very difficult for me to relate with men, and I avoided them if I could. Then one day, an Italian who was visiting Kenya saw me and I think he liked me. He started visiting more often and eventually we got to like each other. He invited me to go with him to Italy, which I did. When we arrived in Italy, he abandoned me and I had to go and seek help from the social services. They put me in a home and provided for my needs. I did not like this situation because I would have liked to be independent and earn my daily bread, but I did not have a choice. Later, I was given a permit of stay and I could start looking for a job.

It was very difficult for me to settle in Italy because I was alone, with harsh weather conditions, different food, different language which made me feel very frustrated in having a cultural negotiator translate for me when I visited various places, and the sense of being cheated by the Italian boyfriend. Eventually, I was able to get a casual cleaning job and all the money I received I send it to my mother because she needs it more than myself.

I have had several problems in settling in Italy, I feel the hostility of people, and I miss my home. I could not find anyone to talk to about my situation. I was not independent and this made things difficult for me. I don't like to depend on anyone at all for anything and I feel humiliated about the whole thing. I just hope I will one day get a better job and be able to provide everything that my mother needs. I will forever be grateful to my mother for making so many sacrifices for my welfare. I want to repay her.

I feel very bitter about many things, but I know I need to be strong and go on. I will continue looking for a better job until I am able to make my mother's life comfortable, as well as mine.

DEMOGRAPHIC INFORMATION

Name ____

Date of Birth _______________ Country of Birth _______________

Date of Arrival in Italy: _______________

Reason of being in Italy: _______________________________

Level of education: _____________________________________

Profession: ___________________ Occupation: _______________

Religious orientation: __________________________________

Language spoken: ______________________________________

Other languages: _______________________________________

Marital status: ____

Children: ____

Family

Age of Father: __________ Occupation of Father: _______________

Age of Mother: __________ Occupation of Mother: _______________

Where they live: _______________________________________

Number of siblings: _______ Their ages: _______________

Their locations: _______________________________________

At the beginning of the session, only the names of the participants will be asked. The other demographic information will be explored towards the end of the interview when the participant will have shared about their family, or the information filled in as they share about themselves, and only those questions which will not have been answered will be explicitly asked.

INTERVIEW QUESTIONS

The following questions are guidelines and may not necessarily be followed to the letter. The participants will be invited to talk about themselves and other issues without limiting them to specific questions. These questions, however, form the basis for the research in that they lead towards seeing how REBT could be applied in the integration process of these participants. Sessions may be multiple, as need requires, and answers compiled in such a way that all of the areas covered by the questions will be addressed.

Please feel free to answer the following questions.

1. Tell me about your nucleus family: your parents, your brothers and sisters, and how growing up was like in your family.
2. Tell me what happens when a child is born and the rituals attached to this event.
3. How is reward and discipline administered in your family?
4. When one is sick in the family, how are they considered and treated?
5. How do you celebrate birthdays, weddings, funerals, initiation ceremonies, and other occasions?
6. If someone in the family has any kind of need, do they deal with it as individuals or does everyone come together to help out?
7. If someone decides to marry, are they influenced by their family members or do they decide independently of everyone else's opinion?
8. Are there collective tasks and activities that your family is involved in? If yes, which ones? How are they carried out?
9. What rights do you believe you have that you feel need to be respected by everyone?
10. How is silence viewed in your family?